To Avoid Catastrophe

To Avoid Catastrophe

A Study in Future Nuclear Weapons Policy

Edited by
Michael P. Hamilton

William B. Eerdmans Publishing Company

Copyright © 1977 by Wm. B. Eerdmans Publishing Co.
255 Jefferson Ave. SE, Grand Rapids, Mich. 49503
All rights reserved
Printed in the United States of America

Library of Congress Cataloging in Publication Data

Main entry under title:

To avoid catastrophe.

   1. Atomic weapons. 2. Atomic warfare. 3. Atomic energy industries—Security measures. I. Hamilton, Michael Pollock, 1927-
UF767.T6   327'.174   77-24983
ISBN 0-8028-1703-3

Contents

Preface Senator Dick Clark 7
Introduction Michael P. Hamilton 15

The Background

I An Unfinished History of the Atomic Age 23
   Gregg F. Herken
II The United States–Soviet Union Arms Competition 45
   Adrian S. Fisher
III The Proliferation of Nuclear Reactors and Weapons 63
   Herbert Scoville, Jr.
IV Energy and the Conquest of Fear 83
   William G. Pollard

Scenarios of Disaster and Hope

V A Terrorist Attack 113
   Brian O'Leary
VI Nuclear War Comes to the Middle East 131
   Robert J. Pranger
VII Sabotage at a Nuclear Power Plant 153
   James J. MacKenzie
VIII Holocaust by Accident 171
   Lloyd J. Dumas

The Future

IX Facts, Morals, and the Bomb 197
   Charles C. West

X	What Can be Done: Some Practical Steps *Thomas A. Halsted*	221
Appendix	Organizations Concerned with Arms Control and Disarmament	239

Preface

It is a measure of this age that the proliferation of nuclear weapons has become a common and credible element of contemporary fiction. In the current novel "The Massada Case," a beleaguered Israeli government, under military attack by overwhelmingly superior Arab forces, suddenly reveals that it has hidden nuclear weapons in several national capitals, including Washington and Moscow, and threatens to detonate these devices unless the Arabs are called off. Mary Hartman, in the popular Norman Lear television production, frets over whether a fellow mental patient is constructing a nuclear weapon in his basement to blow up Ohio.

That these incidents are even believable nowadays is depressing evidence of the extent to which proliferation of nuclear technology has come to be taken for granted. Today, not just the super-powers but a dozen other far less stable countries possess the technology to become nuclear weapons powers. By 1980 there will be some four hundred light-water reactors in thirty-five countries, producing huge quantities of plutonium. As Director General of the International Atomic Energy Agency Sigvard Eklund put it recently, weapon capability is spreading "like a plague."

The super-power confrontation is real enough, with the Soviet Union and the United States facing each other behind enormous numbers of nuclear weapons. But that confrontation displays a certain stability, it has evolved a ritual all its own, with both powers fully aware of the dangers of resorting to a nuclear alternative. There exists a whole pattern of institutions —from "Hot Line" to SALT talks—to prevent this from happening. This explains why it was possible for the United

States to fight a protracted war in Vietnam without using nuclear weapons or being threatened with their use by the Soviet Union. Both nations are acutely aware of the limits to nuclear politics.

The more likely threat to peace arises not from the nuclear capability of the super powers, or even their junior partners, like Britain, France, or China, for whom a nuclear capability serves only as a retaliatory force to frighten potential aggressors. Far more critical is the possession of such capability by the smaller—and often far less stable—states. It doesn't take much imagination to sense the extreme dangers in the mixture of weapons and politics in places like the Middle East, Taiwan, Korea, or southern Africa.

And then there is the entirely separate proliferation danger stemming from possible terrorist acts. There have already been eleven recorded attacks on nuclear facilities. The authors of this book spell out in graphic detail other things that can go wrong. A recent government study concluded that it is not unthinkable that even in the United States, where nuclear weapons are most safely stored, "a well-trained commando unit of about eight to twenty attackers" might steal a bomb. We can only wonder how long it will be before some hijacker, or technically gifted individual, will hold a city hostage.

The problem is thus far more acute than generally realized. Fortunately, there are signs that both the administration and the Congress are becoming alert to the dangers.

United States concern for proliferation has waxed and waned throughout the atomic age. The initial Baruch plan proposals, largely an administration initiative, called for sharing nuclear technology, but were quite naive politically and never had a chance. A far more serious step down the proliferation road was taken by the "Atoms for Peace" program of President Dwight D. Eisenhower. For over a decade this extremely short-sighted policy gave to a technology-oriented Atomic Energy Commission (AEC) a monopoly on licensing sales abroad, a mandate which it executed with uncommon enthusiasm. True, it forbade the export of enrichment or reprocessing technology, but neither the AEC nor the fully compliant congressional committee grasped clearly the inevitable proliferation impact of the reactor technology itself.

While recognizing intellectually that military and peaceful

atoms were identical, United States policy continued to treat them as if they were somehow different. Albert Wohlstetter has noted how the United States has refused to come to grips with the interrelationship between peaceful and military applications of atomic energy and tried "to stop one and to promote the other."

As ex-director of the Arms Control and Disarmament Agency Fred C. Ikle described our proliferation role, "The United States was the principal sinner. We trained thousands of scientists and engineers, and we sent research reactors to many countries—Chile, South Korea, the Congo, Vietnam—and even information kits describing how to make plutonium."

Under this program India received the essential heavy water that enabled it to go nuclear; Argentina got sufficient technology to go almost that far. For some inexplicable reason there was a sort of naive confidence in the "safeguard" system, though, as is often pointed out now, the safeguard is merely an alarm signal, nothing more.

In retrospect, it is incredible that it took the United States and the Soviet Union until 1963 to agree on even a partial restriction on nuclear testing. Fortunately this was followed reasonably soon by the Non-Proliferation Treaty (NPT), with its—admittedly inadequate—system of incentives for states not to go nuclear.

It is fair to say that throughout this period neither in the Congress nor in the public at large was there yet a fully developed appreciation of the dangers of proliferation. In part, this was reinforced by the relatively long period in which the Big Five had enjoyed nuclear monopoly. It was a period, too, in which United States sales policy continued to be dominated by an AEC attitude that stressed sales and neglected the dangers.

Three things stimulated a greater sense of urgency in the early 1970s. First, the 1973 Middle East crisis and the resulting petroleum embargo kindled a renewed drive for nuclear power plants. Then, a year later India detonated a "peaceful" nuclear explosive, an event of incalculable importance throughout the world of India's peers. Finally, there was an undeniable advance in nuclear technology, overwhelming if only for the numbers of participants involved.

At last Congress began to act. Recognizing the shortcoming of having the AEC serve as both promoter and regulator of nuclear energy, it dissolved the agency and split the responsibilities between an Energy Research and Development Administration (ERDA) and the Nuclear Regulatory Commission (NRC). ERDA was supposed to handle research and development, and NRC was to serve as the regulatory body. At the same time, the dissolution of the AEC resulted in the diminished role of the Joint Committee on Atomic Energy, which had lost much of its capacity to regulate the agency. Other committees in both Houses of Congress are now moving to take a closer look at United States nuclear export policy.

Senator John Pastore reflected the Senate's concern about proliferation in 1975 when he introduced the resolution urging the United States to take the lead in seeking international cooperation and strengthening safeguards over nuclear material. Strongly supporting efforts of the International Atomic Energy Agency (IAEA), Pastore urged "an extensive cooperative international effort" to strengthen and improve safeguards, as well as restraint by the suppliers in nuclear transfers and a rigid system of safeguards in the entire nuclear cycle.

Senator Stuart Symington, chairman of the Foreign Relations Committee's subcommittee on disarmament, followed that up last year with an amendment to the Foreign Assistance Act of 1961, an amendment requiring that economic and military assistance to the buyer and seller of enrichment and reprocessing materials, equipment, and technology be cut off, unless a multilateral approach — including full IAEA safeguards — was provided for. Hearings were held, resulting in the most comprehensive survey of the proliferation problem — going well beyond just the matter of weapons — yet carried out by Congress.

That an awareness of the problem was emerging became clear during the 1976 presidential campaign. Possibly in reaction to the Indian explosion, both candidates accorded proliferation a key priority in their campaign. President Ford commissioned an inter-agency study which expressed considerable concern over the dangers of proliferation and recommended against continuing efforts to achieve a reprocessing capability. He asked — in vain, as it turned out — all nations to agree to a three-year moratorium on the sale or purchase of reprocessing equipment. Jimmy Carter was equally outspoken in his concern for proliferation, and both candidates ended up officially endorsing a moratorium on commercial reprocessing of spent fuel cells.

This was a decision long in coming. Although the United States experience with reprocessing had been costly and unsatisfactory, European nations continued to plod ahead with expensive and relatively unsatisfactory systems, and international deals were being made. France had committed itself to supplying Pakistan with a reprocessing facility, and Germany had promised a full fuel cycle to Brazil. Only with the greatest difficulty was the United States able to talk South Korea out of a similar operation.

Already in the early weeks of the new administration, President Carter took steps to reaffirm his commitment to grappling with the dangers of proliferation. These dangers were among the first subjects for a "Presidential Review Memorandum," and for the first time in a long while, the bureaucracy has really turned to analyzing the problem. Unquestionably, thinking on this issue will be much influenced by an exhaustive study on nuclear power issues financed by the Ford Foundation, concluding that there is every reason for a moratorium on the use of plutonium for fuel. President Carter can be confident that Congress is eager to join in solving the problem. Whether they will be able to agree on a method for going about this is quite another matter.

Congress seems determined to push ahead with additional controls on the nuclear export business. A bill, slightly revised from an earlier version in 1976, has been introduced that would establish unprecedented criteria to govern United States exports. It also calls for accelerated international negotiations, and provides for measures to guarantee that the United States remains a reliable supplier of uranium fuels. Significantly, it also prescribes a larger role for the NRC in export policy-making.

The prospects that Congress will take a more active role in proliferation policy have been much enhanced by the reorganization taken in the wake of the dissolution of the Joint Atomic Energy Committee (JAEC). So long as the JAEC was active, outside pressures on policy formulation were remarkably limited. The committee's strangle-hold on policy was based both on its all-encompassing mandate and also on the alleged requirements of secrecy. In the past the principal source of influence on policy has thus been the nuclear energy industry, bolstered by its enormous multinational influence.

Nuclear export policy issues are now to be divided more broadly among a variety of Senate committees. The Armed Services Committee has responsibility for the national security aspects, with primary focus on weapons. The Foreign Relations Committee will look at the international facets of nuclear energy, including nuclear transfer problems. The new Energy and Natural Resources committee will handle the ERDA and NRC authorization bills. And finally, Government Operations will be investigating the broad field of organizing the government for the most effective conduct of nuclear transfer policy.

Although some fear has been expressed that the divided jurisdiction could result in a lack of focus for United States policy, it is in my judgment high time that an issue as vital to our security and well-being as nuclear energy and foreign export policy be opened to broader Congressional oversight.

I have no illusions, however, about the complexity of the issue and the difficulty of formulating policy in this field. For one thing, Congress is still subject to tremendous pressures from the nuclear industry itself. Until now, nuclear energy has been a high-risk, low-profit enterprise, and the industry is extremely reluctant to be subjected to unilateral American controls which might affect its international competitive position.

The Department of State itself is an ambiguous guide to Congress — concerned, on the one hand, with the dangers of proliferation, but equally aware of the need for the United States to mind its image as a reliable supplier. The temporary slow-down in United States fuel deliveries since 1974 has, in their judgment, significantly undermined confidence in the United States, and it is not unlikely that Brazil's decision to purchase the West German technology was in part provoked by this shock.

Also impeding Congressional input into nuclear export policy are the deep disagreements among the members themselves on what to do. There are fundamental differences, for example, over what can be achieved by unilateral United States action. Many members argue that export policy will not be stabilized until it is undertaken in full cooperation between

PREFACE

the suppliers and the recipients. Fortunately, there are some signs of progress in this direction at the London supplier group.

Perhaps the basic precondition to achieving international cooperation, however, is reliable information on which to judge the issues. Here, the nation's scientific community has an essential role to play. Far too often the debate over nuclear policy has become a contest between ideologically and emotionally involved protagonists, quite without regard to facts. But "facts" can be extraordinarily complex and misleading in this field, and considerably more scientific information is necessary before we know quite where we are headed.

The controversy over the West German deal to provide Brazil, which did not sign the Non-Proliferation Treaty, with a full fuel cycle is an excellent example of this. Well-intentioned protagonists argue at length over the fundamental issues of future energy consumption levels, the availability of uranium fuel, and the economics of reprocessing. The United States projection of world energy consumption, for example, is far below that of the Europeans. United States experts also disagree basically with the Europeans on the economics of the reprocessing cycle. And United States specialists are far less certain than their European counterparts of the practicality of the breeder reactor.

Issues of this sort should be manageable and must be an early priority. Reasonable agreement on energy consumption projections should be achievable if the scientific community is better integrated into the process. Somewhere, either in the IAEA or the newly formed London group, these extremely basic issues simply must be addressed. It will be the task of Congress to stimulate these initiatives.

Fortunately, as the Congress moves into this new and critical phase of its efforts to grapple with proliferation, it can rely on unprecedented public support. The public is becoming uniformly alert to the dangers of proliferation, and is agreed that it is the primary threat to the peace. Congress has now to accept this mandate and proceed with earnest measures before these "Atoms for Peace" really do become "Bombs for Sale."

United States Senate
Washington, D.C.

Dick Clark
(D. — Iowa)

Introduction

This is not another "doomsday" book. Rather, it is an attempt to look carefully and honestly at new problems which face us as a result of the discovery of nuclear fission and the proliferation of energy-producing reactors and nuclear weapons, and to offer constructive policies to reduce their attendant dangers.

When the Old Testament Israelites were confronted with apparently insuperable threats to their existence, they discovered ways to avoid catastrophe. On the religious level of understanding, these deliverances were interpreted as God's saving acts and became the basis of their liturgical traditions. On the secular level — a concomitant but not contradictory mode of interpretation — these deliverances can be understood as the successful outcome of a nation making unexpectedly strong efforts to meet dangerous challenges. I hope these essays will help to elicit such efforts in our day.

In planning the book, I thought it would be helpful to have an introductory section of which the first chapter would tell of the discovery and initial use of atomic bombs. Professor Gregg Herken, a scholar in the area, undertakes this task, and emphasizes the political considerations which, from the beginning, determined the nature of the scientific research and development. Adrian Fisher, who personally participated in United States disarmament discussions with the Soviets, takes up the story and illustrates the competitive character of the nuclear policies of the United States and the Soviet Union and provides a description of the dilemmas in contemporary negotiations.

In Chapter III Herbert Scoville gives an outline of the way materials for the construction of bombs are acquired, and a summary of the state of nuclear technology in the nations of the world. The science of nuclear fission also offers us a relatively inexhaustible supply of energy, and Dr. William Pollard, physicist and theologian, completes the background chapters of the book by arguing forcefully for the merits of nuclear reactors as a crucial source for electrical power. The reader must in his or her mind weigh the advantages of nuclear power against the well-known fears regarding the cost and dangers involved, particularly in relation to the disposal of nuclear wastes and the opportunities for the theft of plutonium for the purpose of manufacturing weapons.

It is ironic that the great destructive power of nuclear missiles has probably been the major peace-keeping force between the Soviet Union and the United States, for it is clearly too dangerous for either nation to plan on nuclear war against the other. The concentration of effort and attention to preserving this stalemate, as well as being inordinately expensive, has resulted in a mutual public blindness to the new dangers arising from the acquisition by lesser national powers of atomic bombs and energy reactors. While we concern ourselves with the Russian nuclear threat, we are unwilling to face up to the implications of international proliferation wherein lie the greatest likelihood for nuclear attacks. Like two great dinosaurs we have been so preoccupied with each other that we have been oblivious to the environment changing around us.

The central section of the book is a series of scenarios of possible future disasters. I invite the reader to engage in personal, creative thinking in relation to them. Thus, after you have read the scenario parts of Chapters IV to VIII, stop and ask yourself (or your family, your friends or some discussion group in which you participate) this question: "What steps do I wish our government would take to avoid this calamity?" Ponder that question, inform yourself on alternative answers, let your associates worry about it, argue about the answers, pray about them, dream about them — and then read the authors' recommendations in the second parts of their chapters entitled "reflections." Whether or not you agree with them is less important than the fact that you are consciously involved in an important political and scientific issue of our times. You will now be in a better position to influence others because you have made the effort to think ahead.

INTRODUCTION

The first scenario is about a terrorist plot to gain the release of political prisoners through nuclear blackmail. Most people who have studied terrorism as a means of effecting change consider it of limited usefulness. The moral outrage engendered by terrorism as a means to an end militates against its success. A worthy goal can more easily be lost than gained by methods considered improper by the general public. This is particularly true when terrorists do not gain power as in a coup, for whatever bargain they may be able to strike with those they threaten tends to be of temporary value and will not change the abiding institutional character of the conflict. They are often cold of heart and unwilling to make any moral judgment on the measure of suffering they inflict on their enemies in relation to the suffering they wish to relieve by their acts. Finally, the attraction to dangerous methods often hides a self-destructive element within their psyches which makes them willing to risk their own deaths. Since they are seldom deterred by rational arguments, we may expect terrorists to continue to strike, and Brian O'Leary tells us a chilling tale of a threat involving a nuclear bomb.

In Chapter VI Robert Pranger, an expert on the Middle East, projects his scenario of a nuclear attack in that troubled part of the world. His account is so persuasive that it would be more accurate to say that the nuclear attack he describes grows naturally out of many unresolved political tensions of that area. It is interesting to note that Pranger suggests that some good may arise from such a great evil. Thus a nuclear strike becomes the opportunity for the United States and the Soviet Union to work to resolve those international problems which might be occasions for other nuclear wars. For anyone who believes, as I do, that the proliferation of atomic weapons will continue and a nuclear strike is likely, this chapter offers hope that a political dynamic for change and reform could also emerge with it. A new measure of international justice, both political and economic, may result from fear and self-interest as well as from charity and benevolence.

But if proliferation does continue, the pace at which it proceeds and the quality of safeguards for nuclear reactor sites are concerns of utmost importance. In Chapter VII, written by James McKenzie, the security of a nuclear energy reactor is broached, saboteurs enter and make their demands from within the complex. An eerie situation is posed, and even if the danger to the surrounding country and its inhabitants is not as grave as the public fears, a nuclear threat is cause for special dread.

The topic of sabotage faced me as an editor with two moral and political dilemmas. First, should any story about sabotage be published if it might inspire somebody to attempt it? Are the author and editor of such a chapter unpatriotic and morally irresponsible? Some advised me not to treat the subject at all in a book written for a wide audience, and others, whose work involved designing safeguards and thinking about the dangers of sabotage, did not wish to share their knowledge with me. On the other hand, as this book was in the process of preparation, a number of newspaper stories and magazine articles about sabotage appeared and the topic lost some of its taboo quality.

From my personal experience and involvement in public affairs in Washington, D.C., I have come to believe that secrecy is often a cloak for incompetence and an educated public is an asset, not a liability, to wise government. An informed electorate would be an advantage, for instance, if for reasons of security the government wished to take measures to reduce the likelihood of sabotage and terrorism. If citizens had not had opportunities to learn about sabotage, they would resent such restrictions on their civil liberties. To leave out information which is essential to the understanding of public policy leads to government by edict, by propaganda, by the bypassing of congressional debate, and that has no place in American democracy. I decided that sabotage was a legitimate topic for examination and inclusion.

The second dilemma concerned the quality of a scenario about sabotage. If it was composed by somebody who didn't know much about security and technological aspects of a reactor site, then the story would not be plausible and readers might think that there was no real danger. However, if the story was written by somebody who knew all the secret safety precautions and was himself or herself a nuclear physicist, then the scenario might tell too much! James McKenzie tells a story about sabotage at a power plant and you will have to judge for yourself if he avoided the horns of this dilemma. Potential saboteurs should know that there are secret safe-

INTRODUCTION

guards, in addition to those mentioned in this chapter, which should deter them from their rash endeavors. The general public, however, should be aware that no safeguards are one hundred percent effective, and that a nation, as well as individuals, lives by faith.

The final scenario depicts a truly disastrous situation in which the superpowers engage in an all-out nuclear exchange. If you think this could only be the result of madmen in positions of leadership, then you need to read Lloyd Dumas' story and pay particular attention to footnotes 3 to 13. Do you remember the conflicts, confusions, and false assumptions made in regard to the dropping of the bombs on Hiroshima and Nagasaki? That was an example of the quality of nuclear decision-making by a nation which enjoyed the luxury of being the only possessor of atomic weapons. That American decision did not have to be made under any great time pressure and there was no fear of retaliation. Can you imagine the potential for mistakes under the pressure of making decisions within a matter of minutes when there is a convergence of a technological breakdown and political miscalculation, when there is an issue which has provoked international rivalry and bitterness, and when the opponents are armed with nuclear missiles? Full-scale nuclear war is far from being impossible.

Unfortunately, the United States has never been able to accept a state of parity in relation to Russia's nuclear strength. The Pentagon and Congress seem incapable of resisting the temptation to gain a temporary advantage by the funding and development of new sophisticated armaments. The blame for this can be shared quite widely; with the scientists who do not contain their curiosity for researching new and yet more abominable means of destruction, with the armament industry which seizes upon ideas as means of keeping their industry and profits thriving, with the politicians who lapse into simplistic and anti-communist rhetoric because it aids their elections, and with the general public who have not yet attained the psychological maturity that enables them to live on equal terms with their enemies. Our need to be "one up" rather than to accept parity is so strong that, even though it may impoverish us financially and ecologically, even though it may blind us to the worldwide problems of hunger, even though we pay lip service in our diplomatic rhetoric to other goals, it still dominates our foreign policy. Professor Dumas has some recommendations relevant to this state of affairs in the final pages of his chapter on disarmament.

In the last section of the book two chapters complement each other in their approach. Charles West, a theologian, writes about the relation of nuclear physics to truth as we know it from other sources, and also about the relation of nuclear armaments to the moral character of the world we live in. Thomas Halsted, a man with a broad range of experience, provides a summary of actions which he recommends to reduce the likelihood of the fictional scenarios actually occurring.

* * * * *

In closing, I wish to thank those who, in a variety of ways, have made this book possible. I am indebted to Dean Francis B. Sayre Jr. for the opportunity and encouragement he gave me to spend my time on this venture. The funding for the book came from the Washington Episcopal Cathedral where I work, and also from the Paddock Foundation which has long been concerned in bringing new and controversial issues before the public and the churches for evaluation and action.

A number of people have given generously of their time and their wisdom, first to educate me in the area of nuclear policy, and then to make suggestions for the planning of the book. In particular, I'd like to mention Thomas Halsted and Professor George Rathjens. I am very glad to be able to make public my gratitude to them and also to many voices on the long distance and local telephone who, giving generously of their time and wisdom, became my friends as well as advisors. Nancy S. Montgomery, editor of *Cathedral Age*, provided very important and skilled aid in the editing of texts, and Randa H. Murphy, my efficient and long-suffering secretary, was helpful in tasks both great and small.

The credit for whatever is worthy in the book goes to these people and, of course, to the authors who labored so well in the production of their contributions. The mistakes and inadequacies are my responsibility. I trust the reader will catch something of the sense of excitement and urgency, of fear and hope, which pervades those spending their lives in nuclear matters and which the editing of this book elicited in me.

Canon Michael P. Hamilton

The Background

I

An Unfinished History of the Atomic Age
GREGG F. HERKEN

Genesis of the Atomic Bomb Project

The atomic age began not with a flash over the New Mexican desert or with the destruction of a Japanese city, but with an experiment in a German laboratory, less than a year before the onset of the Second World War. The origin of atomic fission in Germany was as important — or portentous — as the implications of atomic energy itself. It was the all-too-plausible specter of an atomic bomb in the hands of the German *Führer* that would serve as the inspiration for America's atomic research and the impetus behind the creation of the first nuclear weapon by her scientists.[1]

---

[1] Ironically, the fear of a German atomic bomb proved groundless. Due to early misconceptions, the exigencies of war, and Hitler's blind racial prejudice, German nuclear research never came close to achieving success. Scientists of the German atomic bomb project were stunned — even disbelieving — upon hearing the news of Hiroshima. See David Irving, *The German Atomic Bomb: The History of Nuclear Research in Nazi Germany* (New York, 1968).

Gregg F. Herken received his doctorate in history from Princeton University in 1973. From 1974 to 1975 he was a visiting scholar at the University of California, Berkeley, and a research fellow at Berkeley's Institute of International Studies. Since then, he has taught recent American history and United States foreign policy at the University of California, Santa Cruz, and at the San Luis Obispo campus of California Polytechnic State University.

Dr. Herken's practical experience in the area of international relations includes a brief service as an intelligence analyst on the Soviet internal affairs desk of the Central Intelligence Agency in 1971. His particular interest is the effect of technology upon international affairs, and he has contributed to both symposia and anthologies on that subject.

Dr. Herken is currently working on a book which deals with the role of the atomic bomb in American diplomacy and defense planning from 1945 to 1950, entitled The Winning Weapon: The Atomic Bomb in the Cold War.

The roots of America's effort to build an atomic bomb began in 1939, with a letter from two scientists to President Franklin Roosevelt. The scientists, physicist Leo Szilard and mathematician-theorist Albert Einstein, were disturbed by two facts stemming from the discovery of nuclear fission in the previous year: that atomic energy might have military application; and that a fascist state was at that time preeminent in this newly discovered science. The scientists' letter — actually written by Szilard but bearing the signature and prestige of Einstein — spurred the President to create the "Uranium Committee" in the fall of 1939. The committee's responsibility was not to build an atomic bomb but to study the feasibility of one. The Uranium Committee, however, did not view the problem of the military application of atomic energy with the scientists' spirit of urgency, so that it was not until shortly before America's entry into the war that an atomic bomb seemed more than a distant, theoretical possibility.[2]

The Japanese attack on Pearl Harbor ended this lassitude. By 1943, the project to build the bomb — given the code name Manhattan Engineer District — was placed under the authority of the United States Army Corps of Engineers and the personal direction of Brigadier General Leslie Groves. From its inception the Manhattan Project was of an unprecedented scale; but most of the wartime project's problems stemmed from its diverse origins and unique mission. Its subcontractors ranged from the manufacturers of chewing gum wrappers to a munitions giant like Dupont.[3] And the top-secret American project benefited initially from research into atomic energy conducted under a British precursor of the Uranium Committee entitled MAUD. Throughout its lifetime the Manhattan Project would continue to rely upon the talents of an international array of scientists whom an exasperated Groves once characterized as "the greatest bunch of prima donnas ever seen in one place." Yet Groves proved to be an inspired choice as administrator of the entire project, which would eventually spend some two

[2]On atomic research prior to Pearl Harbor, see R. G. Hewlett and O. E. Anderson, Jr., *The New World 1939/1946: A History of the United States Atomic Energy Commission*, I (Univ. Park, Pa., 1962), chapter two.

[3]On the wartime development of the atomic bomb project, see S. Groeff, *The Manhattan Project* (New York, 1967).

AN UNFINISHED HISTORY OF THE ATOMIC AGE

billion dollars to produce the first atomic bomb.[4]

As work progressed toward development of the bomb, the confidence of Groves and of the scientists grew. Intelligence reports from within Germany and the success of allied arms in Europe by 1944 had together largely dispelled the fear that Hitler might be first to have the weapon. But the prospects were good that the bomb would play a significant — even decisive — role in the final battle with Japan.

As the bomb itself moved from hypothesis to reality, moreover, scientists were not the only ones to take an interest in the future of atomic energy. Those in Washington who would bear responsibility for making policy on the bomb were becoming alive to the possibilities of the nascent weapon for the current war — and beyond.

As early as December 1944, Secretary of War Henry Stimson had approached President Roosevelt with the idea of using the atomic bomb as a bargaining point in the diplomatic dealings that would follow the war. Specifically, Stimson suggested that the United States offer to share information on the bomb with Russia in exchange for concessions from the Soviets on political matters in dispute between the two superpowers. The fate of eastern Europe was already one such bone of contention. Roosevelt's death in the spring of 1945 came before the President had decided on how to approach Russia on the subject of the atomic bomb, but not before he had unavoidably linked atomic energy with postwar politics through secret agreements with the British on future cooperation concerning the weapon.[5] These Anglo-American understandings, which included provisions for sharing information and atomic raw materials, would ultimately cause problems for Roosevelt's successor once the war against Japan had ended. However, it was Russia, and not Britain or Japan, that would be the real postwar concern of the administration of Harry Truman.

---

[4]On Groves and the Manhattan Project, see L. R. Groves, *Now It Can Be Told* (New York, 1962).

[5]Concerning atomic policy under the Roosevelt administration, see Martin J. Sherwin, *A World Destroyed: The Atomic Bomb and the Grand Alliance* (New York, 1975).

From Alamogordo to Nagasaki

Truman was told of the Manhattan Project's existence almost immediately after his accession to the presidency. But it was not until later in the same month of April that the President heard the full details from Stimson and Groves. At that time the bomb was scheduled for its first test during the coming summer.

Truman, like Stimson, remained sensitive to the potentialities of the bomb in America's dealings with Russia and postponed his first meeting with Soviet Premier Joseph Stalin so that the weapon's July test might coincide with the encounter.[6] The new President, his advisors, and confidants at the Potsdam conference awaited word from New Mexico on the results of the atomic test.

Groves' "prima donnas" back at the desert test site in Alamogordo, New Mexico, also awaited the witness of their efforts with anticipation and anxiety. One among them had speculated that the fission reaction of the test might engulf the entire state. At 5:30 on the morning of July 16, 1945, the era of nuclear destruction dawned. The blast of the bomb broke a window 125 miles away, turned the desert sand to glass at the point of the explosion, and formed a crater some 1200 feet in diameter. Neither the scientists in New Mexico nor the policy-makers at Potsdam were disappointed by the results of the test. Upon receipt of the coded message from Alamogordo that "the baby had been born," the Americans at Potsdam were, in Stimson's recollection, "immensely pleased." Truman himself was "tremendously pepped up by it," to the extent — British Prime Minister Churchill claimed — that the President now "told the Russians just where they got on and off and generally bossed the whole meeting."[7]

But the advent of the atomic bomb as what Stimson termed a "colossal reality" also made certain problems immediately emergent: whether and how to use the bomb; whether to share it with our allies; and how to control it for the future. Significantly, among the three questions the last two occupied Tru-

---

[6]On Truman at Potsdam, see Harry S. Truman, *Memoirs: Year of Decisions* (New York, 1955), pp. 367-455.

[7]Hewlett and Anderson, *The New World*, pp. 386-392.

man's attention at the closing meetings of the Potsdam conference. Yet the President was unable or unwilling to resolve them at Potsdam. The bomb as a factor in diplomatic as well as military strategy posed its own problems. Truman was fearful that a simple announcement of the bomb's success to Stalin might provoke a request to share in the discovery — a request that he was not ready to honor — and he was concerned, too, that no announcement at all would be interpreted as a slight to America's ally. The President's solution to the problem was seen as clever by some, disingenuous by others. But in all fairness, it was perhaps only representative of the moral dilemma created by the invention of nuclear weapons. Approaching Stalin at the end of one conference session on July 24th, Truman told the Soviet Premier that America had devised a "new weapon of unusual destructive force," without mentioning that it was an atomic bomb.[8] The President had thus technically fulfilled his responsibility of informing an ally without at the same time incurring an obligation to share the bomb's secrets.[9]

Ironically, the most immediate problem posed by the bomb — whether or how to use it against America's enemies in the war — apparently did not concern Truman as much as the question of its future role after the war. The decision to drop the bomb was notable, indeed, for its very lack of ambivalence. The scientists of the Manhattan Project were among the few knowing of the bomb to express doubts concerning its use and the only ones to propose a "demonstration" of the weapon prior to its being dropped upon a city. The scientists' revolt grew as it became evident that the United States would be the only country to have atomic bombs in the war. But the objections of the scientists were only a small and belated voice against the chorus

---

[8] Truman, *Year of Decisions*, p. 458.

[9] Stalin's only response to Truman's announcement was an expression of hope that the United States would make "good use" of the weapon against the Japanese. This dour reaction left at least one observer in the American camp convinced that Stalin "did not grasp the importance" of the President's news. It is hard to imagine, however, that Stalin — whose spies were operating against the Manhattan Project as early as 1943 — was unaware that the weapon in question was an atomic bomb (a contention that recent Soviet publications tend to confirm). Rather, it is likely that Stalin's apparent lack of response was only the first example of atomic diplomacy in "reverse." See the next section of this chapter, "Atomic Diplomacy: A Threat at London."

of opinion urging the bomb's use.[10] The expectation that the weapon would be used had, in fact, silently grown up alongside the project to build it. "At no time from 1941 to 1945," Stimson is quoted as saying, was "it suggested by the President or any other responsible member of the government that atomic energy should not be used in the war." In his memoirs, Truman confirms Stimson's recollection by noting that there was "never any doubt that [the bomb] should be used."[11]

There was, indeed, no compelling argument *against* using the bomb. Any claim to mercy on the part of the Japanese, it was almost universally believed in Washington, had been forfeited by their attack on Pearl Harbor. There were, however, powerful inducements to the wartime use of the bomb beyond the obvious one of forcing Japan to surrender. These included the "idealistic" hope that a present sacrifice might so horrify humanity as to avoid future disasters; the "pragmatic" concern of a few that the two billion dollar investment be proven worthwhile; and — most often cited at Potsdam — the expectation of American policy-makers, including Truman, that the bomb might put an end to the war against Japan before the Russians entered and established a claim in the postwar peace settlement. Apart, these two driving considerations — the military rationale concerning Japan and the political one concerning Russia — reinforced the already existing inclination to use the weapon. Together, their effect was compelling to that decision.[12]

On July 24, the same day that he dodged the issue of the bomb's future role with Stalin, Truman set his signature to the order that two atomic bombs be dropped on Japan. Two weeks later a single bomb, exploded above the city of Hiroshima, killed or wounded more than 100,000 inhabitants of that city. Three days after the bombing of Hiroshima, on August 9, a second bomb largely destroyed the city of Nagasaki and killed some 40,000 Japanese. The two bombs dropped on Japan had been the extent of America's nuclear arsenal at that time. A

---

[10] On the scientists' lobby before Hiroshima, see Alice K. Smith, *A Peril and a Hope: The Scientists' Movement in America, 1945-1947* (Chicago, 1965), chapter one.

[11] Truman, *Year of Decisions*, p. 462.

[12] The pressures behind the decision to drop the bomb are discussed further in Barton Bernstein, ed., *The Atomic Bomb: The Critical Issues* (Boston, 1976).

third atomic bomb, then being assembled, would not have been ready until much later in August. Whether this third bomb would have been dropped upon Japan remains an unanswered — and probably unanswerable — question.[13] The decision concerning its use was made unnecessary by the Japanese surrender on August 14.

The role that the atomic bomb played in compelling Japanese surrender continues to be clouded by doubt more than thirty years after the end of the war. American intelligence reports of the time — based on secretly intercepted Japanese communications — suggest that the wartime leaders in Tokyo were finally pushed toward surrender more by Russian entry into the War on August 9 than by the effect of the atomic bomb. Stalin had promised to enter the Pacific war as soon as possible after Germany's surrender; at Potsdam the Soviet Premier predicted Russian intervention in early August. The peace faction of the Japanese government had been making clandestine efforts to negotiate a surrender as early as the summer of 1944, but was frustrated in its effort by the American demand that surrender be unconditional. It was only with the Russian declaration of war, which ended Japan's hope that the Soviet government might intercede to negotiate a conditional surrender, that a continuation of the War was seen to be futile even by the previous holdouts in Tokyo.[14] The possibility exists that the timetable for Russian intervention was accelerated somewhat by the news of Hiroshima. But the timing of the surrender decision, coming as it did after the Russian entry, compels speculation that the first bomb was probably a significant but not necessarily a decisive factor in ending the war; and that the second bomb was, in fact, unnecessary.[15]

[13]President Truman never publicly expressed doubts about the justification behind the first two bombs, but did reveal some qualms about the use of a third in remarks at the Cabinet meeting of August 10. Truman then had ordered that the atomic bombing of Japan be suspended because, he is quoted as saying, "the thought of wiping out another 100,000 people was too horrible." See John Blum, ed., *The Price of Vision: The Diary of Henry A. Wallace, 1942-1946* (Boston, 1973), p. 474.

[14]On the Japanese surrender, see R. J. C. Butow, *Japan's Decision to Surrender* (Stanford, 1954).

[15]On the use of the second bomb, see J. L. Marx, *Nagasaki: The Necessary Bomb?* (New York, 1971).

Atomic Diplomacy: A Threat at London

One of the early — and important — ironies of the postwar world was that the atomic bomb, whose military application against Japan seemed so successful, failed so dismally in its political application with regard to Russia. As has been seen, the atomic bombing of Japan did not bring an end to the war before Russia intervened and established a claim in Asia, as some Americans at Potsdam had hoped. Despite this initial disappointment, however, the hope and expectation remained in Washington that America's military advantage as represented by the bomb might also be translated into a political or diplomatic advantage in the postwar world.

The subsequent practice of "atomic diplomacy" after Hiroshima actually had two faces. One was the implicit threat of the bomb's use, which inevitably was at the back of every confrontation — however decorous — between the United States and Russia. And the other was the explicit *promise* of cooperation in the bomb's eventual control made to Russia by the United States as an inducement to cooperation in other spheres. There was to both forms of atomic diplomacy a certain element of risk and of urgency; for America's advantage in the bomb was already a wasting asset, destined to end once the Russians — at some unknown future date — developed their own atomic bomb. It was due both to this pressure and to the very real confusion surrounding United States policy on the bomb after Hiroshima that both faces of atomic diplomacy were turned to Russia as the Second World War ended and the Cold War began.

Among the first to suggest that the United States hold out to Russia the prospect of cooperation on the bomb was Secretary of War Stimson, the man who had briefed Truman on the Manhattan Project and who later brought the news of Alamogordo to Potsdam. Stimson's own thinking had undergone several changes by the time he met with the President in mid-September of 1945 to propose a direct approach to Russia on the bomb. Believing before Hiroshima that the United States should demand changes in the Soviet system as the price for collaboration on atomic energy, Stimson on this occasion urged that Truman consider cooperation without strings attached as a gesture that might help to defuse the increasing tension in Soviet-American affairs.[16]

In direct opposition to Stimson's advice was that of Truman's Secretary of State, James Byrnes. Byrnes had been the first to tell the President of America's secret weapon and openly looked upon the bomb as a potent political as well as military advantage. He had been among those at Potsdam who hoped that the bomb would make Russian participation in the Pacific war unnecessary, and he continued to believe after Hiroshima that the United States nuclear monopoly would compel Soviet concessions in diplomacy. Stimson correctly feared that Byrnes, in the peace settlement to be worked out with Russia after the war, would approach those meetings with the atomic bomb "in his hip pocket."[17]

The conflict between Stimson's cooperative approach and Byrnes' atomic diplomacy initially defined the question of what to do with Russia and the bomb for the Truman administration. By the autumn of 1945, Truman was under intense pressure to resolve that issue, having avoided it from Potsdam to Hiroshima. Public and congressional opinion, moreover, was overwhelmingly opposed to any cooperation with Russia that might compromise America's vital "atomic secret."[18] The depth of this concern about the security of the atomic secret — a concept based largely upon a popular misconception of nuclear technology — probably made serious consideration of Stimson's direct approach impossible in the Truman administration, although there is also no firm evidence to indicate that the President himself was ever favorably inclined toward Stimson's proposal. Having rejected Stimson's advice by late 1945, however, the President did not then turn to Byrnes and embrace his version of atomic diplomacy.

---

[16]Concerning Stimson's changing thought on the bomb, see H. L. Stimson and McGeorge Bundy, *On Active Service in Peace and War* (New York, 1947).

[17]On Byrnes' attitude, see "An Interview with James F. Byrnes," Bernstein, *The Atomic Bomb*, pp. 18-21.

[18]On public opinion concerning the bomb, see H. G. Erskine, "The Polls: Atomic Weapons and Nuclear Energy," *Public Opinion Quarterly* (Summer 1963), 172-173.

The first experiment in atomic diplomacy after Hiroshima produced some surprising — and, for Byrnes, disturbing — results. Meeting with his Soviet counterpart at a conference of foreign ministers in London during late September, Byrnes faced a problem similar to that of Truman at Potsdam. While careful to avoid direct reference to the bomb for fear that the Russians might demand a share in its control, Byrnes at the same time made no effort to reassure the Soviets that the bomb was not a threat. Like the mystery whose signal clue was the dog that did not bark in the night, the importance of the atomic bomb at London was its very unobtrusiveness.[19]

The Russians, however, had responded with their own form of atomic diplomacy in reverse. Even in casual conversations with Byrnes at London, Soviet Foreign Minister V. M. Molotov repeatedly brought up the topic that the Secretary of State had declared taboo — the atomic bomb.[20] Molotov's gambit, it appears, was to call Byrnes' bluff; to convince him that Russia was unmoved by America's monopoly of atomic bombs and that the bomb — as an obstacle to better relations with Russia — was actually more a liability than an asset in American diplomacy. The Soviet strategy worked on both counts. It was in London, therefore, that Byrnes learned the lesson he would later recount, namely, that the Russians were "stubborn, obstinate, and they don't scare." Byrnes would also blame the ultimate collapse of that conference upon the indirect influence of the atomic bomb. Thus, he saw in the insistent demand of Molotov for a Russian trusteeship in northern Africa a veiled attempt to get at America's source of uranium in the Belgian Congo. Most importantly, Byrnes now began to believe that, far from making the Soviets more compliant at the bargaining ta-

---

[19] Regarding the practice of atomic diplomacy at London and its unexpected result, see Gregg F. Herken, "Atomic Diplomacy Reversed and Revised," in Bernstein, *The Atomic Bomb*, pp. 135-142.

[20] This sometimes took on humorous, even absurd dimensions. An American intelligence report on one social gathering of foreign ministers records, for example, that a somewhat tipsy Molotov approached British Foreign Minister Ernest Bevin and Byrnes to confide, "You know we have the atomic bomb." Molotov, giggling, was then led away by a grim-faced Soviet security agent. Byrnes, however, apparently saw no humor in such incidents. See Gregg F. Herken, "American Diplomacy and the Atomic Bomb, 1945-1947" (unpublished doctoral dissertation, Princeton University, 1974), p. 121.

ble, the United States atomic monopoly seemed to be one source of their intransigence.[21]

Atomic Diplomacy: A Promise in Moscow

Brynes took the lesson he learned in London home with him to Washington. There Truman had already rejected Stimson's cooperative approach. Now the President learned from his Secretary of State how the bomb as an implied threat had backfired. Truman by this time was leaning toward a compromise solution to the problem of Russia and the bomb. In early October of 1945, he had declared that the United States and Great Britain, America's partner in atomic research, would consider themselves "trustees" of the new weapon until the international control of the bomb could be safely assured. Up to the actual attainment of international control, however, the United States would share with no other nation — not even Britain — the secrets of the bomb.

Though Truman's idea of an open-ended trusteeship was borrowed from both Stimson and Byrnes, it potentially represented a third alternative — a policy of exclusion. The prospect of cooperation remained only that, with no date given for when international control might be achieved. Privately, the President expressed doubts that it could be attained in less than a thousand years.[22] In the meantime, the declaration of a trusteeship meant that the United States would hold on to its monopoly of bombs, with the ever-present threat that implied. By the end of the autumn of 1945, the issue of American atomic policy seemed narrowed down to a choice between international control or a continuing monopoly. If not yet settled, progress at least had been made in resolving the issue of atomic policy. Or so it seemed. The atomic diplomacy practiced by Byrnes with such negative results at London was, in fact, not dead but merely transformed. It was not as a threat but as a promise that

---

[21]Bernstein, *The Atomic Bomb*, pp. 138-139.

[22]On Truman's doubts concerning international control, see Gregg F. Herken, "American Diplomacy and the Atomic Bomb, 1945-1947" (unpublished doctoral dissertation, Princeton University, 1974), p. 93.

the atomic bomb would next appear in Soviet-American relations.[23]

Believing, therefore, that tension over the bomb had been a significant cause of his previous problems with the Russians, Byrnes undertook his own initiative in November of 1945 to settle those problems, using cooperation on the bomb as an inducement. Byrnes' initiative took the form of a proposal to the Soviets to hold a foreign ministers conference dealing explicitly with the question of the future control of the atomic bomb. At this meeting the Secretary of State meant to offer the Russians an ambitious plan which would start with a confidence-building gesture, the exchange of basic information on atomic energy, but could culminate in joint Soviet-American control of the bomb itself. To Byrnes' delight, the Soviets not only accepted the proffered invitation, but, in a meeting at Moscow during December of 1945, also substantially agreed to his proposal.

Byrnes' dream of a renaissance in Soviet-American relations, with the atomic bomb and his own personal diplomacy as inspiration, was destined to be disappointed, nonetheless. It had always been, in reality, a private vision; not fully shared with either the President or the Congress. Learning, therefore, of what Byrnes had agreed to at Moscow only after his return to Washington, outraged members of Congress moved — with Truman's tacit approval — to repudiate the Moscow accords. In their action the President and the congressmen seemed motivated not so much by what Byrnes had accomplished at Moscow as by his methods, particularly his unwillingness to consult with them about the proposal put before the Russians.

Byrnes was ultimately successful in gaining approval from his critics for a much-amended version of the Moscow agreement, but it was at best a Pyrrhic victory. In the aftermath of that ill-fated agreement the whole notion of approaching Russia on the bomb was allowed to lapse; with the imminent shift of discussions on atomic energy to the highly visible arena of the United Nations, its time had passed. It is thus an irony of the atomic age that, after the initial posturings and delays, a direct approach to Russia on the bomb had finally been undertaken — and achieved initially encouraging results — only to be abandoned by the United States.

[23]*Ibid.*, pp. 153-183.

Did the practice of atomic diplomacy at London and the later debacle of Byrnes' abortive turn-about in Moscow add to the tension and mistrust of Soviet-American relations in the developing Cold War? Without access to Soviet records no final answer can be given that question. But the continuing, open-ended trusteeship of the atomic bomb in American hands provided a tangible sign of that mistrust, and a source of chronic contention. And, for as long as mistrust and contention would characterize American relations with Russia, it was the implied threat of the bomb and not the distant prospect of its eventual control that remained paramount.

International Control of Atomic Energy: The Baruch Plan

With the abandonment of the direct approach to Russia at the end of 1945, American atomic policy developed along two separate and diverging paths. One was the continuation of America's open-ended trusteeship of bombs, which excluded friend and foe alike from the weapon's secrets. The other was a declared policy of seeking the international control of atomic energy through the United Nations. One path would be that chosen by the Truman administration as the solution to the still-unresolved problem of what to do about the atomic bomb. In the matter of international control, the form as much as the content of American policy was vital. An offer of cooperation that appeared insincere — or disingenuous — would end the hopes of international control and guarantee a policy of monopoly by default. From this perspective, the appointment by Truman and Byrnes of Bernard Baruch to be America's representative at the United Nations talks on international control may have been fateful.[24]

A seventy-six-year-old financier and park-bench statesman, Baruch had a determining influence upon the American proposal for international control, which came to bear his name. One of his first acts upon assuming his post in the spring of 1946 was to transform fundamentally the draft proposal that had

---

[24]On Baruch at the United Nations, see Barton Bernstein, "The Quest for Security: American Foreign Policy and International Control of Atomic Energy, 1942, 1946," *Journal of American History*, 60 (March 1974), 1003-1044.

been prepared for him by the State Department. This change in wording was also representative of a change in thinking. The emphasis of the State Department document had been upon the possibilities for cooperative action in atomic energy's control; the Baruch Plan would stress at the outset the negative aspect of punishments for violation rather than rewards for compliance. Privately, Baruch and his associates hinted at a more cynical and dangerous motive behind the change: The requirement that Russia reveal her real uranium resources as a prior condition to serious negotiation might, for example, allow the United States to gauge when Russia would get the bomb. It would also open up Soviet society to Western inspection and, hence, to Western ideas.

Though there can be no serious question that Baruch *did* hope for the international control of atomic energy, there is equally little doubt that he intended for such an agreement to be on American terms. Baruch believed that the atomic bomb would remain, in his terms, America's "winning weapon" in either diplomacy or war should relations with Russia deteriorate. Consequently, his reply to critics of the plan, who argued that it was needlessly rigid and provocative, was also a succinct expression of his attitude toward the United Nations talks: "Anyway, we've got the bomb!"

With the negotiations stalemated by late 1946, and under increasing attack both from these domestic critics and from his international colleagues at the United Nations, Baruch decided to force the issue of international control to a final vote, hoping thus to put the onus for its failure upon the Russians. The subsequent ratification of the Baruch Plan in the United Nations by all but Russia and her allies was, however, a hollow victory for the United States; for the collapse of negotiations on international control foreclosed the last alternative to atomic trusteeship and the policy of exclusion. The irony of America's position would later be pointed out by pacifist A. J. Muste: While the West bemoaned the "iron curtain" that separated it from Russia and the Soviet bloc countries, the United States, as chief trustee of the bomb and its secrets, had raised an "atomic curtain" that now cut it off from the rest of the world.

Deterrence Without Diplomacy: The Military Dimension

There was always — from the start of the atomic age — the certainty that the secret of atomic energy's military application would spread. The important question in American minds was when the Russians might get the bomb. Here informed opinion on the answer to that question varied widely. The estimate of most scientists was that the monopoly could last no more than three to five years. Manhattan Project director Groves, however, was convinced that it would take the Russians from seven years to a generation to build a bomb. Significantly, it was Groves' longer estimate — founded upon the mistaken premise that the United States and Great Britain had a preclusive monopoly of the ores needed to build atomic bombs — that most of those involved in making atomic policy chose to believe. Ultimately, Byrnes, Baruch, and the President himself accepted the word of Groves, and not of the scientists.[25]

The expectation that America's atomic monopoly would be enduring was an important argument for those who urged that the United States keep the secret of the bomb, and renewed the hopes of some that the weapon might yet make a difference in America's dealing with Russia. The years before the Soviets got the bomb would be "our years of opportunity," Secretary of Defense James Forrestal wrote in late 1947.[26] Popular accounts of the time also viewed with sanguine enthusiasm the potential of the atomic bomb for changing the face of future wars. Early works on nuclear weapons and military strategy thus spoke of the bomb as an "absolute weapon," and of its putative role in a strategy of "determent" against possible aggression.[27]

In this, as in previous calculations on the bomb, however, there was substantial error and disappointment. Actual defense planning in America proved to be much more conservative in its assessment of the bomb's effect upon warfare — to the extent that American strategists essentially failed to take into account

---

[25]On the myth of the atomic secret and its effect, see Herken, "American Diplomacy and the Atomic Bomb," pp. 30-54.

[26]Concerning Forrestal and military thinking on the bomb, see Walter Millis, ed., *The Forrestal Diaries* (New York, 1951).

[27]Bernard Brodie, ed., *The Absolute Weapon* (New York, 1946).

America's nuclear hegemony during the first two years of the atomic monopoly. As late as the spring of 1948, therefore, the top-secret war plans of the Joint Chiefs of Staff envisioned the complete evacuation of American troops from Europe and Asia at the outset of a general Russian attack. And even the strategic air offensive — using atomic bombs — that would follow the American withdrawal was thought insufficient by the Joint Chiefs for winning a war with Russia without at least three more years of protracted, conventional fighting.[28]

This lag between theory and doctrine in American military planning was attributable to several causes, paramount among which were the conservatism of armed services' leadership, intensified inter-service rivalry after the war, and the practical limits imposed by the very small number of bombs in the atomic arsenal as late as 1948. But the effect of this lag was undisputedly to make the "opportunity" of which Forrestal had innocently written less than obvious. America's military weakness rather than her strength was the theme most common to those reports evaluating Russia's threat to the West.

Nor did America's atomic trusteeship make the Russians any more deferential than they had been at the Potsdam or London conferences. To judge by both word and deed the Soviets seemed unawed — even indifferent — to the threat represented by the atomic bomb. In early 1948 the Russian-backed coup in Czechoslovakia, in which a coalition government was replaced by a pro-Soviet one, graphically demonstrated the difficulty of translating atomic energy into a force useful in international power politics. The subsequent fear of war in the West following upon this Soviet initiative pointed up, as well, the failure of Baruch's "wining weapon" to guarantee even the rudiments of United States security — at least in the public's mind.

It was not until the later crisis over Berlin, in the summer of 1948, that the atomic bomb was finally and officially integrated into American military planning. Only with that crisis, therefore, does the bomb become for the first time an explicit threat aimed at the Soviet Union, as sixty long-range American bombers are dispatched to European bases within a striking distance of Russia. Significantly, even this threat was likely a

---

[28]On U.S. war planning, see G. H. Quester, *Nuclear Diplomacy* (New York, 1970).

hollow one. Due to a dispute over custody of the bomb, it is doubtful that the B29s sent to England at this time actually carried atomic weapons. Moreover, this *beau geste* for the defense of Berlin was ultimately compelled by the Truman administration's realization that it lacked any more suitable means of demonstrating American resolve in Europe. But the transfer of bombers overseas marked a turning point in the atomic age: the inauguration of the modern strategy of nuclear deterrence.[29]

To an extent that only an international crisis made clear — and more by necessity than design — the atomic bomb had become the bulwark of the security that America sought in the world by 1949. In the process those early assumptions about the diplomatic and military advantages to America's nuclear preeminence had been considerably modified, or abandoned altogether. It was not the fruits of victory but the consequences of defeat that concerned the Truman administration in its policy of containing Russia. And here the bomb played a role of primary importance as an instrument of last resort.

In the course of this increasing reliance upon the bomb there was a curious and concomitant tendency among policymakers to ignore the obvious fact that the monopoly could only be transitory. Indeed, the official mind of the Truman administration remained attached to the notion of an enduring trusteeship even when external evidence signaled that its end was approaching — and after public opinion had accepted the inevitability of its demise. Opinion surveys of 1948 thus revealed a majority view that the Russians already had, or would shortly have, atomic bombs. Yet that same year a magazine article by Groves predicted that, even with possession of Manhattan Project blueprints, the Soviets could not develop a bomb before 1955. Contemporary United States intelligence reports estimated, equally, that a Russian bomb was not likely before 1952-53. In fact, the popular — rather than the official — view was more nearly correct.[30]

---

[29]On the significance of the "bombs-from-Britain" strategy, see Walter Millis, *Arms and Men* (New York, 1956).

[30]Leslie Groves, "The Atom-General Answers His Critics," *Saturday Evening Post*, June 19, 1948.

The Monopoly Ends, the Race Begins

The paradox in the policy of escalating dependence upon a diminishing resource was brought to light with dramatic suddenness in September of 1949, when Russia's first atomic test was confirmed. The Soviet bomb arrived just four years after the bombing of Hiroshima; it had taken the Russians only six months longer than the wartime Manhattan Project to duplicate the feat for which Groves, eighteen months earlier, had deemed them "technologically and even psychologically unequipped."[31] The sudden end of America's nuclear hegemony was unquestionably a rude shock to many in Washington, though serious efforts were made to belittle its importance. One immediate effect of the news was to rekindle the earlier debate concerning what to do about Russia.

The circumstances of that debate were, of course, substantially altered by the fact that the Russians now had the bomb, but many elements were familiar. The "whole discussion made me feel I was seeing the same film, and a punk one, for the second time," one former advocate of international control observed of the renewed controversy over American atomic policy.[32]

Discussion of atomic policy within the Truman administration in late 1949 and early 1950 centered on two alternative courses of action in the wake of the Soviet test. One proposed alternative was to reassess the aim of achieving security through a reliance upon nuclear weapons and reopen negotiations on international control of the bomb in the hope that the Russians — now on a more nearly equal footing with the West — might respond favorably. The second approach urged a con-

---

[31] Groves would later pinpoint the error that he and others had made with regard to the Soviet bomb in the course of testimony given —'ironically — before the panel hearing charges against Manhattan Project scientist, J. R. Oppenheimer, a man whom Groves had hired but later accused of being a security risk. The real reason for the unexpected Soviet bomb, as Grove's testimony shows, points to miscalculation and not treason. The General had overlooked the uranium available to Russia in occupied Germany when he calculated that the West had a preclusive monopoly of atomic raw materials. See United States Atomic Energy Commission, *In the Matter of J. Robert Oppenheimer* (Washington, D.C., 1954), pp. 175-176.

[32] A well-informed account of this debate is David E. Lilienthal, *The Journals of David E. Lilienthal: The Atomic Energy Years, 1945-1950* (New York, 1964), pp. 580-582.

tinuation of the previous policy of deterrence through the attainment of nuclear superiority, if not hegemony, with creation of the "Superbomb" — the hydrogen bomb.

There were serious and persuasive arguments made on both sides of the issue. The idea of building the Superbomb — whose potential had been recognized at the outset of the Manhattan Project — was opposed on moral, political, and scientific grounds by some in the administration and by members of Truman's own board of experts on the subject, the Atomic Energy Commission's General Advisory Committee. The hydrogen bomb, one disgruntled scientist complained, represented the "cheap, easy way out," an attempted "return to a state of affairs approximating monopoly."[33] The arguments in favor of the Superbomb, however, had about them a sense of compelling urgency, and behind them a public opinion excited by reports of "atom spies" and Soviet designs of world domination.

The pressure of this domestic opinion, the fear of falling behind the Russians, and the action-reaction phenomenon familiar to observers of the contemporary Soviet-American arms competition all were behind President Truman's decision in January of 1950 to proceed with development of the hydrogen bomb.[34] The controversy behind that decision was neither as prolonged nor as acrimonious as that of the original debate on Russia and the atomic bomb, but that made the decision for the hydrogen bomb no less consequential. With the move to the Superbomb the policy of secrecy and exclusion which the trusteeship had represented was confirmed and continued as a feature of the now-intensified Cold War.

Conclusion: The Illusion of Security

The history of the atomic age thus far has been a microcosm of the modern Cold War. It is a story of reciprocal suspicion, enduring hostility, and — above all — missed opportunities. In-

---

[33]Concerning the background to the decision for the Superbomb, see R. G. Hewlett and F. Duncan, *Atomic Shield: A History of the United States Atomic Energy Commission, 1947/1952*, II (Univ. Park, Pa., 1969), pp. 369-409.

[34]On the scientific debate over the hydrogen bomb, see Herbert York, *The Advisors: Oppenheimer, Teller, and the Superbomb* (San Francisco, 1975).

deed, the way in which American policy on the bomb has proceeded from the start down a path of secrecy and exclusion makes it appear almost predetermined. Had Roosevelt proposed that all the allies — including Russia — work together on the atomic bomb project; had Stimson's direct approach been attempted at the outset; had Byrnes' initiative at Moscow received administration approval and support; had Truman decided to defer the Superbomb pending Russian response to a renewed effort at international control — the history of the atomic age, and of the Cold War, might have been different. At each of these times the reasons for rejecting the alternative of cooperation or negotiation seemed compelling. But the relatively recent evidence of Soviet-American collaboration has cast the common wisdom of earlier days in doubt.

Certainly we know now — if we did not know then — that much of this supposed "wisdom" was based upon illusion: the illusion that the atomic bomb might be a decisive factor in postwar diplomacy, the illusion that America would have a monopoly of bombs for up to a generation, and the illusion that bigger and better bombs meant an increase in our security.

The notion of an enduring monopoly was perhaps the greatest illusion, and a danger that columnist Walter Lippmann had warned against only weeks after the bombing of Hiroshima. "If the [atomic] secret cannot be kept, it is unnecessary to argue whether it ought to be kept," Lippmann wrote at that time. Rather, he concluded, it would be "in the highest degree dangerous to suppose we were keeping the secret if in fact we were not"; for "that could only give us, as it has already given many, a false sense of security and a false sense of our own power."[35] Policy-makers were not alone in sharing this false sense of security. Public opinion pollsters also testified to the extent and consequence of popular faith in American nuclear hegemony. "Many people," one such analyst noted, "even after they had said ... that other countries would find out how to make atomic bombs before long, continued to discuss other questions about the bomb wholly within the framework of our monopoly."[36]

---

[35]*New York Herald Tribune*, October 2, 1945.

[36]Erskine, "The Polls," *Public Opinion Quarterly* (Summer 1963), p. 173.

AN UNFINISHED HISTORY OF THE ATOMIC AGE

Even as security itself became elusive with the end of the monopoly in 1949, the illusion of security remained with development of the Superbomb. That illusion too would be short-lived. Less than a year after the first test of a thermonuclear device by the United States in November 1952, the Russians tested their own Superbomb.[37] The Soviet hydrogen bomb gave added impetus to the Soviet-American nuclear arms race, which has continued at the same fierce level of unrestricted competition until very recently. The effect of that rivalry in the subsequent militarization of the Cold War and through increasing tension between the United States and Russia is a point already made. Receiving less attention here and from historians generally, though, has been the role of the atomic bomb — and the end of illusions concerning it — in creating a legacy of failed expectations and anxiety on the domestic side of the Cold War, at home in the United States.

It is in the context of the fear and disappointment in America surrounding the unexpected Soviet test in 1949, therefore, that the trial and execution of the Rosenbergs for what FBI director J. Edgar Hoover termed the "crime of the century" — the theft of the atomic secret — must be understood. Similarly, the domestic furor from 1950 to 1954 over other supposed "atom spies," culminating in the notorious investigations of the House Un-American Activities Committee and of Senator Joseph McCarthy, had its roots in the painful end of illusion concerning the bomb.

This history of the atomic age is thus necessarily unfinished. From the perspective of the present there would seem to be reason both for hope and for despair. A cause of concern, if not despair, must be the current proliferation of atomic weapons and nuclear technology throughout the world, often in contravention of international agreements. Even more disturbing in the short run is the tendency in both the Pentagon and the Kremlin today to consider that new tactics and advancements in weaponry have made nuclear warfare more acceptable than in

---

[37]A recent book based upon weekly declassified information suggests that America's hydrogen bomb project may even have indirectly helped the Soviets to develop their own Superbomb, in that the Russians could have learned one vital secret of fusion's military application through air-sampling of the first American thermonuclear test. Neither side, however, would have a deliverable hydrogen *bomb* until at least 1954. See Herbert York, *The Advisors: Oppenheimer, Teller, and the Superbomb* (San Francisco, 1975).

the past. Since the destruction of Hiroshima there has been a tacit but worldwide recognition that nuclear weapons are special and that their use represents the crossing of an important threshold. Thus far this threshold itself has seemingly acted as a deterrent, for the bomb has not been employed as a weapon of war since its first use against Japan. The trend in recent military writings and the spread of nuclear weapons to the Third World are perhaps early but disturbing indications that this threshold may now be breaking down.

It would be a mistake, however, to be fatalistic about the future. The progress of recent years toward controlling the arms race — particularly the 1974 Strategic Arms Limitation Talks (SALT) agreement — is surely a cause of hope. The SALT negotiations represent an event that has never before occurred in the atomic age: serious talks between the United States and Russia on reducing the tensions created by competition in arms and on steadying — though not removing — the balance of terror.

The SALT talks, to be sure, hardly presage the kind of multilateral disarmament that would be required for a post-nuclear international order, signifying the end of both the atomic age and of the Cold War. It may be that stabilizing the balance of terror is all that we will achieve in the atomic age — and all we will need to achieve. The increase in the number of nuclear powers and qualitative improvements in nuclear weaponry have not, therefore, changed in any substantive way the lesson that Stimson hoped we would learn from Hiroshima. One of the first to appreciate the ethical questions posed by the advent of the atomic bomb, Stimson wrote in 1947:

> War in the twentieth century has grown steadily more barbarous, more destructive, more debased in all its aspects. Now, with the release of atomic energy, man's ability to destroy himself is very nearly complete. The bombs dropped on Hiroshima and Nagasaki ended a war. They also made it wholly clear that we must never have another war. This is the lesson men and leaders everywhere must learn, and I believe that when they learn it they will find a way to lasting peace. There is no other choice.[38]

---

[38] Henry L. Stimson, "The Decision to Use the Atomic Bomb," *Harper's Magazine*, February 1947, p. 17.

II

The United States–Soviet Union Arms Competition

ADRIAN S. FISHER

This chapter examines the arms competition (or arms race as it is often described) between the United States and the Soviet Union. As the title indicates, it is primarily directed to the competition between America and Russia, although other countries cannot be overlooked. The primary impact of attempts to limit the competition between the two countries has thus far been in measures such as the Treaty on the Non-Proliferation of Nuclear Weapons. This chapter also briefly discusses nuclear weapons and associated delivery systems, although the impact of actual and perceived gaps in the comparative strengths of the two countries' arsenal of conventional armaments is not ignored.

The nuclear arms competition between the United States and the Soviet Union began with the development by the United States of the atomic bomb during World War II, its suc-

---

Adrian S. Fisher is the Francis Cabell Brown Professor of International Law at the Georgetown University Law Center. From 1969 to 1975, he was dean of the Law Center. He is a graduate of Princeton University and the Harvard Law School and has a Doctor of Laws (honoris causa) from Princeton. From 1961 to 1969, he was the Deputy Director of the Arms Control and Disarmament Agency. In that connection, he accompanied Ambassador W. Averell Harriman to Moscow for the final negotiation of the limited nuclear test ban and from time to time has served as the United States negotiator at the eighteen-nation disarmament conference in Geneva. He was serving in this capacity when the United States and the Soviet Union agreed to the text of a non-proliferation treaty.

In his prior government service, he worked as the legal advisor, Department of State; attorney to various government agencies; and law clerk to Justices Brandeis and Frankfurter. From 1954 to 1960, he was vice president and counsel of the Washington Post Company.

cessful test in the spring of 1945, and its use in combat over Hiroshima and Nagasaki in August 1945. (The use of the term "atomic bomb" is a misnomer. The tremendous force of the bomb is not the result of an atomic or chemical reaction. It is caused, rather, by the fission or splitting of subatomic particles.)

During and following the course of the development of the nuclear fission bomb, the United States government initiated intensive studies into the policy implications of its development. There were several such implications, some pointing in quite different directions. First, here was a weapon of such a large explosive power that it might change the face of war. The first bomb dropped on Hiroshima by one aircraft was reported to have the explosive power of 17,000 tons of conventional high explosives. This was an increase of about 2000 in the explosive power carried by a bomber. Second, the United States, for the time at least, was the only country to have this weapon. Third, the experience with the process of nuclear fission showed the possibility of an energy source which was believed to be of great value to a world running short of energy resources. Fourth, and herein lay the cruelist paradox of all, a country which developed the process of nuclear fission for peaceful purposes could, without too much extra effort in either materials or techniques, go on to develop a nuclear bomb. This last point carried with it the painful dilemma of deciding between attempting to deny energy-hungry states access to this new source of energy or facing the prospect of a vast proliferation of nuclear weapons in the hands of many countries, large or small, responsible or irresponsible.

American reactions to these policy considerations were presented in the Acheson-Lilienthal report which recommended the abolition of all national nuclear programs with reliance instead on an international agency which would develop the peaceful uses of nuclear energy for all nations and insure that nuclear programs were not used to make bombs. The program recommended in the Acheson-Lilienthal report was wise and far-sighted, but it was far ahead of its time. By the time the report was translated into a program for presentation at the United Nations (the Baruch Plan, so designated in the name of the man who presented it), it quickly became a victim of the competitions and tensions between America and the Soviet Union. It would be too facile to blame this on what was then known as the "cold war." It is doubtful if such an ambitious program could be put into effect even under the present relaxation of tensions. What the United States perceived as a generous offer to put its own nuclear program (the most advanced in the world and the only one that had produced a bomb) under international control, the Soviet Union perceived as an attempt to prevent it from developing its own nuclear program and weapons. What the United States perceived as an essential requirement for the proposed International Atomic Development Authority to operate free of national control, the Soviets considered to be reneging on the arrangements for the veto to which they had both agreed while working out the charter of the United Nations. There were other difficulties, but it is enough to say that the Baruch Plan got nowhere.

From the first successful nuclear weapons test in the spring of 1945 until September 1949, the United States operated on the assumption that it had a monopoly on nuclear weapons. It was generally recognized that this monopoly wouldn't last forever, but for the present there was comfort in the monopoly and this comfort underlay a variety of policy positions in the United States government. It led various people various ways. It led some sincere supporters of the Acheson-Lilienthal report to believe that this disparity might lead the Soviet Union to accept the generous offer which the report contained. It led others to suggest, and in some cases implement, recommendations to reduce our conventional armed forces capability. It led still others to recommend an extremely hard line in such dangerous manifestations of American-Soviet confrontation as the Berlin blockade. Throughout all these diverse approaches there was a common assumption, oversimplified in some contemporary doggerel: "If things go bad, no matter what, we have nuclear bombs and they have not."

In September 1949, this comforting assumption came to an end, substantially before the time that most believed it would. On September 23, President Truman announced that there had recently been a nuclear explosion in the Soviet Union. As would be expected, the reactions to the sudden departure of this comforting assumption of nuclear hegemony were as varied as those that had been based on it. Those who supported the policies of the Acheson-Lilienthal report recognized that the Soviets, with a full-fledged nuclear weapons program of their own, were not about to agree to put it under an international program. Many argued, successfully, that the United States should reverse the program of dismembering its conventional armed forces which had been supported by its advocates on the basis of a nuclear monopoly which no longer existed. The bitterest arguments were over whether the United States should take steps to maintain its superiority in nuclear weapons over Russia. In the nuclear scientific community this turned into an argument over whether we should press toward the development of a hydrogen bomb. (The term "hydrogen bomb" is somewhat less of a misnomer than the term "atomic bomb" because isotopes of the hydrogen atom are involved in it. Its accurate description would be a nuclear fusion bomb because in it small nuclei are induced to fuse into larger nuclei. It is also called the thermonuclear bomb because of extremely high thermal temperatures required to set off the fusion.) As the hydrogen bomb was developed, it was found that it bears almost the same geometric relationship to the nuclear fission bomb as the latter does to conventional explosives: it is another thousand times stronger. In World War II explosive loads of bombers were measured in tons of high explosives. With the advent of nuclear fission bombs, bomber loads were measured in kilotons, that is, the equivalent of thousands of tons of high explosives. With the development of nuclear fusion bombs, they were measured in megatons, that is, the equivalent of millions of tons of high explosives. The technology of nuclear fusion is such that only a country with a highly developed fission program can engage in it. The paradox of fission is only extended, not compounded: as yet, no economically useful, peaceful purpose has been discovered for nuclear fusion.

The debate on the fusion bomb was bitter. Many opposed it because they considered it an extension of the arms race with the Soviets. Some supported it for the same reason. Most supported it because they were persuaded that the Soviets were embarked on a similar program and they were concerned about our position to negotiate with the Soviets if we were suddenly to discover ourselves in a position of gross inferiority. This latter group had the most influence in advising President Truman, and on January 31, 1950, he announced a decision to work on such a weapon. The assumption of this latter group turned out to be correct. The United States and the Soviet Union both in 1957 of the International Atomic Energy Agency (IAEA), an international agency separate from the United Nations, and which operates without a veto. The IAEA was given authority to give assistance in the peaceful uses of nuclear energy, an authority substantially limited by the fact that it could do so only to the extent that its participating members made resources and technology available. It was also given authority to safeguard any assistance given by it to assure that the assistance was not converted to use in weapons. It was given similar authority to safeguard similar assistance between individual countries, if the agreement for assistance so provided. This forward step was soon followed by disappointment, because very little support was given to the IAEA by the United States or any other country. Time was to prove, however, that its creation was a step of seminal importance.

The second development was the beginning of negotiations to halt all testing of nuclear weapons. While part of the impetus for these negotiations was based on widespread public concern over fallout of nuclear debris, the effect of such a treaty in slowing down the quality race in nuclear weapons and in deterring the acquisition of nuclear weapons by other countries was seen by many as a more significant reason for the treaty. The negotiations got off to a good start. The United States, the Soviet Union, and the United Kingdom, which had by that time detonated its own nuclear device, began regular meetings in Geneva. In order to set the right tone for these negotiations, the parties indicated they would impose a moratorium of one year on all nuclear testing, a moratorium that was later extended, with the right of each country to revoke it subject to prior notice.

The talks shortly ran into trouble, because they brought into sharp focus the issue of verification of arms control agreements. The United States had always insisted that it could enter into no arms control agreement unless it had the means of verifying that parties to the agreement were in compliance. The Soviets did not disagree in principal, although they had a strong tendency to downgrade the issue. The question that arose was how this could be accomplished. Originally this did not seem to be an important issue, because American scientists had issued a report that underground nuclear tests could be detected by seismological instruments, the same type of instrument that

THE UNITED STATES–SOVIET UNION ARMS COMPETITION

detonated nuclear fusion bombs in the early 1950s.

There was one unhappy result of this controversy. Dr. J. Robert Oppenheimer, the chairman of the general advisory committee of the Atomic Energy Commission, was subsequently denied a security clearance because he had opposed the development of the nuclear fusion bomb. Even those who disagreed with Dr. Oppenheimer's scientific evaluation or, in particular, with his amalgam of science and international politics, should feel a sense of shock and outrage at this use of the security process to prevent freedom of expression and to destroy a great scientist.

The final demise of the Baruch Plan came at a time when many influential figures in the United States government were already having serious doubts about it. The plan, they had been saying for some time, only dealt with nuclear weapons, where the United States was ahead, and did not touch the problem of conventional forces, where the Soviets had an immense advantage over us. When the shock of the Soviet nuclear detonation wore off, and particularly after the decision to go ahead with the development of the fusion bomb made it unlikely that the United States would be inferior, at least in terms of nuclear weapons capabilities, this point of view received increasing support. As a result, when the Sixth Session of the General Assembly of the United Nations met in Paris in the fall of 1951, the United States made a proposal that reduction of conventional forces and nuclear forces should be negotiated in the same forum.

This proposal, which involved general disarmament, has been under negotiation ever since — in one form or another — and with occasional dramatic interruptions. It has been under negotiation in various places (the United Nations specially held conferences in London and Geneva); it has even had spin-offs which have resulted in substantial agreements. But the basic problem of across-the-board reduction of all armed forces, conventional as well as nuclear, has not as yet been solved.

The period between 1952 and 1960, outside of a widely publicized break between the Secretary of State and the chief disarmament negotiator, was marked by four significant developments, some favorable, some not.

The first was the proposal made by President Eisenhower of an "Atoms for Peace" program. This led to the establishment

THE UNITED STATES–SOVIET UNION ARMS COMPETITION

identifies earthquakes, and that tests in other environments could be identified either acoustically, by picking up the fallout which resulted, or by similar means. Shortly after the talks had begun, American scientists indicated that seismological instruments could not distinguish an underground test from the numerous earthquakes that took place in various areas of the Soviet Union and that the only way in which underground nuclear tests could be detected and identified was through on-site inspection of designated areas which seismological readings indicated were suspicious. To this the Soviets gave a flat no and the talks were stalled.

The third development was the breakdown of the talks on comprehensive disarmament then going on in Geneva in a forum consisting of five members of NATO and five members of the Warsaw Pact. The breakdown was caused by the walkout of the Soviet representative followed by his Warsaw Pact colleagues. It came after the U-2 incident and was probably a part of the changing relations which followed that incident, including cancellation of the Paris summit meeting. The Soviets were insisting on a program of general and complete disarmament over a period of three years and accused the Americans of stalling and seeking espionage capabilities under the guise of verification. Interestingly enough, the Soviets did not walk out of the test ban talks, then going on simultaneously in Geneva but with different negotiators.

The fourth development was the orbit of Sputnik. The Soviet Union was the first to get into space. It did not take much imagination to see that a nation with a capability of putting an object into orbit had a capability of intercontinental rocket delivery. This resulted in a shock quite similar to the one the United States went through after the first Soviet nuclear test. We were in danger of being behind, something we could not tolerate. The result was the "missile gap," which reverberated down through the 1960 Presidential campaign, and whose consequences still affect the arms competition between America and Russia.

The first twenty months following the inauguration of President Kennedy on January 20, 1961, were a mixed bag as far as the American-Soviet arms competition was concerned. A confrontation took place between President Kennedy and Chairman Khrushchev in Vienna in the summer of 1961 which was vigorous to the point of being brutal. This was followed by the construction of the Berlin Wall, and the termination of the moratorium on nuclear testing by the Soviet Union through the institution of a massive series of nuclear tests, including one in the thirty megaton range which some scientists predicted could easily be extended to a 100 megaton bomb. On the other hand, the talks on banning nuclear tests did continue, although to no particular avail, and the United States and the Soviet Union were able to agree to formulae under which the general disarmament talks could continue. This they did in March 1962; the conference by this time included eighteen countries. The test ban talks were duly incorporated in this conference.

The turning point in the arms competition came as the result of the Cuban missile crisis. A great deal of contemporary, and now some revisionist, history has been written about this crisis, and there is debate between these two schools as to whether this turning point was for the good or for the bad. But that it was a turning point should not be denied.

In his final letter to Khrushchev, President Kennedy made the following statement: "Perhaps now, as we step back from danger, we can together make real progress in this vital field [disarmament]. I think we should give priority to questions relating to the proliferation of nuclear weapons, on earth and in outer space, and to the great effort for a nuclear test ban."

This invitation for serious talks to limit the arms competition was not unanswered. On December 19, 1962, Chairman Khrushchev wrote President Kennedy suggesting that the two countries reconsider the problem of a nuclear test ban. Khrushchev indicated his view that the American insistence on on-site inspections was solely for the purpose of placating members of the United States Senate; he also said that he was prepared to consider two or three on-site inspections per year, but strongly implied that they would be purely symbolic. This response, however, was sufficiently encouraging to lead to an intensive round of renewed negotiations at higher levels on both sides. This round failed because of American determination to find out what the inspections involved before agreeing to a number, and the Soviet determination to agree on a number of inspections while the nature of those inspections, real or symbolic, be left vague.

The breakup of the negotiations left many believers in the

limitation of the arms race disconsolate. However, another chance for a second but significant choice soon presented itself. Primarily as a result of British intervention, reports came in that the Soviet Union might be receptive to a treaty limiting nuclear tests in environments where on-site inspection was neither necessary nor feasible, that is, tests in the atmosphere, outer space, under water, or even underground if fallout went outside of the territory of the country. President Kennedy made a public offer to this effect in a speech at American University on June 10, 1963. Chairman Khrushchev made a grudging acknowledgment in a speech in East Berlin on July 3; a delegation headed by Averell Harriman went to Moscow in mid-July, and a treaty was agreed to by the end of that month.

The signing of the treaty was a cause for some rejoicing, but with definite limitations. The rejoicing was due to the fact that the United States and the Soviet Union had finally made the first step in reducing their arms competition by agreeing not to conduct a type of atomic weapons test that they would otherwise have conducted. The limitations were due to the fact that the treaty permitted underground tests providing they did not vent to a degree in which the radioactive debris was detectable outside of the country conducting the test. This led to the prediction by many that the number of underground tests would be substantially increased (they were) and to the prediction that it might be more difficult to get a nuclear test ban covering all tests.

Following the negotiation of the Limited Test Ban Treaty, efforts to reduce the arms competition between America and Russia went into a fallow phase. Elaborate discussions continued on the competitive plans before the conference for general and complete disarmament, with particular reference to the percentage of reductions of various types of armaments, including nuclear delivery systems, during the first stage of such a plan. While these spirited debates concerning reductions were going on, both sides were rapidly increasing their nuclear warheads and the means of delivering them. In January 1964, President Johnson in a message to the conference at Geneva suggested a "verified freeze of the number and characteristics of ... strategic nuclear offensive and defensive vehicles" while negotiations went on for their reduction in a broader context. A United States representative at the Geneva negotiations pointed out in April 1964 that his country had recently announced that it had 750 operational intercontinental ballistic missiles, a number which had doubled since the current phase of the Geneva disarmament conference had begun. He pointed out that further increases were planned by the United States, assumed that the Soviet Union was planning similar increases, and argued that it might be wise to stop the increases and to allow the debate to continue as to how deep the decreases should be.

The impact of the freeze, however, was upon the production, not the deployment, of nuclear delivery systems and the United States insisted that it be verified. This would involve inspection of production facilities and here the old problem of on-site inspection again proved insuperable. It is probably the case that the time was not ripe for these negotiations for two reasons.

In the first place, the Soviets were preoccupied with the Federal Republic of Germany and concerned that the Republic might somehow either develop nuclear weapons or work out an arrangement with the United States under which the Republic could start a nuclear war between America and Russia. Every Soviet representative would say this in almost identical words. In this oft-repeated position there was constant reference to World War II casualties. It might have been easy to dismiss this as a propaganda gimmick except for the fact that there had been twenty million dead as a result of the German invasion of Russia in 1941 and the resultant fighting, and it was not hard to understand the Soviet feelings on this subject.

These feelings were exacerbated somewhat by the fact that the United States was then actively pursuing negotiations for a Multilateral Nuclear Force (MLF) composed of key countries in NATO, including Germany, which might — in some way that was not defined — have access to nuclear weapons. At this stage, from 1964 well into 1966, the United States was actively pursuing the negotiation of a Treaty on the Non-Proliferation of Nuclear Weapons at the Geneva disarmament conference. America wanted such a treaty every bit as much as did Russia, albeit for slightly different reasons. The United States believed that its objectives of non-proliferation of nuclear weapons could better be obtained by a cooperative effort with the Soviets than by unilateral American pressure. But for the Soviet Union the subject of the non-proliferation treaty was Germany. So, as long as the negotiations were going on for a MLF in which Germany might play a dominant role, the non-proliferation discussions might be an interesting exercise in forensics and semantics, but they would not amount to a real negotiation.

By late summer and early fall a combination of pressures from the Congress of the United States and changes in European attitudes resulted in the dropping of the MLF. After that, progress toward the substantive articles of a Treaty on the Non-Proliferation of Nuclear Weapons proceeded expeditiously. Only one problem remained to be solved—verification, which had dogged all disarmament negotiations so far and which had only been avoided in the test ban by limiting its scope so that no international verification machinery was required. This is where the creation of the IAEA a decade earlier — although a disappointment at the time — proved to be of critical importance. An international control organization had already been created and was functioning, albeit at something less than half speed. It was not too difficult to provide in the treaty that this organization should be used to verify that peaceful nuclear activities of parties to the treaty should not be diverted to making nuclear explosive devices. One delay in establishing a safeguards system was caused by finding an acceptable formulation for the role of regional nuclear organizations — in particular EURATOM, the atomic arm of the European Economic Community — in the safeguards process. An acceptable formulation was worked out, however, and the treaty was signed on July 1, 1968. It has not worked perfectly as at least one country — India — has developed nuclear weapons since it went into effect, but the situation is undoubtedly better than it would have been had the treaty not been implemented.

With the coming into effect of the non-proliferation treaty, one of the obstacles to negotiations on the freeze (soon to be called by another name) disappeared. The other two had either already disappeared or were in the process of disappearing. The first difficulty which had caused the most discussion at Geneva — on-site inspection of production facilities on nuclear delivery systems — was no longer as great a problem. In a series of high-level exchanges in the early winter of 1967, the emphasis had been changed from a freeze on production of strategic nuclear delivery systems to a limitation on further deployment.

Also the United States had indicated its willingness to accept verification *by national means* of any agreement which might be reached. This rather cryptic term was never spelled out, but any reader of *The New York Times* (and presumably of *Pravda*) would conclude that it included satellite observation by both parties of the territory of the other.

All signs indicate that a substantial number of Soviet decision-makers felt that they were behind in the field of nuclear delivery systems. But by July 1968, they apparently felt that this situation no longer existed, and they were prepared to begin Strategic Arms Limitation Talks (SALT).

At this stage it is necessary to make a diversion by way of explanation. There is no agreed quantitative indicator by which the deceptively simple terms "ahead" or "behind" may be measured. There are a variety of competing formulations. The first is the total number of strategic delivery systems. Critics of this basis of comparison will raise questions of size: How big a nuclear weapon can it deliver? (The current jargon for this is "throw weight.") The rejoinder will be that the weapon may be *too* big (overkill) and that size (throw weight) is not even relevant unless it is related to the accuracy of the delivery system. Then will follow the assertion that what is relevant is the number of deliverable warheads and that great consideration should be given to the number of multiple, independently targetable warheads (MIRVs) to be delivered by a single missile.

The arguments concerning the validity of these various bases of camparison have gone on indefinitely and will probably continue in apparent disregard of the lack of relevance of the issue when each side has more than enough power to destroy the other. The important thing is that on July 1, 1968, the Soviet Union felt that it was no longer in a position of inferiority and was prepared to start talking.

The discussions began on November 17, 1969, and resulted in two agreements which became effective on October 3, 1972. The first was a Treaty on the Limitation of Anti-Ballistic Missile (ABM) Systems which provided, in effect, that each party was limited to two ABM systems, one of which should be around its national capital. This treaty was amended on July 3, 1974, to reduce the number of ABM systems to one each. To date the United States has deployed no ABM systems and has no plans to do so. The Soviet Union still has an ABM system deployed around Moscow.

The second agreement, an interim agreement, had to do with the limitation of strategic arms and had a duration of five years. Here the parties agreed essentially to freeze at existing levels the number of strategic ballistic missile launchers on each side and to permit an increase in submarine ballistic missile launchers up to mutually acceptable level. Within certain limitations, modernization and replacement are permitted.

A realistic appraisal of the way in which these two agreements have operated can be obtained by studying the analysis of American and Russian strategic force levels in mid-1975 which Secretary of Defense James Schlesinger presented to Congress:

	USA	USSR
OFFENSIVE		
ICBM Launchers[1]	1,054	1,590
SLBM Launchers[2]	656	700
Intercontinental Bombers[3]	498	160
Force Loading Weapons	8,500	2,800
DEFENSIVE		
Air Defense		
Surveillance Radars	67	4,000
Interceptors[4]	405	2,500
SAM Launchers		10,000
ABM Defense		
Launchers		64

1. Excludes launchers at test sites.
2. Excludes launchers on diesel-powered submarines.
3. Excludes bombers configured as tankers and reconnaissance aircraft.
4. These numbers represent Total Active Inventory.

The size of these figures certainly justifies the concern expressed by the American representatives in 1964 that the two countries should immediately start to prevent further increases. Yet these agreements are not without substantial benefits. The result of the ABM treaty is effectively to remove the ABM concept from the strategic equation. The fear of decision-makers, Soviet and American, that massive ABM deployments protecting ICBM missile sites were a possible precursor to a first strike, with the held-back protected missiles available to counteract a retaliatory strike of the enemy, was removed. Such a positive step takes us quite a long way toward accepting the concept of the stable deterrent. The restriction of offensive delivery systems to a certain rough equality (sufficiency for both being perhaps a more felicitous term) even at very high levels is also a positive step.

There are at least two deficiencies. The interim agreement does not deal with the quality race in a way which prevents the development of destabilizing first strike weapons. And it expires on October 3, 1977.

A framework for the negotiation of a subsequent agreement was announced on November 24, 1974, at the Vladivostok meeting between President Ford and General Secretary Brezhnev. This accord indicated that an agreement should provide for a ceiling on each side of 2400 strategic delivery vehicles (ICBMs and bombers) with freedom to change the mix. The accord also provided that there could be 1320 of the missiles carrying MIRVs, although it placed no limit on the number of MIRVs those missiles could carry. The accord also provided that these ceilings will remain frozen for ten years, although negotiations to reduce them could begin sooner.

The Vladivostok accords have received a mixed reaction. Many feel that if the high quantitative ceilings set by the accords merely become floors from which to launch a qualitative arms race and if the agreement, in effect, becomes a "hunting license" to assure approval of more costly and unneeded arms, its harm will exceed its value. Others feel that the accord does represent a step forward in that both sides have indicated agreement on ceilings, albeit high ones. They hope that, if properly used, the accords might be a starting point for a turnabout in the arms race, providing the basis for eliminating uncertainties about intentions, for reducing spending on arms, and for systematically reducing the levels of strategic nuclear forces on both sides.

To date, however, no formal international agreement has been made to carry out the provisions of the Vladivostok accords. The reason has apparently been a dispute over whether the ceilings proposed by these accords should include two weapons systems, the Backfire bomber under development by the Soviet Union and the cruise missiles under development by the United States. The Backfire bomber is a high-performance airplane which, even without refueling by air tanker, could reach the United States although it could not return to Russia. In this regard it should be noted that the Backfire, of which so far only a small number exist, has a role not dissimilar to many American and NATO aircraft in Europe which can reach Russia on one-way missions.

The cruise missile is a subsonic aerodynamic vehicle which travels at low altitudes (making detection difficult) and which, due to highly developed guidance systems, has an accuracy greater than current ICBMs. It is designed in two modes, one to be launched by an aircraft and the other through the torpedo tubes of an attack submarine. Published data estimates its range as being between 1200 and 2000 nautical miles. Many supporters of arms control have opposed the development of these missiles on the ground that they may present insuperable difficulties in verification.

One of the issues which has been holding up the conversion of the Vladivostok accords into a formal international agreement has been disagreement as to whether these two delivery systems count against the proposed number of 2400 strategic nuclear delivery systems. The United States takes the position that the Backfire should count against the Soviet number, but the cruise missile should not count against ours. The Soviets take exactly the opposite position. There the matter rests. The negotiations have been dormant since early 1976, some suggest because of the political situation in the United States.

Another matter still pending is the Threshold Nuclear Test Ban Treaty and its companion, the recently renegotiated Treaty on Underground Nuclear Explosions for Peaceful Purposes. The first of these two treaties bans underground nuclear tests with a yield of over 100 kilotons. The second, as renegotiated, prohibits any individual underground peaceful nuclear explosion greater than 150 kilotons and any group of individual explosions with a total yield exceeding 1500 kilotons (1.5 megatons). Neither of these signed treaties has been ratified by the Senate and therefore neither has come into effect.

These agreements have come under severe criticism. The principal basis of criticism of the first treaty is that it appears to be an abrogation of the position of the United States that we are prepared to ban all nuclear tests that we can verify. Almost all agree that the limit of 150 kilotons is well above the limits of verification by seismic means, and probably a majority of those who have followed the subject would also agree that our detection and identification capabilities by seismic means have developed to a point where we can accept a ban on all nuclear tests. Gains to American security through a cessation of the quality race in nuclear weapons would greatly outweigh the dangers from the possibility of evasion by the Soviet Union through small clandestine tests.

The second treaty has also been criticized because it puts a seal of approval on peaceful nuclear explosions even though it is admitted that nuclear explosives intended for peaceful applications and explosives for weapons applications are indistinguishable.

At the end of 1976 the state of the nuclear arms competition was at a sufficiently high level to place an increased emphasis on the stability of weapons systems. Probably the best way to define a stabilizing weapons system is to define what it is not, that is, by defining a destabilizing weapons system. A destabilizing system is one which is much more effective if used in a first strike than if used in retaliation. The development of MIRVs was destabilizing. Assume three MIRVs to a land-based missile (a modest assumption); in this case the country that launched a first strike might take out three opposing missiles and nine warheads with one strike. The logic of this is obvious to both sides and the destabilizing factor might tilt the scales in time of extreme tension. One would hope that decision-makers would not engage in any such cataclysmic act, but the stakes are so high that it is unwise to introduce any factor that tilts in that direction.

Sometimes a system is destabilizing because of technological uncertainties that surround it. This was behind the basic opposition to the ABM. If a full-fledged ABM were installed, the side installing it could not safely assume that it would really work and would have to take other measures to assure a retaliatory capability. The other side, however, could only assume that it would work very well and would have to build up its missile capability in order to break through it.

A good example of a stable missile system is the nuclear submarine-launched missile. Under present technology they are practically invulnerable and are designed to be most effective in a retaliatory second strike. Strategic planning has to be on the basis that it is there. That the other side knows it is there, one would hope, prevents it from ever being used.

The freedom to change the mix is one of the best factors of the Vladivostok accords and in the minds of some more than makes up for the high levels contained in those accords. Prompt negotiation along the lines contemplated by these accords is called for. This should be accompanied by a renewed effort to obtain a comprehensive test ban. If these two efforts are undertaken, an attempt should be made to obtain wider adherence to the Treaty on the Non-Proliferation of Nuclear Weapons. The chances of success in this latter effort would then be greatly increased.

III

The Proliferation of Nuclear Reactors and Weapons

HERBERT SCOVILLE, JR.

Historical Perspective

In 1945, flushed with the success of having accomplished the technical feat of developing the first nuclear weapons, the United States euphorically believed that other nations would find it difficult to repeat that performance and that they could be persuaded to renounce the option of acquiring weapons. Unfortunately, this wishful thinking was rapidly dispelled. Attempts at eliminating nuclear weapons from the arsenals of mankind failed, and in 1949, only four years later, the Russians tested their first nuclear weapon. The British, who, of course, had access to nuclear technology in cooperative programs with the United States during World War II, tested their own first weapon in 1952. The French, barred from access to weapons design information, nevertheless began nuclear testing in 1960, and finally the Chinese followed suit in 1964.

Herbert Scoville, Jr., was born in New York City in 1915, received his B.S. at Yale in 1937, and after study at Cambridge University for two years received his Ph.D. from the University of Rochester in 1942. He became involved in programs studying the effects of nuclear explosions, first as senior scientist at the Los Alamos Laboratory, and from 1948 to 1955 as Technical Director of the Arms Force Special Weapons Project in the Defense Department.

From 1955 to 1963, he was with the Central Intelligence Agency, first as Assistant Director for Scientific Intelligence and later as Deputy Director for Research. From 1963 to 1969, he was Assistant Director for the Arms Control and Disarmament Agency, actively involved in negotiating the non-proliferation treaty.

Since 1969, he has been associated with the Carnegie Endowment for International Peace arms control program and has been an officer of the Arms Control Association and of the Federation of American Scientists. During the past seven years, he has written many articles and testified before Congressional committees on nuclear security matters. He is the author with Robert Osborn of Missile Madness.

The first tests of Russia, the United Kingdom, and France, like that of the United States, involved implosion devices using plutonium as a fuel, but the Chinese, possibly because they had Soviet assistance in the production of enriched uranium-235 (U-235), used that fissionable material instead. There is no evidence that any of these countries ran into any major technical difficulties in designing their initial explosive; the basic secret was out when the United States had conducted a successful first test that showed it could be done. After these straightforward beginnings, all five nations have carried out extensive development programs leading to weapons using fusion together with fission reactions to produce thermonuclear weapons with very much higher explosive yields. Although peaceful nuclear power programs were, except in the case of China, carried out simultaneously, all of these countries carried out independent programs specifically aimed at procuring weapons.

In May 1974, India tested its first nuclear explosive, which it claimed was part of a peaceful nuclear program but which was obviously designed to demonstrate to the world that India was capable of building nuclear weapons of its own. Unlike the other countries, however, India acquired the fissionable plutonium for its first explosive from the CIRUS reactor ostensibly built as a part of a nuclear research program but capable of producing from four to six kilograms of plutonium per year. Nevertheless, the Indians almost certainly always had in the back of their minds that this could be tapped for the eventual production of weapons. They obtained the CIRUS reactor, a forty-MWt,[1] natural-uranium, heavy-water reactor (HWR), in 1956 from Canada under an agreement that it would be used only for peaceful purposes. The heavy water was furnished by the United States under a similar understanding with the Indian government. However, this was before the concept of the peaceful uses of nuclear explosives had achieved much attention, and later Canadian statements that this proscription applied equally to peaceful nuclear explosives (PNEs), since these could not be distinguished from weapons, were pointedly ignored by the Indians. The Indians informed the United States government that no United States material was involved in the

[1] The power of nuclear reactors is expressed in megawatts thermal (MWt) or in megawatts electric (MWe) in the case of power reactors. Since the electrical efficiency of a power reactor is about twenty-five percent, the MWt is about four times the MWe.

production of the plutonium used in their explosive. While the United States originally took this declaration at face value, recent evidence indicates that some of the original heavy water was still in the reactor while it was producing the plutonium used in the Indian explosion. India has refused to become a party to the Treaty on the Non-Proliferation of Nuclear Weapons (NPT), which it denounced as discriminatory: so there were no International Atomic Energy Agency (IAEA) safeguards on that part of their program. They also used native ore and built an independent fuel reprocessing capability so that they could acquire the material for their nuclear explosives without relying on any outside assistance. Thus, the Indian government claimed that their peaceful nuclear explosion did not violate any international undertaking. India is now the sixth country having a nuclear weapons capability, although it has not yet exploited this for military purposes and still insists it has no intention of doing so.

Israel is the only other country which may have a nuclear weapons capability today. In early 1976, a public CIA briefing revealed an estimate that Israel had ten to twenty such weapons, an estimate which is consistent with the plutonium available from its small research reactor, located at Dimona and originally supplied by France to operate at a power level of about twenty-five MWt. While hinting at a potential weapons capability, Israeli officials have avowed they would not be the first to introduce nuclear weapons into that part of the world. Whether they actually have weapons or not, they are probably only a turn of a screwdriver away from such a capability.

Nuclear Fuel Cycle

In order to understand the mechanics of acquiring a nuclear weapons capability, it is useful to examine the various elements in the nuclear fuel cycle which are required both for nuclear power and for nuclear explosives. The cheapest and quickest way for a country to obtain nuclear weapons is the direct approach of building a plutonium production reactor without attempting to use the power simultaneously produced. A country can also enrich natural uranium to weapons grade quality, following the Chinese example, but this is expensive and difficult to do, particularly for a small country. On the other hand, it can use the indirect approach of producing the plutonium as a by-product of a nuclear research or power program following the Indian precedent. Use of the indirect approach also allows deferral of the final decision on the acquisition of nuclear weapons until a much later time and avoids early political repercussions that such a decision would undoubtedly incur. If the explosive itself is developed ostensibly for peaceful purposes, as India did, this could still further blunt political opposition.

The key elements in the nuclear power fuel cycle are shown in Chart I. The central element is the nuclear power plant or reactor which generates electricity and simultaneously produces plutonium, a key weapons material. The input part of the fuel cycle starts with the mining of the uranium ore, refining this ore, and then either fabricating the natural uranium metal directly into fuel for certain types of reactors or first enriching it to increase the U-235 content from the 0.7 percent in natural uranium to between two and four percent. Enrichment can be carried out all the way to ninety percent material, which can then be used directly in weapons.

The output from the reactor is spent fuel containing unused uranium, plutonium — a basic weapons material — and a mixture of highly radioactive fission products. This can be either stored or reprocessed to separate the plutonium and any unused uranium, which in turn can, if needed, be fed back into the fuel fabrication part of the cycle. The radioactive fission products must be stored as wastes in such a manner as to prevent their release into the biosphere for thousands of years. The separated plutonium is in a form readily convertible into weapons. The general principles of fission weapons design are widely known, and the technology of building at least a crude weapon is not beyond the capacity of a moderately advanced nation, once the plutonium or fully enriched uranium is available. However, the thesis that weapons can be made in a basement by a high-school student is a gross oversimplification.

At the present time, there are two basic types of power reactors which are being widely built or considered for use around the world. The most common is the light-water cooled and moderated enriched uranium fueled reactor (LWR) designed originally by the United States, but now being marketed by the Federal Republic of Germany and France as well. The enriched uranium fuel contains only two to four percent U-235, so that it cannot be used directly in nuclear explosives, which require on the order of ninety percent U-235. Enrichment from this two to four percent level to weapons-grade material still requires extensive facilities, but far lesser ones than would be needed to enrich natural uranium even to the two to four percent level.

Chart I

NUCLEAR POWER FUEL CYCLE

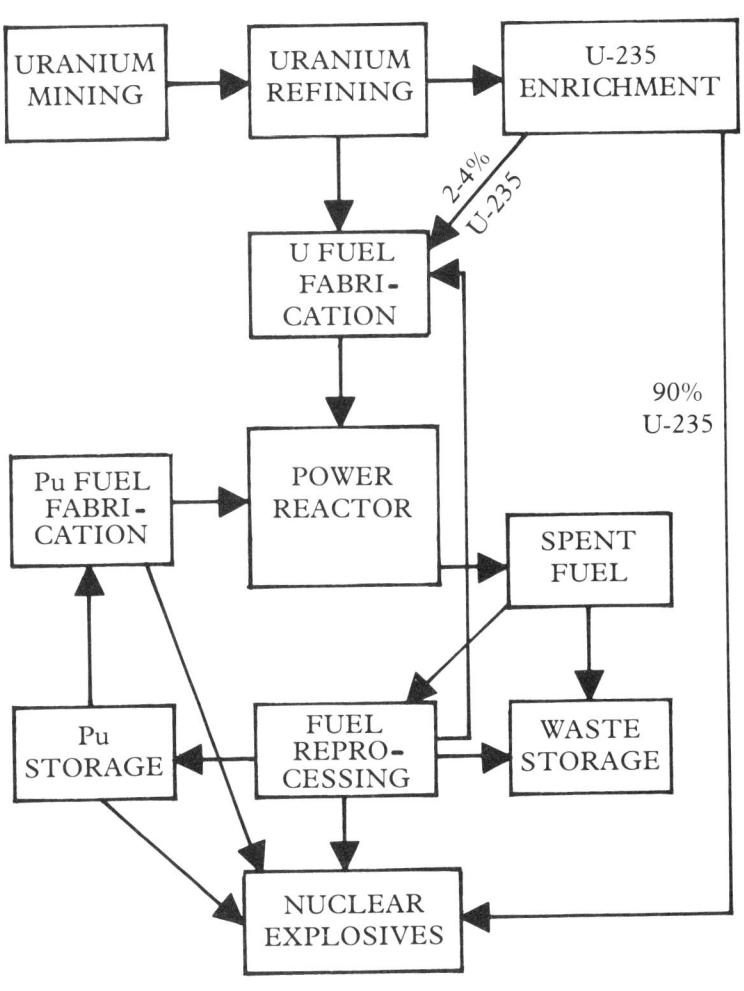

The second major type of reactor currently in use, the HWR, was developed by Canada and uses natural uranium with heavy water as a moderator and coolant. Unlike the LWR, which is refueled on a batch process, normally at intervals of a year or more, the HWR uses continuous refueling, which makes the withdrawal of some spent fuel containing plutonium easier. It also makes it possible to keep the fuel in the reactor for shorter periods of time so that the quality of the plutonium produced is somewhat better for weapons purposes.

Other types of power reactors which are now in existence or are being built outside of existing nuclear weapons countries are the boiling-water reactors (BWR), which use enriched U-235, and the gas-cooled reactors (GCR), but the economics of these types are generally considered inferior to either the LWR or HWR, and no future significant procurement of these types is anticipated. However, considerable work is going on on the development of so-called breeder reactors, which use plutonium as fuel but produce more plutonium than is consumed. At the present time, the United States breeder program is moving ahead at a very slow pace, far behind schedule, and it is not clear that it will ever be a practical approach in this country. European developers are more optimistic on breeder reactors, and at least a few will probably be in operation in the next ten years. These types of reactors present much more serious risks with respect to nuclear proliferation since they use plutonium as fuel, and until this plutonium is placed in the reactors, it is in a form which can be readily diverted to weapons. There are also proposals for recycling plutonium into the light-water reactors, and this would present some of the same problems, but at the moment the economics of this are still uncertain, and recycling will probably not become truly practical until plutonium is also needed for breeder reactors.

The spent fuel rods which have been used in a reactor contain plutonium intimately mixed with highly radioactive fission products so that this spent fuel must be stored for at least three months and often for a year or more in a deep-water trench before it can be treated to separate the plutonium and any unused uranium from the dangerous waste products. This is done in a chemical reprocessing facility using remote handling techniques and heavily shielded chambers. Once it has been separated from the fission products, plutonium can be relatively

THE PROLIFERATION OF NUCLEAR REACTORS AND WEAPONS 69

easily handled and converted into weapons material. Thus the major proliferation risks do not occur in the nuclear power plant per se but in the reprocessing facility. As long as the material is still associated with fission products, there is no great danger that a nation or a terrorist group will convert the material into explosives. While the technology of chemical reprocessing is generally publicly available, it is not an easy operation for an undeveloped country to carry out. The fabrication of the remote handling equipment and the construction of an efficient and safe reprocessing plant is difficult, although it might not be too hard to build a small inefficient laboratory facility to separate out enough plutonium for a single weapon. This latter approach would be quite appropriate for the material from a research reactor.

Because chemical reprocessing is the most critical point in the nuclear fuel cycle, it must be carefully controlled if further proliferation is to be prevented. Since there are always some process losses, the safeguarding of reprocessing facilities is difficult. Fortunately, at the present time, there is no requirement in the power cycle for chemical reprocessing of the spent fuel; the plutonium cannot yet be economically used to produce more power. Since reprocessing would at best only cut down on the natural uranium requirements for reactors by twenty percent, the economics do not favor plutonium recycling at present prices of uranium. Furthermore, current reprocessing techniques do not significantly alleviate the waste storage problem.

The United States does not have a commercial reprocessing plant in operation, and both President Carter and former President Ford have called for the deferral of reprocessing and the recycling of plutonium. Fortunately, at the present time, there are relatively few chemical reprocessing plants outside of the nuclear weapons states. India has one small plant which was used to provide the material for its first explosive, and a fairly sizable plant, soon to be in operation. Nothing is publicly known about Israel's reprocessing capability, and Argentina has a small plant of uncertain status. However, plans are afoot for additional plants to be built in a number of areas, and decisions on providing the technology for such plants are critical to the control of proliferation and will be discussed later.

Once the plutonium has been separated from the fission products, it must be placed in a storage area with tight physical security to prevent its seizure by unauthorized groups. It might be wisest to store all plutonium in nuclear weapons nations or at least outside disturbed areas until it is needed to be fabricated into fuel for subsequent use in reactors. Fortunately, accounting for stored plutonium or fuel rods is relatively easy so there is little danger of secret diversion during storage.

Plutonium fuel fabrication is another stage that must be carefully controlled. Since there are inevitably some scrap losses in making the fuel rods, accountability is not perfect in this part of the cycle, making safeguards difficult. Although the fabricated fuel is associated with other materials, such as uranium, it nevertheless still remains a relatively simple task to convert it into plutonium for use in a weapon. Thus, until the plutonium is again put back into the reactor and fission products generated, there is a potential danger of its being diverted to explosives. Safeguards and physical security must be very stringent at all times.

The other part of the fuel cycle which involves risks of proliferation is the enrichment plant by which natural uranium, which contains 0.7 percent U-235, is enriched to the two to four percent needed for reactor fuel. Such a facility can be used to enrich the fuel all the way to weapons-grade material, so careful observation is needed to prevent misuse of the plant. The most common type, in fact the only type now in commercial operation, is the gaseous diffusion plant, which entails a very large capital investment and a great expenditure of electric power. Such plants are only feasible for very large nations and exist only in the United States, the United Kingdom, France, the Soviet Union, and China. Furthermore, a plant that is operating to enrich material from two to four percent cannot easily change its operating procedures to produce weapons-grade material. For these reasons gaseous diffusion plants do not present excessively serious proliferation risks.

However, there are other methods for producing enriched uranium. The most highly developed of these alternatives is centrifuge separation. This technique does not require large quantities of power and so is more suitable for use by smaller, less advanced nations. Even so, it still requires large numbers of elements or stages: for example, thousands of centrifuges, which can normally only be manufactured in a highly industrialized nation. Perhaps the greatest risk might come if a nation took material with two to four percent enrichment designed for a power plant and further enriched it in a relatively small secret centrifuge plant to acquire material for weapons. Such an operation would run a significant risk of being discovered by foreign intelligence.

A third enrichment process, the so-called nozzle technique, is still unproven and is only in the development stage in Germany and South Africa. This requires even more power than the gaseous diffusion process and therefore is only feasible in nations which have an excess electrical power capacity. Because this process is being developed in South Africa and because recently the Germans agreed to provide such a plant to Brazil, a potential future nuclear weapons country, it has aroused considerable public attention. However, if a plant using this technique is designed for two to four percent material, it would be very difficult to change the operation to produce U-235 for weapons. As a consequence, the dangers from this type of plant have probably been exaggerated.

Finally, there is a new process on the horizon, the separation of uranium isotopes by using laser beams. While the feasibility of this new technique is as yet unproven, it is potentially very dangerous from a non-proliferation point of view because, instead of being a multi-stage process, it permits essentially complete separation of U-235 from U-238 in a single stage. This makes it very adaptable to the small production needed for an embryonic nuclear weapons program. It also is potentially inexpensive and uses very little electrical power. If this process proves feasible and the technology becomes generally available, then the prevention of further spread of nuclear weapons will have been made very much more difficult.

Storage of the spent fuel after it comes out of the nuclear reactor is relatively easy since the material is quite compact and dangerous to handle for long periods, thus presenting little security risk. Initially, the fuel is kept in deep-water canals, and if it is decided not to reuse material in the fuel, it could be stored in underground vaults of relatively small volume. However, after the fuel has been reprocessed, the plutonium is readily convertible to weapons and must be carefully protected against theft or diversion until it is refabricated into fuel and replaced in the reactor. The time lag between reprocessing and employment in a reactor should, of course, be kept as short as possible;

the reprocessing should never be carried out until there is a clear need for the product. After the fission products have been separated from the plutonium and uranium, waste storage presents somewhat different problems than for the fuel rods themselves. The highly radioactive materials can be concentrated into compact form simplifying their storage, but the relatively large volumes of residues with small but nevertheless dangerous amounts of long-lived radioactive materials pose a more difficult problem. However, waste disposal should not be an insoluble roadblock for the nuclear power industry — providing that it is willing to spend the necessary money and exercise the required supervision for periods which can last for hundreds or even thousands of years. Careful and continuous monitoring of the storage areas will be necessary and occasional repackaging may be required in the event of accidental leakage.

In sum, large parts of the nuclear fuel cycle are not major potential sources for the diversion of fissionable material into a weapons program. Until the plutonium produced in a reactor has been separated from the fission products, it is not readily available for diversion into weapons. Therefore, reprocessing should only be carried out when proven absolutely necessary; at the present time, there is no obvious economic need for this. However, once plutonium has been separated from the fission products, rigorous control must be maintained over its storage and handling until it is put back into a reactor. The only other facilities that are potential proliferation hazards are the uranium enrichment plants, but at the moment these do not present a serious risk. However, if laser separation ever becomes practical, then another dam curbing the spread of nuclear weapons will have been breached.

Nuclear Power Programs

The continued growth of the nuclear power industry is at the moment very uncertain because it is being affected by two opposing forces. First the world energy shortage, made more graphic by the recent oil embargo and by the escalating price of fossil fuels, has created tremendous pressures for the expansion of nuclear power as an alternative source. These pressures, however, have been counter-balanced by public concern over

THE PROLIFERATION OF NUCLEAR REACTORS AND WEAPONS 73

possible nuclear accidents, over environmental damage, and over the dangers that these programs will become a ready source of material for nuclear explosives. A major contributory effect has been the reduction in the overall energy requirements brought on by the skyrocketing costs of energy — including nuclear energy — the depression, and to some extent, increased conservation. These factors have resulted in a drastic slowing of the expansion of nuclear power from the predictions of a few years ago. The most recent estimates of world nuclear power made in 1976 by the Edison Electric Institute were 218,000 MWe by 1980 and 1,120,000 MWe by 1990. It is likely, however, that even these estimates, already reduced from earlier ones, will not be achieved.

Regardless of what the precise nuclear power generation capacity will be, there is no question that it will be large and that tremendous quantities of plutonium will be produced as a by-product. Each 1000 MWe creates about 230 kilograms of plutonium per year in a light-water reactor, the most common type, and 370 kilograms in the heavy-water type. Research and plutonium production reactors of the same power level can produce even more plutonium. Since less than ten kilograms are required for a weapon, the potential for nuclear weapons production is obviously very great. However, the overall world figures can be misleading because a large part of this power generation will occur in existing nuclear weapons countries — such as the United States, France, the United Kingdom, and the Soviet Union. To evaluate the proliferation risks, it is, therefore, necessary to look at the potential in individual countries that might in the future be considering acquiring a nuclear weapons capability.

India already has a significant nuclear power capacity of about 800 MWe which produces about 200 kilograms of plutonium per year. This capacity will roughly double by 1980 unless its major foreign suppliers, Canada and the United States, withhold assistance. (Canada has already done this and American policy is now under review.) India has a small fuel reprocessing plant, which produced the plutonium used in India's first "peaceful" nuclear explosive, and a second larger one will shortly be in operation. Since India has a supply of native uranium ore, heavy water, natural uranium reactors, and a chemical reprocessing capability, it has all the elements necessary for an independent nuclear weapons program. Regardless of outside aid, India can, if it chooses, continue its present program of building nuclear explosives on a small scale. These would almost certainly be used for weapons since there is no apparent economic justification for a peaceful explosives program in India. Although these weapons can perhaps provide India some world prestige, it is hard to see how they can add to its security. India will always be vulnerable to a Chinese nuclear attack, and geography alone makes it difficult for it to have a credible nuclear deterrent in response. India has no need for nuclear weapons to deal with its other potentially hostile neighbor, Pakistan, and in fact could force that country into acquiring nuclear weapons of its own. A nuclear Pakistan would be a much greater threat to India than the current non-nuclear one.

Pakistan, which is not a party to the NPT, has a small nuclear program composed of a 125-MWe HWR producing thirty kilograms of plutonium per year. It is now attempting to expand this program so that by 1990 it could have 4900 MWe installed and be in a position to produce about 1500 kilograms of plutonium a year. At the moment, it does not have any means to reprocess the fuel, but recently the French government agreed to supply it with a chemical reprocessing plant. The United States is currently trying to persuade Pakistan and France to cancel this agreement because of its proliferation risks. Although this plant would be under IAEA safeguards, it would provide Pakistan with a potential for producing weapons. If India continues to follow its present course of acquiring a nuclear weapons capability, then it seems almost certain that in time Pakistan will follow suit. Since there is little economic justification for it to have a reprocessing plant, Pakistan's acquisition of such a facility from France is almost certainly the first step toward a nuclear weapons option. While it is not technologically advanced, it is clear that with the foreign assistance being provided, a small nuclear capability is well within its grasp.

Iran is the other nation in the mid-Asian area which is developing a potential for acquiring nuclear weapons. However, it is a party to the Non-Proliferation Treaty and has thus accepted safeguards on all its nuclear facilities. The program is still in its early stages, being at present limited to research and training,

THE PROLIFERATION OF NUCLEAR REACTORS AND WEAPONS 75

but Iran has laid out ambitious plans for nuclear power ten to twenty years from now. It has already contracted with the Federal Republic of Germany and France for four LWRs and is negotiating with the United States for more. It has been estimated that it could have 10,000 MWe in place by 1990, but undoubtedly this program will fall behind schedule. In addition to reactors, Iran has bought into Eurodif, the Western European gaseous diffusion plant being built in France, in order to have an assured supply of enriched uranium, but this, of course, would be outside Iran's national control. It has also been negotiating with the United States, France, and Germany for a reprocessing plant to be installed in Iran, and if any of these negotiations are successful, Iran will have all the elements necessary for a weapons program. However, the United States is attempting to have any reprocessing done outside that area or at least to internationalize any facility for that purpose. Since the whole program is under safeguards, Iran would have to abrogate the NPT or secretly divert material to acquire weapons. If both India and Pakistan obtain weapons capabilities, Iran might feel forced to take such action, but this could then place its nuclear power program in jeopardy since it would have no internal supply of enriched uranium.

Israel's nuclear power program is very small since other nations have been reluctant to provide it with facilities without having assurances that Israel has no weapons program anywhere — an assurance it has refused to give. It has also refused to sign the NPT. Unfortunately, however, back in the late 1950s the French supplied Israel with a small 25-MWt reactor capable of producing enough plutonium for about one bomb per year. This reactor, located at Dimona, was initially very secret and has never been under any IAEA safeguards so that the disposition of the plutonium produced is unknown. For a time the United States carried out private inspections to insure that the plutonium had not been diverted to weapons, but apparently this has not been done for a number of years. There is no known chemical reprocessing facility in Israel, but a small laboratory-type operation capable of separating enough of the Dimona plutonium for a few bombs could easily be concealed. An announcement was made by a CIA official in early 1976 that it was estimated that the Israelis had ten to twenty bombs.

In the summer of 1976, United States officials announced

the completion of negotiations for supplying Israel with a large (600 MWe) power reactor. This would be under strict IAEA safeguards and the spent fuel would be withdrawn from Israel to prevent its ever being used in a weapons program, but no safeguards would be demanded for the rest of Israel's nuclear program. The failure to get such safeguards is likely to make Congressional approval of this export very difficult to achieve. The recent refusal of Israel to allow a Congressional delegation to visit Dimona will not make this easier.

Egypt, also not a party to the NPT, has no significant nuclear program at the moment, but the United States has offered to supply it with a power reactor in a parallel move with that to Israel. The provisions would be the same, but unlike Israel, Egypt has as yet no other important nuclear facilities that should be safeguarded. This proposed export is so closely linked with that to Israel that its fate currently hangs very much in the balance.

Brazil and **Argentina** are the two countries in the Western Hemisphere which have the potential for acquiring nuclear weapons and have given signals that they might do so at some time in the future. Both have refused to sign the non-proliferation treaty and have placed roadblocks in the way of their membership in the Latin American Nuclear Free Zone. By 1980, Brazil could be producing about 150 kilograms of plutonium a year from its first power reactor, but even more importantly, it has recently signed an agreement with Germany to acquire all parts of a nuclear fuel cycle. This will include not only reactors but also a U-235 separation plant using the untried German nozzle process and most critically a chemical fuel reprocessing facility. Brazil is reported to have available both uranium and thorium ores so that within the next twenty years it could have an independent national program. The German deal involves very extensive IAEA safeguards with provisions against using the transferred technology in other unsafeguarded plants within Brazil. However, once an entire complex is in operation, Brazil could abrogate its agreements under some pretext and proceed with an extensive nuclear explosive program. This would likely involve the sacrifice of any further foreign assistance to its nuclear power program.

While Argentina started earlier than Brazil and has had a 300 MWe power reactor and a small reprocessing plant in opera-

THE PROLIFERATION OF NUCLEAR REACTORS AND WEAPONS

tion for a couple of years, this program has been beset by political difficulties and is now of an uncertain status. However, once these are overcome, Argentina could move quite rapidly toward a nuclear capability and will probably do so in an attempt to match its neighbor Brazil.

While **Canada** and to a lesser extent **Mexico** have important nuclear power programs, neither of these countries has given any indication of any desire to acquire nuclear weapons capability. Canada could have done so many years ago, but instead has been in the forefront of those nations seeking to control and eliminate nuclear weapons. It recently exercised restraint by refusing to continue assistance to India in the aftermath of the Indian explosion. Both countries are parties to the NPT, and Mexico was a leader in establishing the Latin American Nuclear Free Zone. There is no evidence that either Canada or Mexico will change their attitudes toward nuclear weapons in the foreseeable future.

Japan is in the midst of a very large nuclear power program stimulated by its desire to reduce its dependence on Middle Eastern oil as an energy source. It already had more than 5000 MWe, and this will increase threefold by 1980. It has a small reprocessing facility and has proposed construction of an even larger one, but it is having difficulty finding a site for such a plant because of local environmental opposition. It is entirely dependent on outside sources for its uranium ore and for the enriched uranium for its LWRs. After a six-year delay, caused primarily by internal political complications, Japan, finally, in the spring of 1976, ratified the non-proliferation treaty. It has always accepted IAEA safeguards on all its programs and never seriously contemplated acquiring nuclear weapons because of the strong popular aversion to them as a result of Hiroshima and Nagasaki. It seems unlikely that in the foreseeable future this policy will be changed. Even the Indian explosion did not create pressures for Japan to follow suit; in fact, it was most outspoken in condemning the Indian action.

Both **South Korea** and **Taiwan** have small nuclear power programs which will be capable of producing significant amounts of plutonium by 1980. At the present time the nuclear programs of both countries are under IAEA safeguards and both have ratified the non-proliferation treaty, but in the case of Taiwan the continued connection with the IAEA is uncertain because it was ousted from membership in the IAEA when mainland China was admitted in 1972. It is hoped, however, that the present quasi-relationship with the IAEA can be maintained, and Taiwan will remain under IAEA safeguards. Taiwan has been building a laboratory capability for processing fuel but as yet has no definite plans for a large facility. Recently, it was rumored that Taiwan was secretly diverting plutonium to a weapons program, but after official statements by the United States government, Taiwanese officials have volunteered to forego reprocessing.

South Korea has one 550-MWe pressurized-water reactor (PWR) which will soon be in operation and another projected in 1980. It had proposed to acquire reprocessing technology from France, but under pressure from the United States dropped this plan.

South Africa is a major supplier of uranium ore but has not yet expanded its nuclear power program beyond the research reactor stage. However, it has developed a native uranium enrichment capacity, probably using the jet nozzle method, so that it could be in a position to have a nuclear weapons capability at an early date based on enriched uranium rather than plutonium. South Africa is not a party to the NPT, and neither its uranium ore production nor enrichment program is under safeguards. The acquisition of nuclear weapons by South Africa would have little apparent military value and could have serious political costs; threats to use them could lead to retaliation by one of the nuclear powers supporting black African nations.

Spain is not a party to the NPT, but has a very extensive nuclear power program, all the material of which is under IAEA safeguards. It already has three reactors with about 1000 MWe capacity in operation and plans for about 10,000 MWe by the mid-1980s. It already has in spent fuel a stockpile of more than 1000 kilograms of plutonium and a small pilot plant for reprocessing in operation. Thus, a potential for nuclear weapons is already available to Spain. It has some native uranium ore, but since it does not have any means of enriching uranium for its reactor fuel, its power program might be in jeopardy if it suddenly decided to procure nuclear weapons.

A number of **other European countries** have significant nuclear power programs, but none is a likely candidate for becoming a nuclear weapons nation. Sweden and Switzerland

THE PROLIFERATION OF NUCLEAR REACTORS AND WEAPONS 79

both have sizable power reactor installations but have not moved toward acquiring a fuel reprocessing capability, although they have the technological capability to do so. A number of NATO nations — particularly the Federal Republic of Germany and Italy — have large programs, including small reprocessing plants, but they have ratified the NPT and placed all their materials under IAEA safeguards. Other NATO countries have smaller, but nevertheless significant, programs. There would be strong internal and external pressures against any of these acquiring nuclear weapons unless such weapons became widely available throughout the world. Similarly, several Warsaw Pact countries have nuclear power facilities obtained with assistance from the Soviet Union, but again there would appear little likelihood that any would go the nuclear weapons route. Yugoslavia is also in the early stages of a nuclear power program, but it has not given any indication it would consider acquiring a weapons capability.

Australia has a native supply of uranium ore and has recently indicated that it might enhance the economic value of this asset by building an enrichment plant based on centrifuge technology. To date, it has not advanced its nuclear power program beyond the research stage because of the widespread availability of other sources of power. It has become a party to the NPT, and there is no evidence that it is seriously considering acquiring nuclear weapons.

There are many lesser developed countries around the world that have nuclear research programs and have even given consideration to modest nuclear power installations. None of these, however, would seem to have the capability of acquiring nuclear weapons in the next ten to twenty years unless these were provided by a more advanced nation. Nuclear power is an economically questionable source of energy for countries with limited energy requirements, since it becomes more and more expensive as the scale of the plant decreases. Other sources, such as solar energy, do not have this disadvantage.

The nuclear weapons capabilities of various countries are summarized in the chart on the following page.

Chart II

COUNTRIES WITH NUCLEAR WEAPONS CAPABILITIES

Current Nuclear Weapons Countries (6 + 1?)
 US*, USSR*, UK*, France, China, India, Israel(?)

Current Technological Capacity for Nuclear Weapons (13)
 Argentina, Belgium*, Bulgaria*, Canada*, Czechoslovakia*, Democratic Republic of Germany*, Federal Republic of Germany*, Italy*, Japan*, Netherlands*, Spain, Sweden*, Switzerland.

Technological Capacity in 10-20 Years for Nuclear Weapons (15)
 Australia*, Austria*, Brazil, Egypt, Finland*, Hungary*, Iran*, Mexico*, Pakistan, Philippines*, South Africa, South Korea*, Taiwan*, Thailand, Yugoslavia* (Excludes countries which might acquire weapons through research reactor programs.)

Potential New Nuclear Weapons Countries in 10-20 Years (9)
 Argentina, Brazil, Egypt, Iran*, Pakistan, South Africa, South Korea*, Spain, Taiwan*

*Party to non-proliferation treaty

In addition to existing nuclear weapons states there are about thirteen nations which now have the technological capacity to procure nuclear weapons, and within the next ten to twenty years about fifteen additional countries could be added to that list. If nuclear power continues to spread widely throughout the world, nuclear weapons will not be beyond the capabilities of an ever larger number of countries. However, despite this increasingly dangerous situation, it is surprising that to date only six — or possibly seven if Israel has such capability — have made the decision to develop and acquire nuclear explosives. About nine others might be classed as potential nuclear weapons states in the next ten to twenty years. One hundred nations have become parties to the Treaty on the Non-Proliferation of Nuclear Weapons by which they have renounced any intention of exercising that option. However, a few of these nations cannot be ruled out as potential nuclear weapons countries. Nevertheless, even in the present climate, in which nuclear weapons are advertised as the cornerstone of military and political strength by the superpowers, there are apparently strong pressures inhibiting countries from taking this step. The risks and costs inherent in a nuclear capability are seemingly more widely recognized than might be expected.

Therefore, any program to limit the further spread of nuclear weapons must emphasize their disadvantages and, indeed, the necessity of a deterrent to the acquisition of nuclear weapons. The leaders and people of nations around the world must understand the limited military and political value of nuclear weapons. Nuclear weapons have only one sensible purpose — to deter another nuclear country from using or threatening to use such weapons — and this is not a practical objective for small countries since a limited nuclear capability can be a magnet for nuclear attack rather than a deterrent. A few first-generation weapons will inevitably be vulnerable to a first strike by an enemy; they will also be prone to accidental detonation. Thus, an embryonic nuclear armed nation could well be the first to suffer nuclear devastation. Small nations are wiser to rely on the nuclear umbrella of the larger ones.

The two superpowers, the United States and Russia, have a special responsibility to create a climate in which the political and military value of nuclear weapons is downgraded. However, the continual competition between these two countries expressed by adding more and more nuclear weapons to their arsenals, and their repeated statements that nuclear inferiority can lead to political weakness — despite stockpiles of tens of thousands of bombs — make the achievement of such a climate unlikely. Threats to use nuclear weapons in a response to conventional attacks are weakening the inhibitions of potential nuclear weapons countries. Instead, the superpowers should be pledging not to use nuclear weapons against any party to the non-proliferation treaty which has foregone the nuclear option. They should be cutting down on their stockpiles of strategic warheads rather than adding more advanced and dangerous types. They should agree to stop all nuclear explosive testing as a demonstration of their seriousness to exercise restraint.

But this new climate will not arrive in a day. Therefore, it is also important to buy time by placing controls on the availability of weapons materials throughout the world. This is particularly true in the next ten years as national decisions are being made everywhere on the acquisition of nuclear power to cope with the widespread energy shortage. Alternative non-nuclear routes to energy sufficiency should be strongly encouraged. All nuclear assistance or trade should be safeguarded and limited to only those countries that are either parties to the non-proliferation treaty or have accepted safeguards on all their nuclear programs. The reprocessing and storage of plutonium in a form readily usable in weapons should be restricted to locations where the risks of seizure by non-nuclear countries or dissident groups is at a minimum; preferably, these should be kept under international control. The development and particularly the spread of laser enrichment technology should be regulated to prevent this potential new source of weapons material from becoming a major threat to world security.

With a program of physical controls to buy time combined with a major effort to develop better world understanding of the drawbacks and risks of having nuclear weapons, there is still some hope that the world can be spared another nuclear holocaust and can eventually be free of nuclear threats. But the next ten years are critical.

IV

Energy and the Conquest of Fear

WILLIAM G. POLLARD

". . . for fear is nothing but surrender of the helps that come from reason."
Wisdom of Solomon 17:12

There must have been a time when primitive man shared with all the other animals of forest and steppe a paralyzing fear of fire and fled in terror from it whenever it broke out. But at some point man came through to the other side of fear and instead of running from fire, brought it right into his living quarters and thereafter tended and nurtured it. Uncontrolled outbreaks of fire

---

William G. Pollard received his doctorate in physics at Rice University in 1935 and began his academic career as professor of physics at the University of Tennessee. He received a leave of absence in 1944 to work on the Manhattan Project as a research scientist. In 1947 he was appointed executive director of the Oak Ridge Associated Universities in Tennessee, a position he held from 1946 to 1974, and a staff member of its Institutes for Energy Analysis until his retirement in 1976. Dr. Pollard has received numerous honorary degrees and awards and has served as chairman of the southeastern section of the American Physical Society, as Fellow of the American Physical Society, of the American Association for the Advancement of Science, and of the American Nuclear Society. He was formerly a trustee of the University of the South where he taught in the graduate school of theology.

Dr. Pollard was ordained to the priesthood in the Episcopal Church in 1954. Since that time he has served at several Episcopal churches in Tennessee as well as being a deputy to the General Conventions in 1958, 1961, 1964, and 1967. Dr. Pollard was chairman of the House of Deputies Committee on National and International Problems in 1964 and 1967.

Dr. Pollard's publications include Chance and Providence (Scribners, 1958), Physicists and Christian (Seabury, 1961), Man on a Spaceship (Claremont Colleges, 1967), and Science and Faith—Twin Mysteries (Thomas Nelson, 1970). Dr. Pollard contributed a chapter entitled "God and His Creation" for the book This Little Planet, Michael P. Hamilton, ed. (Charles Scribners, 1970).

continue to be fearful events, and each year fire takes a large toll of human life and property. Yet it has so enriched human life and enlarged its possibilities that we have largely conquered our natural fear of it and use it gratefully with as much caution as we can manage.

When railroads were first introduced in the last century they were accompanied by widespread fear. Their locomotives belching smoke and fire and hissing and puffing steam were a terrifying sight when first experienced. Later at the turn of the century when electricity began to come into use, it too was accompanied by widespread fear. It was a new and unfamiliar force, invisible and mysterious, and it inspired deep and unarticulated fears. There was, of course, a real basis for some of this fear. Electricity is in fact quite dangerous, and a healthy fear of it has resulted in great strides since its introduction in devising measures for using it safely. Man has found ways of conquering his natural fears of steam and electricity so that they no longer paralyze him into refusing great gifts of nature for his welfare.

Now we have just begun to use another previously unknown energy resource which has aroused in the public a whole new spectrum of fears. Nuclear energy has come on the scene just as the crisis of shrinking reserves of fossil fuels has begun to be felt. Yet the prospect of a heavy reliance on it is beset by the fear of nuclear weapons with their awesome and terrible destructive power and by the fear of generating the huge quantities of radioactive substances which necessarily accompany it with their lethal radiations persisting for centuries. Much of this fear is genuine and well grounded, but some of it is misplaced or needlessly exaggerated. It is the purpose of this essay to examine this new spectrum of fears of nuclear energy in some detail and to suggest ways in which the paralysis which they naturally induce may be overcome.

The first practical nuclear power plants were developed for naval submarines, and these became the basis for the United States light-water reactors (LWRs) which are now so extensively deployed in electric utility systems. The energy source for all these reactors is the fission of the light isotope of uranium of atomic weight 235 (U-235). This isotope makes up only 0.7 percent of natural uranium and it must be enriched to around three percent in isotope separation plants for use in

ENERGY AND THE CONQUEST OF FEAR

LWR power plants. At the present rate of building new plants, there is only enough uranium in the world in ores of moderate quality to fuel such plants for another fifty years or so. Thus, if it were necessary to rely only on naturally occurring U-235 to fuel our growing nuclear power systems, nuclear power would be only a temporary interlude in the world's energy crisis. This, however, is fortunately not the case. The real potential of nuclear power lies in converting the 99.3 percent of uranium-238 (U-238) in natural sources into plutonium, an equally good fuel for nuclear power plants, in a quite different power reactor known as a fast breeder.

A small-scale prototype breeder reactor has been operated in the United States for over two decades, and a full-scale breeder power reactor is now operating successfully in France. The United Kingdom and the Soviet Union have underway huge development programs for this form of nuclear power. A full-scale demonstration breeder power plant is now under construction at Oak Ridge. Considerable research and development remain to be done before commercial breeder reactors are widely available for electric power generation, but the prospects for success at moderate power costs are reasonably well assured.

The gaseous diffusion plants originally constructed during World War II to provide highly enriched U-235 for weapons have since been operated to produce less highly enriched uranium for research and power reactors in this country and abroad. The natural uranium in the form of a gas is enriched in the light isotope as it flows forward through the plant, while the balancing reverse stream is depleted in it. The depleted plant "tails," generally running 99.8 percent U-238, are condensed to a solid in large steel drums each containing somewhat over nine tons of uranium. By now 20,000 such drums have accumulated around the three gas diffusion plants and their number is increasing each year.

Once breeder reactors have been extensively deployed they will use this reserve of U-238 as the feedstock for conversion into plutonium fuel. I am indebted to my colleague in the Institute for Energy Analysis of Oak Ridge Associated Universities, Alfred M. Perry, for the following calculation of the magnitude of this energy resource. With ten passes through breeders, seventy percent of this uranium can be converted into fuel plutonium. That amount of plutonium is sufficient to generate the same amount of electricity as 450 billion tons of coal or one and a half trillion barrels of oil. This means that we in the United States have in hand already mined, processed, and purified, a reserve of at least as much and possibly considerably more than all the recoverable coal in the United States, or as much as all the recoverable oil in the whole world. A lengthy transition period from LWRs to breeders will be required to produce enough plutonium to make them self-sustaining, but when that stage has been reached, this reserve of depleted uranium would be sufficient to keep the United States going at the present rate of electrical generation (about two trillion kilowatt hours per year) for another 500 years. Yet this immense energy reserve, if all brought together in one place, would occupy only about thirty acres. Moreover, by the time breeder power plants have become commercially deployed, this vast reserve of depleted uranium will have been more than doubled through fueling LWRs between now and then.

This providential energy resource will certainly be used by mankind as reserves of fossil fuels decline. The maintenance of human civilization and the freedom which abundant energy makes possible will demand that we use it. At this early stage, however, there are a variety of deep-seated fears surrounding all forms of nuclear power. For some people these fears are so intense that they urge a renunciation of nuclear power in general and of any further development of breeder reactors in particular. In what follows, these fears will be considered under four general headings. The objective in each case will be to distinguish real from exaggerated or misplaced fears. The latter will in time cease to play a role. For the valid fears, the problem is to find ways for dealing with them. Throughout the whole course of his pilgrimage as a species, man has had to cope with and overcome the debilitating and paralyzing effects of fear. To a large degree human progress has been dependent at each step along the way on the conquest of fear.

The Fear of Nuclear Weapons Proliferation

Ever since the first nuclear bombs were exploded at Alamogordo, Hiroshima, and Nagasaki, man has lived under the fearful threat of nuclear annihilation. For a brief period nuclear weapons were a monopoly of the United States, and a major effort was made in the United Nations under Bernard Baruch to internationalize them under a plan in which all nations would bind themselves not to develop, manufacture, or use nuclear weapons. Now, thirty years later, the massive arsenals of the United States and the Soviet Union confront each other atop intercontinental missiles. The United Kingdom, France, China, India, and apparently Israel have all acquired nuclear arsenals of their own. The status of other countries with respect to further proliferation is described in detail in Chapter III.

Any nation which is determined to have nuclear weapons of its own must first acquire a source of nuclear explosives. There are three ways in which a country could plan to do so. The first alternative would utilize U-235 of ninety percent enrichment or better. For this the nation would need to purchase from another nation or design and build its own isotope enrichment plant. China acquired such a plant from Russia during the period of their détente. Brazil is acquiring one from West Germany. Isotope separation plants are presently such massive undertakings that few other nations are expected to choose this alternative, unless smaller plants requiring much less electric power, such as centrifuge or laser systems, become practical.

The second alternative is to use a research reactor or specially designed production reactor to convert U-238 into plutonium. In order to follow this alternative, a remote controlled, heavily shielded reprocessing plant must also be on hand to separate chemically the plutonium from the extremely radioactive fission wastes and the remaining uranium. Many nations already have research reactors sufficient to produce plutonium slowly over a number of years and so accumulate enough material for a few bombs. India used a Canadian research reactor in this way and separated the plutonium in its own reprocessing plant. Pakistan has had the necessary reactor for years and is now acquiring a reprocessing plant from France. United States intervention prevented South Korea from acquiring such a plant from France. Brazil is obtaining a reprocessing plant in addition to the isotope separation plant from West Germany. Israel, Argentina, and South Africa have built small reprocessing plants of their own.

The third alternative is the one of gravest concern for the

expansion of the nuclear electric power industry. Under this alternative, nations bent on acquiring nuclear weapons would need neither reactors nor reprocessing plants. They would plan instead on diverting or stealing small amounts of plutonium from plants reprocessing spent fuel from nuclear electric generation, especially in the future from plants reprocessing breeder reactor fuel and uranium breeding rods. Reprocessing plants at Hanford and Savannah River have been extracting plutonium for weapons in large quantities for many years. Spent fuel from nuclear electric plants has simply been stored in place since no commercial reprocessing plants are yet in operation in the United States, but this accumulation of spent fuel will eventually have to be reprocessed. Reprocessing is an integral component of breeder reactors and will eventually result in large amounts of separated plutonium in process of refabrication into fresh fuel elements for the power reactors.

This third alternative makes the fear of nuclear weapons a potent factor in the decision to use our vast energy reserve of depleted uranium for the generation of electric power. The prospect of a worldwide "Plutonium Economy," as the National Council of Churches calls it, would, it is feared, make plutonium so universally plentiful that the world would have to abandon any further hope of slowing down the proliferation of nuclear weapons. The threat of weapons proliferation is indeed a basis for real and valid fear. If there were any feasible and practical way to prevent it, the nations of the world would be justified in accepting a considerable sacrifice to do so. But apart from the general question of nuclear weapons proliferation, the contribution of nuclear electric generation to this problem is not as simple and clear-cut as it has frequently been made out to be. In order to reach a rational basis of judgment on this issue, three basic aspects of this problem will be considered.

The first point to make is that plutonium produced in breeder reactors for electric power is not necessary for weapons. Not a single nuclear weapon in existence today contains any nuclear explosive derived from a nuclear power plant. The approximately 30,000 warheads in the United States nuclear arsenal contain plutonium made in the production reactors at Hanford and Savannah River, not reprocessed power plant fuel. It is evident that whether or not we decide to generate electric power from the vast energy resource in depleted uranium which is now providentially in our hands, the proliferation of nuclear weapons can and unfortunately probably will proceed. Any nation which decides it must have nuclear weapons will not be deterred by a United States decision not to develop breeders for electric power. Up to now they have all found ways to achieve this objective without using power plant plutonium, and these same ways will be open to other nations in the future.

The second point to make is that the plutonium produced in power reactors is not as desirable for bombs as that produced in research or production reactors. For low-cost nuclear power it is necessary to burn up as much of the plutonium in the reactor fuel elements as possible. This involves exposing unburned and newly bred plutonium in the reactor to neutrons for much longer times than in the other reactors. As a result around thirty percent of the weapons grade plutonium-239 is converted by neutron capture to heavier isotopes of atomic weight 240 and 241. Plutonium-240 emits neutrons spontaneously and this greatly complicates the controlled triggering of a bomb containing it. Plutonium-241 is much more radioactive than the other isotopes and this results in internal heating which is a problem in a bomb stockpile held for long periods. The amount of plutonium from this source required for a critical mass in a bomb is around twice as much as that with weapons grade plutonium-239.

As a result of these complications, it seems probable that nations which have already acquired nuclear weapons when power plant plutonium becomes accessible for diversion will not turn to this new source, but will instead continue to rely on their present sources of weapons grade plutonium. Nations which do not have nuclear weapons by that time might decide to attempt a nuclear weapons program based on the possibility of stealing plutonium from breeder reactor reprocessing plants or fuel element fabrication plants. But there is a third complication. If they did so they would still have to assemble a sizable group of scientists, engineers, technicians, and high level craftsmen and provide them with buildings, expensive equipment, and instruments for their task. Several years of concentrated effort would be required for success. Once such a group had been launched and had begun to consider design alternatives and long-term benefits, it seems quite possible that they would try to dissuade their government from its initial decision to rely on being able to steal power plutonium. Although they certainly could make bombs from power plutonium, their task would be considerably simplified and better assured of success if they could have weapons grade plutonium. With a sizable investment already made in the bomb group and facilities, the addition of a small production reactor and reprocessing plant would not much more than double it. Any such nation might well decide that its long-term interests would not be well served by making its weapons dependent on diverted power plutonium. This would be especially true if it foresaw as a likely development increasingly stringent international measures to safeguard power plutonium against diversion.

In any event the practical effect of a decision not to employ a vast providential energy resource to generate electricity for the benefit of man is to relegate this resource to exclusively destructive purposes. The record of proliferation to date insures that its use for an increasingly potent arsenal of weapons will continue regardless of how we decide to handle its constructive use. One is reminded of the Deuteronomic injunction, "I call heaven and earth to witness against you this day that I have set before you life and death, blessing and curse; therefore, choose life that you and your descendants may live" (Deut. 30:19). The purpose of this injunction was, of course, to produce a clear-cut decision for the blessing and against the curse. Its actual effect in the subsequent history of Israel was, however, the realization of both blessing and curse either alternately or simultaneously. It is this ambiguity of human choice which now surrounds the question of nuclear energy. We have already, to our peril, chosen the curse of nuclear energy with its vast potential for death and destruction. Are we then, for the fear inspired in us by the curse, to renounce the blessing with its equally vast potential for life in an increasingly energy-hungry world? Or can we find the strength to conquer this fear, as we have other energy-inspired fears in the past, and resolve to do everything in our power to increase the blessing and diminish the curse?

There is much more that can be done to insure that power plutonium is not used for bombs. My colleague Alvin Weinberg, Director of the Institute for Energy Analysis, has argued persuasively for a siting policy for all breeder reactors which would confine them to large nuclear "parks." Such a park would have its own reprocessing and fuel fabrication plants, waste storage facilities, and ten or more reactors generating electric power. For a considerable period no plutonium would

ENERGY AND THE CONQUEST OF FEAR

leave the site. A large nuclear power center could be provided with maximum security against sabotage or theft, and could be operated by an elite corps with long-term continuity and a developed tradition of excellence. Such a nuclear park would be not only physically isolated but socially isolated as well. The maintenance of its security would interfere with the freedom of the general public no more than sensitive military installations do now.

This is but one of a number of steps which can be and doubtless will be taken to insure that power plutonium is secure and used only in reactors generating electricity. Another already in operation is the safeguard inspection network of the International Atomic Energy Agency. Critics point to its present inadequacies, but the safeguard network is not a fixed thing. It is in process of development and is continually being improved and strengthened as experience with it grows and weaknesses are discovered and corrected. In all the approaches to this problem we take, the inherent inferiority of power plutonium for weapons will be of much assistance.

The specter of a growing number of nations with nuclear arsenals of their own and the consequent prospect of an outbreak of nuclear warfare is genuinely terrifying. But valid as this fear is, we must not let it paralyze us to the point of rejecting the blessing of a vast new energy source. It is important to do all in our power to minimize the curse, but it is equally important that we press forward with a firm determination to maximize the blessing.

Fear of Nuclear Explosions

Nuclear energy is indelibly stamped in the psyche of mankind with the vision of the awesome fireball and mushroom cloud of an atomic bomb exploding in the atmosphere. As a consequence there is a deep-seated subconscious conviction that every nuclear power plant is a tamed atomic bomb which might go off at any moment with devastating effect in an accident arising from some technical defect or human error. It is this widespread and deeply felt fear which is responsible for the emotional public concern for the safety of nuclear power plants.

There is a genuine basis for concern for the safety of nuclear power plants, but for the present generation of LWRs it does not arise from the possibility of such an explosion. A *nuclear* explosion in a light-water reactor is a physical impossibility by a wide margin. The real concern centers rather in the intense radioactivity of the wastes which have already been generated in an operating power plant. When the reactor has been completely shut down, these radioactive wastes trapped within its fuel rods continue to generate heat at a rapid rate. This heat must be removed as rapidly as it is produced. Normally this is accomplished by continuing to circulate the water through the core that generated the high pressure steam when the reactor was operating. In order to guard against the rare event in which this primary water circulation was accidentally knocked out, each American LWR is provided with a completely independent Emergency Core Cooling System (ECCS) which will flood the hot core independently of the primary system.

The fission wastes in the fuel elements of a modern nuclear power plant which has been generating electricity for some time at a rate in excess of a million kilowatts have the same radioactivity as 10,000 tons of radium. They are a mixture of many radioactive species ranging in lifetimes from hours to years. The internal heat generated by their radioactivity immediately after the reactor is shut down is intense. If both the primary and emergency cooling systems should simultaneously fail, the bare core mounted inside its pressure vessel would rise very rapidly to a white hot heat and reach a temperature sufficient to melt the uranium oxide fuel, the zirconium tubes containing it, and the variety of compounds formed by the fission waste elements. Such an accident is called a "core meltdown" and its prevention is the primary objective of reactor safety measures.

Let us try to visualize the consequences of such a core meltdown. The core of each LWR is mounted inside a massive eight- to ten-inch thick steel pressure vessel within which water (in pressurized-water reactors or PWRs) or water and steam (in boiling-water reactors or BWRs) circulates under very high pressure. This is surrounded by a seven- to ten-foot concrete radiation shield for protection of the operating personnel and the surrounding plant environment. Beyond this barrier the entire plant is enclosed in a domed containment shell strong enough to sustain a direct hit by a 707 jet aircraft. If inside its pressure vessel the bare hot core should melt, it would drop in a molten pool to the bottom of the pressure vessel, and there begin melting its way through the thick steel pressure vessel. The resulting molten core-iron mass would then drop to the concrete foundation and begin melting its way through that, releasing as it did so great quantities of carbon dioxide gas. The accumulation of this gas might build up a sufficient overpressure to rupture the containment shell and allow some of the volatile radioactive fission wastes to escape with it into the surrounding air. When the concrete foundation had been penetrated, the resultant, molten core-iron-concrete mass would begin to melt through the soil and rocks below.

After a year of such melting, the short-lived fission wastes would all have decayed away, and the residual radioactivity would be less than a tenth that in the original core meltdown. The radioactive wastes would now be diluted in a large red-hot mass of lava deep below the plant site measuring up to forty feet across and sixty feet high. At this point it would begin to solidify into a glass-like ceramic pillar in the ground.

This is a description of the worst kind of reactor accident that nuclear power plant designers and operators contemplate. It does not involve an explosion of any kind or a release of radioactivity to the atmosphere around the plant unless the containment shell is breeched by overpressure within it. On the other hand it would be a calamity for the utility owning and operating the plant. Not only would the plant itself be a total loss, but its isolation and protection from its surroundings would be an expensive, long-term obligation. There could be some leaching of radioactivity by ground water flowing around and through the cracked ceramic pillar. But by the time such contaminated water reached a distant spring, well, or stream, it would probably be diluted and decayed to a point at which it would not constitute a health hazard.

A detailed method of estimating the probability of failure in individual components of complex systems for a variety of accident chains has been developed for United States Minuteman missiles and the NASA Apollo missions. This method of "fault tree" or "event tree" analysis has been applied by Norman Rasmussen of the Massachusetts Institute of Technology to determine the probability of various accidents, including those resulting in a core meltdown, in American PWRs and BWRs.

Its greatest value is in identifying weak spots in such accident chains which can guide designers to incorporate safety improvements in future plants. But the method also yields the best available estimates of the probability of various kinds of accidents in existing plants. The conclusion is that a core meltdown in such a PWR plant would not be expected to occur more often than once in 15,000 to 25,000 years, or in a BWR plant once in 25,000 to 35,000 years.

This is about all that can be said with any confidence about nuclear safety. It does not, however, satisfy the large number of people who visualize such an accident as a catastrophic explosion dispersing radioactive wastes over a large area surrounding the plant. The persistence of this image and the elemental fear which it involves are so deeply ingrained that it has become essential to deal with the question of explosions regardless of how far-fetched the subject might be. If it were not for this widespread public fear, it is doubtful that the subject of nuclear power plant explosions would ever have been seriously considered. But the pressure on those conducting nuclear safety studies to prove the impossibility of such an explosion has been tremendous. As a result they have been forced to explore remote possibilities which they would hardly have taken seriously in the absence of such pressure.

The only possibility which has emerged from this exploration is a steam explosion. When small droplets of white-hot molten metal or rock plunge into water, steam is generated, not in the usual manner by boiling, but instantaneously and explosively. This phenomenon has been observed experimentally in the laboratory. Using such laboratory experiments as a basis, computer models have been devised which go far beyond observed conditions. With this model it is possible to generate conditions which might result in a steam explosion of sufficient violence to blow off the massive head of the steel pressure vessel and propel it with enough momentum to penetrate the thick concrete radiation shield and then the super-strength dome of the containment shell above it. Following this violent breach, much of the radioactivity in the core would be blown out into the atmosphere above the plant and drift as a radioactive cloud in the direction of the prevailing winds.

This is just the kind of accident those who are fearful of nuclear plants have envisioned as the typical and expected accident. It is difficult to argue with such fears. The fact is that the probability is so small that it is comparable to that for a large meteor hitting Times Square. Even that miniscule probability rests on the results of a computer model which has been stretched well beyond the limits of its experimental base.

Up to the present we have had, including naval reactors, over 2000 reactor-years of operating experience with PWRs and BWRs without a single accident releasing appreciable radioactivity to the external environment. The Rasmussen study suggests that there would be at most one core meltdown in the whole world during the period that naturally occurring U-235 is relied upon for electric power and the chance of its happening will be continually lessened as new safety measures are incorporated in future plants. After that quite different safety considerations, including the possibility of a nuclear excursion following a core meltdown, will apply to the breeder reactors which will replace the present LWRs.

There are many other manmade systems in the modern world — dams, refineries, chemical plants, jet aircraft — which are far more hazardous than nuclear electric plants. Those who single out such plants as the penultimate technological threat can only do so on the basis of profoundly held but irrationally exaggerated fears.

The Fear of Radiation

The first atomic bombs and the extended period of atmospheric testing of increasingly sophisticated nuclear weapons after World War II have made people acutely aware of radiation and its dangers. Like electricity it is invisible and mysterious, and the thought of it inspires fear. It is one of the fears which surrounds the whole matter of nuclear power. The idea that a nuclear power plant is a tamed atomic bomb which might accidentally explode at any time leads to visions of widespread public exposure to lethal radiation with many sick and dying people, a widespread outbreak of cancer, and a succession of genetic monsters among the descendants of those involved. Lurid descriptions of such scenes have been given in numerous books and movies over the past thirty years. The fact that the impression they create is demonstrably false does not stop their continued appearance. The grossly exaggerated and unreal fears these descriptions have inspired in the public have become a serious handicap to the development of nuclear power. A review of what is known about the effects of radiation on human health should serve to placate most of this fear.

The original measure of radiation dose is the Roentgen, named for the discoverer of x-rays. It is a measure of the ionization produced in a unit volume of air. Nuclear radiation consists not only of x-rays or gamma rays but also may involve, depending on the source of the radiation, neutrons, beta rays (high speed electrons), or alpha rays (high velocity helium atoms). The damage done to human tissue by these different types of radiation can be measured by a single unit, the *rad* for radiation exposure, or the *rem* for absorbed dose, which include appropriate adjustments for the different kinds of radiation.

There is no question that radiation in sufficient amounts is dangerous. A dose of 1000 units of radiation throughout the body is lethal. The victim dies within a week to ten days from damage to the lining of the intestines and blood vessels throughout the body, leading to extensive internal bleeding. A dose of 3000 units kills in two to three days. A radiation dose of 300 units damages the blood-forming tissues in the bone marrow and the immune system, leading to high susceptibility to infection. Those receiving such a dose have initial nausea and slight capillary bleeding, but with good medical care can be brought through a critical period of twenty to thirty days after which the immune system and bone marrow have started recovering. In another two months they are fully recovered with two exceptions. For years afterward the exposed person will have chromosome aberrations in the peripheral blood lymphocytes whose clinical significance, if any, is not clear. There will also be a significant increase in the probability that the radiation dose will eventually, up to thirty years later, lead to cancer, particularly leukemia. Otherwise there is every evidence of complete recovery.

By far the largest sample of humans who have been exposed to radiation doses in the range of 100 to 500 units are the survivors of the 1945 bombs at Hiroshima and Nagasaki. A large number of them have been identified and the dose which they received has been quite reliably determined from where they were at the time of the explosion. Regular and thorough clinical examinations were begun in 1947. Several radiation-related clinical disorders have been observed in recent years in these examinations. Compared to the unexposed population, the most notable disorders have been increased occurrences of leukemia and lenticular opacity. Most of them show radiation characteristic aberrations in peripheral blood lymphocytes. An increased incidence of thyroid carcinoma has been found at autopsy but not before. Those who were children at the time show a slight impairment of growth and development. Those exposed in the uterus at an early stage of pregnancy and at a high dose show some increased incidence of microcephaly and mental retardation. Just recently some increased incidence of breast and lung cancer is being found in this group which may be the result of radiation. The most surprising result of this extensive thirty-year study is that no increased incidence of any known genetic abnormality has been observed among the descendants of the exposed population.

The population for this study consisted of 285,000 in Hiroshima and Nagasaki who were alive on October 1, 1950. In this exposed population there have been up to the present time 415 more deaths attributed to cancer, of which 192 were from leukemia, than would have occurred in an equivalent unexposed population of the same size. This means that five years after the bomb blasts, each individual exposed to them had a 99.85 percent chance of *not* dying from cancer and a 99.93 percent chance of *not* dying from leukemia within thirty years after their radiation exposure. This is a far cry from the lurid descriptions of radiation catastrophe which have become so common. Excess deaths from all diseases other than cancer were 406.

In this country there have been a few radiation accidents which have provided some additional information. A chain-reaction accident at Los Alamos in an experiment with plutonium just after the war produced a large burst of neutrons which resulted in the death of the experimenter soon after and smaller exposures to others in the vicinity. One of them, who was fifty-nine at the time, recently died at age eighty-nine before developing symptoms attributable to the radiation. In another criticality accident in Oak Ridge in 1958, five maintenance men received mixed-neutron-gamma doses of 235 to 365 units, and three others much smaller doses. They all showed typical radiation-induced chromosome aberrations but until recently seemed otherwise fully recovered. Recently, however, one of the five has died of lung cancer and another has developed a bone marrow abnormality of currently obscure diagnosis. One of the three who received a low dose of thirty units has just had an operation for colon cancer. It is not possible to determine to what extent, if any, the radiation dose they received over eighteen years ago may have contributed to these developments.

These studies have been backed up by extensive controlled animal experiments in America and abroad during the last twenty-five years. Oak Ridge maintains a colony of 165,000 mice for such studies, and some individual experiments have required over five years and as many as 500,000 mice to complete. Both somatic effects, especially leukemia and other cancers, and genetic effects have been studied under carefully controlled conditions as a function of radiation dose. Doses much below fifty units require too many mice and too long a time to obtain statistically reliable results for cancer induction or genetic effects, although some pathological effects can be detected at doses as low as ten units. The observed effects up to 500 units are more pronounced at higher doses but generally not proportionately so. These experiments confirm the delayed increase in leukemia and other cancers now being observed among the Japanese atomic bomb survivors. They have also shown increases in the natural rates of various genetic mutations. A significant finding in these genetic studies is, however, that such effects are largely confined to cases in which mating occurs soon after radiation exposure. If mating is delayed beyond the time when the sperm which received the radiation are still viable, the genetic effects are greatly reduced. Perhaps this is one reason for the failure to observe genetic effects in the descendants of the Japanese survivors.

This brief summary covers most of what is known scientifically about radiation effects. What we would like to know is the effect of very much smaller doses. All mankind and indeed all living things have been continuously immersed in a natural radiation environment throughout the whole course of evolution. Partly this is due to cosmic rays coming into the earth from outer space and partly to natural radioactive elements — potassium, uranium, thorium, and others — in rocks and soil. The average exposure in this country is about 0.1 unit per person per year, but this is subject to wide variations. For persons

ENERGY AND THE CONQUEST OF FEAR

living at sea level in wood houses it may be half as much, and for those in Denver and environs twice to three times as much due both to altitude and soil and rock composition. There are many communities in India built on radioactive monazite sands whose inhabitants have received up to one unit per year for many generations. In addition to this natural radiation, the average United States resident received from medical x-rays an additional 0.07 unit per year. Compared to these exposures, the entire nuclear power industry in the United States adds less than 0.000001 unit to average annual exposure, and even persons living continuously next to the fence of a nuclear power plant receive less than 0.005 unit additional radiation per year.

Various theories have been advanced as a basis for calculating the effects of low levels of radiation by extrapolation from animal data at high levels. The most common of these is the "linear hypothesis" which suggests that if a dose of 100 units is known to increase the probability of a given cancer by one percent then a dose of 0.1 unit would increase that probability by 0.001 percent. Others have suggested a threshold below which the effect is zero because cellular processes repair the damage as fast as it is produced. Still others argue for biological processes which might make the effects proportionately greater at low doses than at high doses. The results of calculations made with such theories are often presented with an impressive show of scientific expertise, even to the point of calculating the exact number of cancer deaths which would occur in a large population as a result of a very small exposure. Such calculations feed upon and nourish widely held popular fears but have no basis in verifiable scientific knowledge. To the extent that their speculative character is not clearly stated, they are dishonest and harmful. For total doses much below fifty units the only honest conclusion is that we do not know and have no way of finding out what the effects really are.

Life is at best a hazardous enterprise. It is threatened by many agents in our environment other than natural radiation exposure. The causes of cancer appear to be many and varied. They range from diet and sunlight, through a wide assortment of both natural and manmade chemicals, to viruses and other unknown agents or causes. If one's chance of contracting leukemia before death from other causes is one in twenty, then it is merely pathological to fear any kind of environmental stress which can at most increase this chance from 0.05 to 0.0501. It is certainly meaningless to single out low-level radiation as an object of special fear among all these other causes. In the words of Psalm 53, "They were afraid where no fear was." In the unlikely event of nuclear warfare, and the certainly miniscule possibility of a maximum nuclear power plant accident, the threat would be real for those exposed to large doses of radiation. Even then, however, as the atomic bomb survivors in Japan have demonstrated, the majority would not develop cancer or other radiation-induced ills in their subsequent life spans. The fear of radiation in the grossly exaggerated forms which have become so prevalent only produces a needless paralysis of action for realizing the blessing from the immense reserve of nuclear fuel already at hand.

Fear of Radioactivity

The one really substantial fear inescapably tied to nuclear power is that of the enormous quantities of radioactive materials necessarily produced in direct proportion to the energy generated. Radioactive fission products are an inescapable result of fission energy. There is no way to have one without the other. Yet this means that in order to have nuclear energy, man must learn how to handle safely and dispose of trillions of times as much radioactivity as he ever experienced before World War II. It is an awesome prospect indeed and it merits the deepest concern.

Oddly enough, a major factor in insuring the safe handling of radioactive wastes is the extreme intensity of the radiation which they emit. It is simply not possible to handle them at all without extreme precautions involving massive radiation shields and remotely controlled devices. At every step — from the removal of spent fuel from the reactor, its temporary storage in deep water tanks near the reactor, its removal from storage and transportation to a reprocessing plant, subsequent storage after reprocessing, to later solidification and final disposal — at each one of these steps everything must be done remotely behind massive shielding. The arrangements for doing so involve such major and expensive engineering feats that exceptional safety is an automatic by-product. Moreover, of all environmen-

ENERGY AND THE CONQUEST OF FEAR

tal hazards, radiation is the most easily and accurately detected. The entire sequence of operations in waste handling is precisely and continuously monitored so that immediate warning is given of any mishap and the engineering design of each facility already includes means of coping with any mishap.

In the thirty years since World War II vast quantities of intensely radioactive wastes have been handled with complete safety. All such wastes, however, are still held in temporary storage. Military wastes continue to be retained in deep underground storage tanks as liquids. The wastes from nuclear power are still stored as unprocessed spent fuel. This last is partly the result of economics, since nuclear power reprocessing plants are commercial and must depend on the utility industry for their profitable construction and operation. None is currently in operation but one or two soon will be. This situation is also the result of a reluctance by the licensing agencies of the government to allow plutonium to be separated and reused for fear of weapons proliferation. The only exceptions to this current situation are the wastes from many underground weapons tests which, of course, remain deep underground at the points where they were generated on the Nevada test site.

For over ten years now, technically satisfactory means for the permanent disposal of these radioactive wastes have been fully developed and tested. The plan for such permanent disposal consists in converting the liquid wastes at high temperature into a glass-like ceramic cylinder about one foot in diameter and ten feet long. This is done ten years or more after removal from the reactor, by which time the short-lived fission products have all decayed, and those that remain are only one-thousandth as active as the fresh wastes. These ceramic cylinders are then buried permanently in specially prepared and geologically suitable formations at least 2000 feet below ground. The preferable geologic sites are deep salt mines because these are formations which have had no ground water for millions of years and because bedded salt is particularly suitable for removal of the residual radioactive heat. But other geological formations would also be suitable and are being studied.

Several reasons are responsible for the delay in proceeding with permanent disposal. Partly they are psychological and political. When word gets out that a particular site is being considered, strong opposition has developed from the governor, state legislators, and members of Congress in the state involved. Another reason has been a reluctance of the federal agency involved to fund disposal when tight budgets have seemed best applied to more urgent needs. However, such procrastination has by now created considerable public concern as to whether waste disposal is technically feasible. As a result it has now become urgent that we proceed with the permanent disposal of the large accumulation of military wastes. Thus, the Energy Research and Development Administration received a strong Congressional and Ford Administration mandate to proceed with all reasonable haste in the execution of such a program.

Public concern with the permanent disposal of nuclear wastes has centered on two issues. One is the thought of burying in the earth's crust a man-produced contaminant believed to be entirely foreign to it. The other is the idea of burdening future generations with a radioactive legacy with which they might not be able to cope because of ignorance. With respect to the first concern, it is necessary to realize that when the sun and planets were formed four and a half billion years ago, the earth and other planets grew out of material containing large quantities of radioactive wastes generated in previous stellar explosions. It is only because of this that the earth still contains uranium, thorium, and other natural radioactive elements. By now the entire mantle of the earth is white hot from the heat generated by these wastes during the last four billion years. But it is this radioactive heat that gives the earth's surface its dynamism and plasticity. Only because of it does the earth's crust exhibit plate tectonics, continental drift, mountains, earthquakes, and volcanoes. We shall never add radioactive wastes to the earth's crust which are more than a minute fraction of those already there, although our additions will initially be more concentrated. Clearly, however, man-generated radioactivity is not a foreign addition to the natural radioactivity already in the earth.

Drilling or mining in the waste burial sites must be prohibited for several centuries. Normal surface activities on the sites could, however, continue unimpeded since no radiation would penetrate the intervening earth from the cylinders buried 2000 feet below. After 300 years, even if one of the cylinders were removed and brought to the surface, it would be a serious radiation hazard only for persons remaining within a few feet of it for extended periods. After 600 years there would be no hazard whatever unless a person pressed his hands on the surface and held them there for an extended period, or unless the cylinder were ground to a fine powder and inhaled. The reason for this is that the radioactivity remaining after this period is due to residual plutonium and other elements heavier than uranium not removed during reprocessing. These elements decay radioactively by emitting alpha particles (nuclei of helium atoms) which are entirely absorbed by a sheet of paper or a few inches of air. It is difficult to imagine a motivation for removing any of these ceramic rods from their deep burial, even if all memory of their nature and origin had been lost, and even more difficult to imagine why anyone would want to grind them into a fine powder. Statements so frequently made that the wastes are very dangerous to future generations for 250,000 years (ten half-lives of plutonium) clearly represent grossly groundless fears.

A related fear of radioactivity centers on the element plutonium. When Dr. Glenn Seaborg, the discoverer of plutonium, realized that its alpha particle output was nearly 200,000 times that of U-238 from which it was produced, it drew from him the awed comment that it must be "the most toxic substance known to man." This was a natural and understandable hyperbole at that time when scarcely any plutonium had been produced and we had no experience with it. It is not, however, a factual statement, as will be seen, and doubtless was not intended to be when it was made. Nevertheless, those desiring to arouse fears of plutonium quote it frequently.

Plutonium is a metal very similar to uranium and like all heavy metals is chemically toxic in sufficient quantities. It is not, however, such chemical toxicity which is important for it. The overwhelming hazard is from the alpha particle radiation which it emits over long periods. Once permanently incorporated in bone, liver, or lungs, those tissues are continuously irradiated thereafter by the burden of plutonium which they carry. Extensive experiments with dogs have determined the body burdens of plutonium which lead to corresponding probabilities of developing bone cancer in ten to fifteen years. An indirect measure for man can be estimated from workers, mostly women, who applied radium to watch dials many years ago before the danger was realized. Body burdens of radium were later determined on many of these workers and correlated with the frequency of subsequent bone cancer. More recently similar data have been obtained from uranium miners who developed lung cancer from breathing the radioactive gas radon. Although the radiations from radium and radon are quite different from those of plutonium, an effort has been made to allow for these differences in establishing occupationally safe maximum body and lung burdens of plutonium for those who work with it.

The walls of the gastrointestinal tract are impervious to plutonium so there is little hazard from ingesting it. The greatest potential hazard seems to be from inhaling a fine dust of plutonium or its compounds. Dust particles in the lungs which are not eliminated naturally in time remain and continuously irradiate lung tissue. Another route for body entry would be through contaminated wounds. Since World War II, twenty-five men who worked at the Los Alamos Laboratory have retained from one tenth to ten times the maximum body burden and up to twenty-six times the maximum lung burden of plutonium. In 1965 a fire at the Rocky Flats, Colorado, plutonium plant generated fumes as a result of which twenty-five additional workers now have more than the maximum burden of plutonium in their lungs. Lung cancer might have been expected in some of them after ten or fifteen years but so far it has not developed in any of them. To some extent this is surprising since the incidence of lung cancer in the general population is now rather high. In 1973 seventeen out of 100 deaths in the United States were from cancer of all types so that some cancer deaths would be expected in any group exposed to radiation entirely apart from this cause.

New fears of plutonium have recently been fanned by a theory advanced by A. P. Tamplin and T. B. Cochran which concludes that the established maximum permissible lung burdens are too high by a factor of several thousand and that plutonium is, therefore, far more hazardous than has been thought. Their theory has been discredited by both British and American scientists knowledgeable in the field, and the fifty cases of lung burdens from Los Alamos and Rocky Flats clearly refute it. Nevertheless, those who wish to play on nuclear fear have seized upon it and continue to quote it as a scientifically reputable conclusion.

Plutonium is certainly a hazardous substance which like other hazardous substances must be handled with due caution.

ENERGY AND THE CONQUEST OF FEAR

But it is certainly not "the most toxic substance known to man," as Dr. Seaborg said soon after its discovery. Potassium cyanide and lead arsenate are at least as toxic as plutonium and are fatal in a few days rather than years later. Botulism toxin and anthrax spores are many times more toxic than plutonium. In the last thirty years hundreds of tons of plutonium have been produced and fabricated into weapons without a single cancer death so far from bodily intake among the workers who handled it.

The grossly exaggerated plutonium fear syndrome has now been adopted as the official policy of the National Council of Churches in the United States. The background document for this action, "The Plutonium Economy," addresses with great alarm all of the fears discussed here. It seizes upon Dr. Seaborg's statement, the Tamplin-Cochran theory, the fear of weapons proliferation, and the fear of the legacy of nuclear wastes in their most exaggerated forms. Many quotations misleadingly out of context are included, and it calls plutonium a "manmade element" (which it certainly is not) which it is wicked for man to introduce into the scheme of things. It is highly regrettable that this widely representative Christian body should have allowed itself to become such a non-Biblical purveyor of fear. It is even more regrettable that this action was taken without any mention of or sensitivity to the vital energy needs of nations and peoples far less fortunate than the United States.

Plutonium must be, can be, and is being handled with great caution. We must and can see to it that it is not diverted to weapons and that those who work with it do so in safety. As with other hazardous substances which we have learned to live with, we can institute precautions which make accidents exceedingly rare as the experience of the last thirty years has demonstrated. But we cannot do any of this if we allow ourselves to be paralyzed by fear. The most significant theological perspective on nuclear energy is the conquest of fear.

Other Fears and Hopes

In addition to the fears of nuclear energy as such, there is the fear of high technology in general of which nuclear is a symbol. Expressions of revulsion are increasingly heard against the highly organized and complex technological structures which are so rapidly sweeping the whole world. Spokesmen for such viewpoints are Jacques Ellul with his "worship of technique," Lewis Mumford with his "mega-machine," Buckminister Fuller, Ivan Illich, and a growing number of others. There is a feeling that technology has become so all-pervasive and out of control that it is no longer the servant of man but has become his master. Everyone is forced to conform to the requirements of the "System" in order to have any effective participation in society. The System is made up of enormous, impersonal multinational corporations and equally vast and impersonal government bureaucracies. It is run by a technological elite increasingly remote from and unintelligible to the average person. Employment in it requires a growing array of specialized skills which can only be acquired through rigorous and demanding training programs. Those who are intellectually, manually, or emotionally unwilling to pursue such training are forced to drop out of the System.

Nuclear energy has become a symbol of this general malaise. There is, indeed, a good reason for this status. Nuclear electric power is large scale, complex, and scientifically and technically extremely demanding. One of the most articulate spokesmen for this point of view is Amory Lovins of the Friends of the Earth.[1] He expresses a strong distaste for electricity in general and especially for its generation in large central station plants with either fossil fuels or nuclear fission — even with fusion if that should ever prove possible. "The social implications of centralized electrification, too, are as disquieting as its capital intensity: it is the most complex and slowest kind of technology to deploy, is remotely administered by a highly bureaucratized technical elite with little personal commitment to their clients, is vulnerable to large-scale and extremely expensive technical mistakes and failures, and is entirely at the mercy of a few people." In contrast, what he calls the "soft technologies" of solar, wind, and organic conversion are admirably suited to the basic ends of heating, cooking, lighting, and pumping which most people need. These are "small-scale, simple, low-technology, decentralized, non-electrical." This path

---

[1] Amory B. Lovins and John H. Price, *Non-Nuclear Futures: The Case For an Ethical Energy Strategy* (Cambridge, 1975).

ENERGY AND THE CONQUEST OF FEAR

leads to social values of decentralization and self-sufficiency, and to a more pluralistic and less coercive system offering a wide scope for social diversity. This plea for a recovery of small-scale technologies which can be the servant rather than the master of man has also been made persuasively by E. F. Schumacher in his book *Small is Beautiful*.

At the April 1975 European Nuclear Conference in Paris, M. H. Siebker of Brussels expressed this same viewpoint in a paper "How Much Energy, For Whom, For What, at What Price?" The following passage from this paper is quoted from the conference proceedings:

> Our countries do not need more energy; they need detoxification from consumption addiction; they need a cultural revolution. More social justice is one prerequisite for this; others are regionalization, decentralization, the cutting down of political and societal structures to dimensions a human being can identify with. And it means education for life, for creativity, rather than being focused exclusively on job preparation.

There is much to be said in favor of these viewpoints. The high-technology society which has been developing in just the last half century and has now come upon us full-blown is certainly not an unmixed blessing. It has brought with it severe environmental and social stresses, profligate wastefulness of fuel and other nonrenewable resources, and often frivolous patterns of consumption. We are already beginning to pay dearly for environmental protection, and new initiatives are urgently needed to conserve energy and curb waste. But the inner dynamics and inertia of this movement in history do not suggest the feasibility of an abrupt reversal of established trends or a radical restructuring of the System. The situation is reminiscent of the agrarian movement of the 1920s and 1930s which strove so unsuccessfully to reverse or at least slow down the accelerating rural-urban migration patterns of the time. The current nostalgia for a vanishing world is understandable but is not likely to be successful in combatting the trends which it deplores.

The idea of decentralized, widely dispersed electrical generation has great appeal. In addition to the ideal of self-sufficiency, it offers the possibility of utilizing the waste heat from the electricity produced in useful and energy-conserving ways. But it should be recognized that this is just the way we started in this country. Electrical systems were small and local even to the point of individual hotels and large buildings. Numerous farms before rural electrification had their own wind-driven Delco electric systems. But the care and maintenance of such systems was a continual and demanding task, and when they broke down one simply did without electricity until they could be repaired and put back in operation. The growth of our large interconnected national electric grid was a natural evolution from such decentralized systems and was gladly welcomed as it came. Underdeveloped countries will doubtless begin to have electricity in rural areas in the same way, but in time the same course of evolution would be expected for them too. Except for isolated instances, a reversal of this course back to widespread decentralization seems most unlikely.

A persistent hope held strongly by those opposed to nuclear energy is that if we can just pull through the next twenty years or so on domestic coal and imported oil, there will be a breakthrough in solar energy or fusion research which will make nuclear fission power and especially breeders unnecessary. Such hopes are based almost entirely on a childlike faith in what science and technology can accomplish if only they are given adequate financial support and a little more time. They are not, unfortunately, grounded in any informed evaluation of technical or economic realities. Solar energy will undoubtedly play an increasingly important role in hot water heaters and the heating of houses and other buildings. Through the production of biomass, particularly in the tropics, it can play a vital role in the production of liquid and gaseous fuels to take over as natural gas and petroleum become unavailable for burning. But for the generation of electricity in any significant quantity, neither solar energy nor fusion can be counted on at any time in the future.[2] It is vital that the false character of these hopes be widely understood in order that the essential role of breeder reactors in the future energy economy of mankind can be fully appreciated. It is irresponsible to hold out hopes which one

---

[2]For further information on these crucial points, the reader is referred to my own evaluation of the long-range prospects for solar energy in the July-August 1976 issue (pp. 424-429) and the September-October 1976 issue (pp. 509-13) of the *American Scientist*. For the prospects for fusion, the three articles by William D. Metz in the 25 June (pp. 1320-23), 2 July (pp. 38-40, 76) and 23 July (pp. 307-09) 1976 issues of *Science*, and especially the editorial by Philip H. Abelson in the latter, are highly recommended.

does not understand in a matter of such vital importance.

One of the extremely attractive features of nuclear electricity is its negligible effect on the environment. A nuclear power plant is quiet, architecturally pleasing, and sealed off from its external environment. The only appreciable environmental effect is the disposal of its waste heat, but this it shares with any alternative mode of generating electricity. The fission wastes from it are necessarily sealed off from the environment at all stages of processing and their ultimate disposal is so far underground as to remove them permanently from the biosphere. Only in the mining of uranium ore is there environmental disturbance, and this is many times less than the mining of the same energy content of coal. In the long range when breeders have been fully deployed and fed from our stockpile of depleted uranium, even this environmental insult will be eliminated. In view of this it is disconcerting that such groups as the National Resources Defense Council and the Sierra Club oppose nuclear energy on environmental grounds. They are driven by the groundless fears previously discussed to work against their own professed objectives. The only way to defend our precious coal resources from needless squandering and to avoid major environmental threats while still meeting minimum needs for electricity is to apply our best efforts toward the utilization of the immense resource of depleted uranium already in hand. These groups should be in the forefront of support for nuclear electricity.

Early in this century when the accelerating use of coal was beginning to create intolerable pollution in many cities, we discovered that we had vast reserves of oil and natural gas and gratefully converted from coal to these cleaner and much more convenient fuels. Now just as our domestic supplies of oil and natural gas are beginning to shrink, a new and unsuspected source of energy has been revealed. This sequence of events strikes one as amazingly providential. Yet in spite of that feeling, many still shrink from its implications. Many of the most sensitive analysts of the current human predicament, with whom I otherwise feel the closest affinity, nevertheless imply the hope that "something else" will come along to save us from what they regard as the dread prospect of nuclear dependence. They acknowledge fully (in contrast to the idealists who want us to make out with practically no energy) the desperate need for energy in meeting the most elementary human needs of a human population of seven or eight billion persons which will be upon us at the end of this century. But still they shrink from the contemplation of nuclear electricity as the only way out. They too are victims of the same unresolved fears which have recently invaded the public domain. Yet once again in the human saga, as he has before, man must conquer his fear in order to avail himself of a new providential source of energy. It is the hopeful objective of this essay to provide some assistance for the difficult passage to the other side of fear as we all face the challenge of nuclear energy in a world which desperately needs it.

Scenarios of Disaster and Hope

V

A Terrorist Attack

BRIAN O'LEARY

The Scenario: New Year's Eve 1999

I was nervous, just like a boy again. It was the anxiety, the fright of fourteen years ago coming back — the flash, the burns, death, and the nagging uncertainty of what the radiation would do to those of us who survived.

Hiroshima and Nagasaki weren't enough, I thought, pacing the floor. It had to happen again. And this time it had been New York.

I poured myself a gin and tonic and walked out to the balcony overlooking the surf which lapped against the Na Pali cliffs about four miles to the west. Clouds were peeling off Mt. Waialeale and the rainbow to the east was bright now, the sun shining through the rain. Wet tropical aromas filled the air.

Hanalei never looked more beautiful but somehow I couldn't feel it. Guilt, maybe, memories of our collective inac-

---

Brian O'Leary received a B.A. in physics from Williams College in 1961, an M.A. in astronomy from Georgetown University in 1964 and a Ph.D. in astronomy from the University of California, Berkeley, in 1967. From 1967 to 1968, Dr. O'Leary served as scientist-astronaut with the National Aeronautics and Space Administration. Since that time, he has taught on the faculties of Cornell, Caltech, the University of California at Berkeley, and the University of Massachusetts; he is currently a member of the research staff of the Physics Department at Princeton University.

Dr. O'Leary is a writer on science policy and space exploration. In 1975, he served as an energy consultant for the United States Congressional House Committee on Energy and the Environment. He is the author of The Making of an Ex-Astronaut, named by the American Library Association as the Best Young Adult Book of 1970. Since 1965, his main research areas have included the physics of planetary atmospheres, surfaces and interiors, and science and public policy with emphasis on space exploration and energy policy.

tion when the threat was made and now the lonely but comfortable and aesthetic retirement on the island of Kauai.

I walked in from the balcony on the twentieth story of Hanalei Towers and up to the mirror. A few grey strands of hair covered the worst of my skin cancer (I was one of those "foolish" individuals who cared to continue spending time in the sun after the attack). I looked all of my sixty years and then some.

I gulped the rest of my drink and then started to scold myself for drinking alone. The dirigible was late, though, and I was nervous.

People had various ways of dealing with guilt. After the United States dropped two atomic bombs on Japan in 1945, some of the scientists and bomb craftsmen in the Manhattan Project spent the rest of their careers trying to assuage their guilt by warning of the hazards of nuclear proliferation.

Now it was our turn. Until 1986 we had been too young to listen or understand. We had heard stories and seen films of the horrors of Hiroshima and Nagasaki but the political realities of these tragedies had dulled our senses. None of us had visited Hiroshima and Nagasaki after it happened. Some of our senior colleagues did, but they could not explain it to us.

In contrast, my memories of the last quarter of the twentieth century were vivid. I remember the hearing room on the third floor of the Dirksen Senate Office Building, a snowy day in January 1976. As a consultant to the Government Operations Committee, I sat behind Senator John Glenn who listened silently and solemnly to the testimony of Jerome Frank, a psychiatrist.

"Why," asked Frank, "is it so hard to maintain adequate controls over the spread of nuclear reactors? The explanation lies, I believe, in the psychological unreality of the dangers."

Witness after witness in these hearings described the futility of preventing the spread of nuclear weapons made with the technology and materials intended for peaceful purposes.

It was depressing, a can of worms. My gaze on the snowflakes from the hearing room in winter 1976 diffused into daydreams of the tropics, of a better world perhaps, the Hanalei of my retirement. The problem was too ponderous and intractable for me or for anybody else.

Former Atomic Energy Commission Chairman David

A TERRORIST ATTACK

Lilienthal had testified during those hearings that the United States should do nothing less than stop all nuclear exports and assume moral leadership in preventing proliferation. He felt that, as the world's foremost provider of nuclear technology, the United States could give the world a chance to avoid a headlong collision with nuclear terror.

Other witnesses had disagreed, stating that Germany, France, and other nations would go ahead anyway in a highly competitive international marketplace. All that could be done, they felt, was to discourage the international spread of those parts of the nuclear fuel cycle from which bombs could be made and to implement strict international safeguards.

It was all academic, though. Little happened to stop the spread. Theodore Taylor, Manhattan Project bomb architect and another witness, had predicted at the 1976 hearings that it was likely that somehow, some way, before the end of the century, a nation or terrorist group would successfully divert fissionable material and explode an atomic bomb for destructive purposes.

He had been correct.

I poured another drink and walked out to the balcony. The sun was about to sink into the Pacific. The dirigible would be coming in through the high-arching rainbow to the east, riding the trade winds from Honolulu. It would contain three of the alumni of our State Department working group who had been involved in the futile negotiations leading to the horror of 1986.

This was all my idea, perhaps to assuage my guilt (*our* guilt?), to see the coming of the millennium with those who helped make the policies which may or may not have contributed to the event. It would be a winter break from our crusades to eliminate all nuclear materials and facilities from the earth, a chance to get together to ponder what went wrong.

* * * * *

In spring 1986 a Brazilian group who called themselves the Revolutionary Vanguard sent an extraordinary threat to the White House. At that time I was a professor of public policy and, as a member of a State Department emergency task force of a working group on terrorist threats, was immediately called to Washington to help deal with the threat.

The telegram simply stated that a nuclear bomb would be exploded in a major American city within forty-eight hours unless the United States government could successfully convince the Brazilian government to release fifty prisoners affiliated with the revolutionary group.

The difficulty in dealing with this threat was that there were no more communications from the group. Intelligence neither confirmed nor denied the authority of the threat, so I leaned in the direction of caution for several obvious reasons.

Over the previous two years, the Brazilian government had changed hands twice. Now ruled by a military junta, repression of other groups was severe. Plants designed to reprocess spent fuel from nuclear reactors were now actively producing plutonium which began to be stockpiled for atomic weapons. The 1975 Brazilian safeguards agreement with West Germany, the nation exporting nuclear material to Brazil, had been broken in the revolution of 1984 when the new government declared a policy of nuclear parity with Argentina.

When the Brazilian nuclear reprocessing plant was again seized in the 1985 overthrow, several technicians fled to underground villages in the Amazon Jungle with a few hundred pounds of plutonium — enough to detonate dozens of nuclear bombs. The new government did not seem to put a high priority on the internal nuclear threat — at least until now — and the United States suddenly found itself right in the middle of it, perhaps because of its support of the new regime.

There was no question in anyone's mind that the Revolutionary Vanguard could explode a nuclear device and could deliver it almost anywhere in the world. As far back as 1976, the MITRE Corporation, a Virginia think tank, warned that nuclear materials in the hands of a terrorist group "would give it a power of blackmail over the world at large and the United States in particular without precedent in history."[1] Between 1969 and 1975, ninety-nine threats of violence were directed against commercial nuclear facilities.

Since that time, international efforts to curb nuclear proliferation could not keep pace with the breakneck speed of the spread of weapons grade plutonium and nuclear material. By 1980, seventeen nations had the capacity to produce atomic

---

[1] MITRE Corporation, "The Threat to Licensed Nuclear Facilities," MTR-7022 (McLean, Va., 1975).

weapons from materials reprocessed from rods in nuclear reactors. Only ten kilograms of plutonium or twenty kilograms of highly enriched uranium are needed to fabricate a crude atomic bomb with a devastation potential similar to that of Hiroshima.

With tons of such material unaccounted for in worldwide inventories and with highly varying monitoring and security practices, most experts agreed it would only be a matter of time before a terrorist group could pose a convincing threat. Stealing such small amounts of nuclear material was no great challenge, particularly in those nations where the line between government and terrorism was fuzzy and always changing. The International Atomic Energy Agency (IAEA), though charged with applying safeguards that detect efforts by governments to divert nuclear materials from peaceful to military purposes, had no jurisdiction over securing materials from theft or sabotage by terrorist or criminal groups. That was the responsibility of each nation, but if the governments of some nations changed hands among various revolutionary groups, sometimes with violence, how could nuclear facilities be consistently safeguarded against theft and diversion?

The options available to terrorists ranged from overt attack to clandestine diversion by an "insider" in the face of inadequate physical security which could be expected during chaotic times. Fabricating and delivering a crude atomic bomb from stolen nuclear material was also a relatively simple task. For decades, the technology for developing atomic weapons was well understood and readily available in the open scientific literature and the engineering has been well within the grasp of underdeveloped nations and motivated terrorist groups in much the same way knowledge of conventional explosives spread among these groups earlier in the century. With a completed bomb weighing perhaps 100 kilograms, the options a terrorist group would have for delivery and detonation worldwide are numerous.

Many of us in the emergency task force had discussed possible methods of a terrorist attack, citing as examples the 1972 Olympics in Munich, skyjackings, Middle East terrorism and the more recent nuclear threats which, fortunately (and remarkably), had proven hollow. Maybe it was for that reason — a case of amnesia — that neither the administration nor the general public seemed to have the will to pay the necessary serious attention to these threats, where some precautionary measures would at least have reduced the likelihood of their success. The Revolutionary Vanguard was a well-coordinated group. I felt they were serious about their threat and that the United States should have at least gone through the motions of putting pressure on to release the prisoners.

Should have — but it was United States policy not to negotiate with terrorist groups. The controversial hard line policy was designed to deter future threats and live with the current threat, come what may. In other words, the United States would not give in to blackmail.

So the decision in our reply was firm and the President made a press release saying that "we will not be blackmailed." My memory haunted me of a similar statement President Richard Nixon had made in 1973 in response to a terrorist threat from Khartoum. The result was that two Americans and one Belgian held hostage were killed by terrorists.

As we all recall, during the crisis of 1986, the President did leave the golf course to issue a number of emergency proclamations for civilian protection — none having any real safety value. The FBI and CIA were alerted to track down the terrorists worldwide, and an emergency United States session was called to request that the Brazilian government and their police take extreme investigative procedures. He went on national television to reassure the people that the danger was not as great as might be feared.

The emergency task force of the working group, then, had little to do but wait. Intelligence reports had told us nothing. Four arrests had been made of suspected leaders of the terrorist group — one in London, one in West Germany, and two in the United States, but no immediate clues or links could be found. We knew that the International Atomic Energy Commission was about to release a report stating that their inspections showed that 150 kilograms of weapons grade plutonium had, in fact, been unaccounted for in the inventory of the Brazilian reprocessing plant. This was consistent with witness reports of the Revolutionary Vanguard's successful seizure and theft there during the 1985 overthrow of the government. The IAEA kept inventories and made inspections but had no jurisdiction over the physical security of the plant.

All I could do was to speculate about the numerous permu-

A TERRORIST ATTACK

tations of possibilities for a successful terrorist nuclear attack — in 1968 Taylor had calculated 10^{70} possible ways, a number so large that it could not even be counted by all the high speed computers in the world in a time as long as the age of the solar system!

I had reminded the group of Dr. Frank's premonition one decade earlier that people lack an accurate perception of the consequences of a nuclear attack: "Humans have incredibly sensitive equipment for detecting light, sound, orders, and objects touching the skin, but none for detecting radiation. Moreover, except for the inhabitants of Hiroshima and Nagasaki and the handful of people who have seen test explosions, no one has experienced a nuclear explosion. Hence, it is little wonder that the dangers of nuclear proliferation, while recognized intellectually, have so little effect on the behavior of national leaders."

After a twenty-four-hour vigil, some of us in the emergency task force went back home after being briefed by the Secretary of State that the problem would probably go away and that he and the President would continue to apprise us of developments.

But that night, March 18, 1986, it happened. As I was lying in my bed in a twilight sleep at ten minutes before midnight in my New York apartment, an unmistakable flash illuminated the room and the horror was immediately upon us.

"What the . . . " were my wife's last words as the shock wave of the blast galed glass into her head. I rolled to the floor with a last memory of the thunderous, throaty, crackling roar, before losing consciousness for several hours.

My son saved my life with an extraordinary first aid effort. I came to in a pool of blood looking at his face as he applied a tourniquet to my arm. He seemed okay but bewildered.

The portable radio was on (Newark wasn't destroyed) and sirens wailed from all directions. The room was full of rubble, my wife dead. The grim memory visits my dreams, day and night — the horror of fourteen years ago.

Terrorists from the Brazilian Revolutionary Vanguard had delivered a five kiloton bomb to an explosion 3000 feet above Manhattan, killing 400,000 persons and inducing another two million or so cases of cancer (nobody really knows how many — was my skin cancer caused by this? I don't know). The bomb was dropped by an agent who hired a Cherokee airplane in New Jersey. He died too. The bomb containing ten kilograms of plutonium had been smuggled into the United States aboard a banana freighter in 1985, and there was no suspicion of its existence. A clean, simple, effective terrorist attack which wiped out ten blocks in midtown Manhattan changed the world.

We now have the benefit of hindsight, the genesis of the greatest human disaster in the history of the world being contained in 2000 volumes of reports. In 1985, two employees of the Brazilian Nuclear Reprocessing Facility — later identified as members of the Revolutionary Vanguard — were able to obtain enough knowledge of handling plutonium and enough information about the design of the plant to lead a twenty-five-man attack into the bowels of the plant during the Brazilian April revolution. With electrical power out and the militia concentrating on urban areas, it was relatively easy to overcome the guards and steal storage tanks containing 150 kilograms of weapons grade plutonium waiting to be shipped to Brazilian nuclear power plants and to their newly formed nuclear arsenal.

Using a hand truck, then a pickup truck, the tanks were driven into the Amazon jungle where three highly paid technicians with university engineering degrees spent the next several months fabricating the bomb (one of the technicians had a masters degree in electrical engineering from MIT with a specialty in pyrotechnic circuits). A West German technician who was present during the attack filed a report to the International Atomic Energy Agency (IAEA) describing the events and estimating the amount stolen. The incident made international headlines and pressure on the new government was met with verbal assurances of stern action, but with little immediate follow-through because of poor organization. The junta was barely able to rule the hinterlands of Brazil. Some of the urban leaders of the Revolutionary Vanguard were identified and arrests were made.

Meanwhile, the overwrought and understaffed IAEA could not quickly respond to the international pressure to assess the loss of plutonium. They issued a statement that its inventory and inspection procedure would take "some months" to complete. The new Brazilian government was reluctant to cooperate with IAEA inspectors, and the IAEA did not consider a few hundred pounds missing to be "of utmost urgency" because of

A TERRORIST ATTACK

tons of missing nuclear material each year reported by their inspections worldwide. It was quite widely known, for example, that the Indian government diverted about one ton of nuclear material each year from its commercial nuclear facilities for explosive purposes.

By September 1985 the first Brazilian Revolutionary Vanguard bomb was completed and placed in the hull of a banana freighter in Rio de Janeiro bound for New York. The 100-kilogram cylinder looked like a trash can. Inside were ten kilograms of plutonium surrounded with TNT and electronic gadgets. At arrival, the bomb cannister easily passed dock inspection along with other trash cans and headed for the Nardone Fruit Company in Bayonne, New Jersey, in a ten-ton truck.

The truck driver, Ricardo Pasquez, was an employee of the company and a member of the Revolutionary Vanguard who fled Brazil and immigrated to the United States during the Revolution of 1985. A burly young pilot and engineer, he was designated by the Revolutionary Vanguard to carry out any threat to the United States which it felt would help gain for the group political power and international recognition.

That feeling became inflamed when two of the leaders of the Revolutionary Vanguard were captured near their Amazon headquarters and executed, without trial, by a firing squad of the new ruling junta on March 4, 1986. Efforts by the CIA and FBI to follow the government's leads to infiltrate the group's Amazon hideout were just beginning but were not in time; the headquarters changed and the "bomb factory" (one small thatched hut) was found by government officials the day after the March 18 disaster.

Upon explicit coded orders sent by a messenger flown in from Rio de Janeiro the day before, on March 18, 1986, Pasquez rolled the cannister from his Jersey City garage into his station wagon, drove to the Newark airport, rented a Cherokee single engine airplane, rolled the bomb onto the front passenger seat of the airplane, took off, and headed over Manhattan. Consulting a map and his airspeed and altitude in a routine he had rehearsed several times, he flung open the right-hand door of the aircraft, threw two switches on the top of the cannister, and rolled it out. Ten seconds later, the bomb exploded, evaporating the airplane and Pasquez and devastating midtown New York.

How could this all have happened? After all the rehashings, the books written, and documentaries finished, it now seems simple. In fact, the incredible had really occurred, Taylor was right, and the catastrophe had happened. Few people seemed to understand.

Two milestones marked the most critical steps. The first was the use of nuclear energy, first unleashed in the crude bomb exploded in Alamogordo, New Mexico. The second occurred some thirty years later, when the framework for expanding the international nuclear club was founded by the perception that the best way to produce electricity would be by nuclear power reactors and that the most economical fuel was plutonium reprocessed from fuel burned in those reactors.

What did not seem obvious to us in the 1970s was that all this was unnecessary, that international nuclear deals were hastily struck with illusory expectations. Just then — when it was getting to be too late to do much about it — it was becoming increasingly clear that nuclear power as a long-term energy source involved incalculable hazards, was uneconomical, and would be replaced, in time, by solar power.

But, in the international community, there developed a sense of near-panic, perhaps in part due to the refusal of the United States and five other nuclear powers to stop stockpiling enormous quantities of nuclear weaponry. After thirty years of this type of domination, other nations wanted a share of the action. What better way to do this than enter the nuclear club under the pretense of acquiring the nuclear technology for peaceful purposes? Companies in the exporting nations fattened their tills, several billion dollars' worth — with each impending deal, with reprocessing technology thrown in as a "sweetener," and each deal was sealed in a package of bilateral safeguards agreements — easily broken once the technology was acquired.

So obvious, in retrospect. But during the 1970s none of us really seemed to be able to do much about it, or wanted to be able to do much about it. It was all so depressing and there were more positive things to think about, even though the evidence, even then, stared us in the face.

In 1973 India exploded an atomic bomb with materials produced in an experimental reprocessing plant which they had bought from Canada. The Indians explained this was a test intended for peaceful nuclear explosions, in spite of allegations by experts that these devices are uneconomical — let alone unsafe — for any envisioned peaceful use, such as canal digging.

* * * * *

A pastel twilight cast a dim reflection off the ocean gnawing at the Na Pali cliffs. Towering puffballs over Mt. Waialeale to the south and east indicated that it was, as almost always, raining at the summit. I was reminded of the mushroom cloud I never saw but felt.

I looked at my watch. It was almost seven o'clock in Hawaii, which meant just a few minutes before the next millennium would arrive on the East Coast. I turned on the television set and watched a frost-huddled crowd await the dropping of the traditional ball — a benign ball — from a clock on the side of a skyscraper in rebuilt Times Square. I shivered.

Walking back out to the balcony, I saw the dirigible in the east. Such bitter irony — my cancer, my wife's death, a death and illness toll exceeding that of any event in the history of the nation — all for a technology meant to produce electricity.

Bitter irony because hanging high above the dirigible to the east were ten bright stars — satellite solar power stations in orbit 22,000 miles above the equator providing 30,000 megawatts of electricity for California, the equivalent of thirty nuclear power plants. Nuclear power unnecessary after all! It had all been a bad dream, the legacy of our misconceptions earlier in the vanishing century.

Reflections

What can be done to avoid this dreadful scenario or any of 10^{70} possible other ones? There are, I believe, several corrections in public policy which the United States could follow to reduce the risks. In the following few paragraphs, I will describe some areas which need immediate attention. Most of this material is from an internal staff memorandum I prepared for members of the Senate Government Operations Committee, for whom I was a consultant in January 1976.[2]

[2]Much of this material is based on data drawn from the United States Senate Government Operations Committee Handbook, "Facts on Nuclear Prolifera-

The first point concerns understanding those aspects of the nuclear fuel cycle which are most susceptible to theft, diversion, and use as nuclear weapons material. The nuclear fuel cycle consists of those industrial processes necessary for the civil use of nuclear power. It includes the mining of uranium, milling of uranium ores, various chemical processing steps, enrichment of natural uranium-235 (U-235), fabrication of nuclear fuel, use of the fuel in power reactors, reprocessing of used fuel to recover residual nuclear materials, and disposal of long-lived radioactive wastes. Of the various points along the fuel cycle, enrichment, reprocessing, and fabrication are most susceptible to theft or diversion for use as nuclear weapons.

Producing the nuclear materials required for nuclear explosives is considered much more difficult than designing and building the explosives themselves. Three types of material can be used as the core material for nuclear explosives: uranium that is highly enriched in the isotope U-235; plutonium, which can be made by capturing neutrons in U-238, the abundant isotope in natural uranium; and U-233, which can be made by capturing neutrons in natural thorium. None of these so-called "weapons grade" materials exists naturally in significant quantities.

A country that wants to acquire the materials necessary for making fission explosives now has several options, at least in principle. The option which would appear most attractive to a particular country would depend on many technological, political, military, economic, and other considerations.

There are also risks that non-national organizations, including terrorists, might covertly direct or openly steal weapons grade nuclear materials from civilian or military nuclear fuel cycles and make their own nuclear explosives, or even steal complete nuclear weapons. Such thefts could be made from facilities or vehicles that are inadequately protected from armed theft or diversion by "insider" members of a group. Such nuclear threats are not subject to deterrence by the threat of nuclear retaliation. Physical security safeguards in the United

---

tion" (1976), as well as from Congressional testimony by Dr. Theodore Taylor, Chairman of the Board, International Research and Technology Corporation; Herbert Scoville, Jr., Executive Director, Arms Control Association; and Lawrence Scheinman, Director, Peace Studies Program, Cornell University.

A TERRORIST ATTACK

States and, very likely in other countries, are not yet adequate to prevent theft from all places where substantial quantities of weapons grade materials exist.

Fortunately, this situation is now changing very rapidly in the United States, as a result of recent actions by the Atomic Energy Commission, and now continuing under the authority of the Nuclear Regulatory Commission and the Energy Research and Development Administration. Unfortunately, the safeguards in several other nations are presently inadequate to be assured of protection against nuclear theft by terrorist groups.

It is clear that the most vulnerable points in the nuclear fuel cycle, from a safeguards point of view, are reprocessing, fuel fabrication and enrichment, and the transportation routes between nuclear facilities. Assuming that we must live with nuclear power on an international scale, the most tractable technological solutions must necessarily involve minimizing the number of fuel facilities (particularly those not under international auspices), co-locating such facilities to avoid the transportation of fissionable materials, and implementing extremely careful detection and inspection procedures, along with tight physical security, to discourage theft and diversion.

Solutions in the following areas must be found:

Enrichment: The control of technology for U-235 separation is at least theoretically still possible, but the situation is rapidly getting out of hand. More and more countries are approaching a basic capability. The South Africans already have a pilot plant. The Germans, Dutch, and British are working on a combined facility, and recently, the Germans agreed to supply the Brazilians with a separation facility. Therefore, the realistic hope of curbing proliferation of U-235 is probably not through the control of technology, although it may be desirable to maintain secrecy on the laser process to buy time. Instead, it lies in developing more economically reliable international sources of supply of enriched uranium fuel, thus discouraging independent national capabilities. The economic justification for such an approach is very strong, but time is running out for action if we wish to avoid a number of small potential sources of weapons grade U-235 being built around the world.

Reprocessing: The fact that reprocessing appears to be economically unjustifiable on the modest scales most nations envision for their nuclear futures raises the possibility that the best form of control is not through bans on technology exchange, which might be impossible to enforce, but through a positive program of internationally managed centers to satisfy the reprocessing requirements of many different countries. These centers could also have fuel fabrication and storage facilities co-located in them. This would be a sound economic approach, would reduce the safety problems from the radioactive materials involved, and, most importantly, would decrease the risks that the processed plutonium could be diverted or stolen and turned into weapons. The availability of such centers would reduce the pressures to supply assistance in the construction of national facilities. Then if a country pursued the national course, they would be raising the warning flag that their intentions may be directed toward a weapons capability, and suppliers would have better justification for withholding assistance.

Safeguards: Tight security against theft of fissionable materials throughout the world is mandatory. The International Atomic Energy Agency (IAEA) will need to be strengthened to cope with the rapidly increasing number of countries and facilities which will be involved. The current IAEA system of safeguards suffers from several major deficiencies which require prompt attention to minimize the hazards of proliferation. Among them are:

- Non-participants and abrogators of the IAEA safeguard provisions of The Treaty on the Non-Proliferation of Nuclear Weapons (NPT) could stockpile fissionable nuclear material and build nuclear weapons. A solution would be for the United States and other nuclear suppliers to discourage nations from developing or importing nuclear fuel facilities (uranium enrichment, plutonium reprocessing, and fuel fabrication plants), primarily on economic grounds, by providing inexpensive, reliable fuel services needed for development of peaceful nuclear power programs without those steps in the fuel cycle which involve producing fissionable material. The establishment of international fuel enrichment, reprocessing, and fabrication centers is one possible solution.

- The negotiation of the NPT/IAEA Safeguards Document resulted in an incomplete safeguards system in which only certain points in nuclear facilities can be monitored and in

A TERRORIST ATTACK 127

which human intervention is minimized. This contradicts the IAEA statute, which provides for "access at all times to places and data" and, therefore, should be reassessed in future negotiations. Moreover, the technology required for implementing such a system has not yet been applied. Once applied in each participating nation, improved accounting procedures may be adequate to ensure a satisfactory system of safeguards, but, until then, the situation is uncertain and potentially grave.

- Secrecy in current inspection procedures may raise suspicions among some nations that inequities are occurring in IAEA safeguards. These procedures should be opened to the extent needed to avert such suspicions.
- The IAEA has no jurisdiction over the physical security of fissionable nuclear materials, nor does it have the charge to discourage export of such materials to those nations that do not meet its security standards. The IAEA needs strengthening along these lines — at least to the extent of discouraging exports to nations deficient in physical security.
- The IAEA should consider separating its promotional and regulatory functions to ensure institutional integrity in implementing its international safeguards system.

One major problem with imposing tight safeguards on nuclear facilities and shipments would be the possible development of a police-state atmosphere which could lead to stepped-up espionage, invasion of privacy, and other related human problems. The effect would be particularly critical if a terrorist nuclear attack were successfully carried out. What could be the response? It is likely that a public outcry would result which would tighten clamps and create a post-catastrophe police-state throughout the world. One result might be that the generation of nuclear power, at least in some areas, would have to come to an abrupt halt at a time some nations could ill afford to be deprived of a sizeable fraction of their energy. These considerations suggest prudent policy planning to cover contingencies and, at all costs, to discourage (or disallow) the development of those parts of the nuclear fuel cycle which produce weapons grade material.

Perhaps a more fundamental point in curbing the hazards of the proliferation of nuclear technology is the question of whether the world needs nuclear power at all. Aside from the threat of terrorist or national use of nuclear weapons fabricated from materials intended for peaceful power, there are the problems of the safety of nuclear power plants, radioactive waste disposal, and the questionable economics of nuclear power. All these factors have given rise to widespread political debate about the efficacy of nuclear power in the United States.

In a time of energy shortages and dependence on foreign oil, the United States has begun to pursue a policy of developing long-range energy sources and energy conservation. The hope among many experts is that fossil fuels and uranium might be replaced by clean, renewable, and economically competitive sources by the turn of the century. Prime candidates for electrical power generation are satellite solar power stations constructed from nonterrestrial resources and power plants making use of temperature differences in the oceans. Unfortunately, the Energy Research and Development Administration has not been quick to pursue these new initiatives and, in many ways, behaves as though nuclear power will be the inevitable source for the future.

Finally, the question of United States policy toward international terrorism is currently under debate. The policy has been, and remains, no concessions, no negotiations. Such a policy, designed to deter future terrorism, is inflexible. It could be an "invitation to murder" in some cases where the terrorist group might perceive it would benefit from the publicity given to its cause.[3] Where the threat is potentially enormous, as in the case of using nuclear materials for bombs, it would seem essential to adopt a flexible negotiating policy in dealing with terrorists, contrary to current United States policy.

In summary, I believe the United States could take the leadership in curbing nuclear proliferation which perhaps is the greatest current threat to mankind. Several general steps are needed:

- International moral leadership, perhaps adopting David Lilienthal's nuclear export embargo with an affirmation that nuclear technology is economically marginal (at best) as a means of producing electricity and is ultimately unsafe. In foreign policy, the active discouragement of other nations from developing those parts of the nuclear fuel cycle which are sus-

---

[3]See Judith Miller, "Bargain with Terrorists?", *The New York Times Magazine,* July 18, 1976, p. 7.

ceptible to weapons production — reprocessing and enrichment.

• The insistence on strict international safeguards standards through the expansion of the size and scope of the International Atomic Energy Agency.

• The development of safe alternative electrical energy sources for widespread use by the early twenty-first century and the encouragement of energy conservation in the meantime.

• The adoption of a more flexible foreign policy in dealing with terrorist groups in which the gravity of the threat is carefully considered.

• International agreements to drastically reduce the existing stockpile of nuclear weapons, a "vertical proliferation" of nuclear overkill of which the United States is the leader.

VI

Nuclear War Comes to the Middle East

ROBERT J. PRANGER

This is a story about how nuclear war came to the Middle East. Events are fictitious. Description of nuclear capabilities and effects are actual. The sequence of events, however, is quite possible if peace negotiations should break down totally in the next few years. This story is written in an effort to gain some foresight into how a nuclear calamity might be prevented in the Arab-Israeli conflict. At its end an effort at hindsight will be attempted in order to determine what went wrong and why the conflict moved to the point at which an Arab city was destroyed by an Israeli atomic bomb. Since the scenario is fictitious, however, this effort at hindsight is actually a form of foresight — none of this need ever happen. It is hoped that by using fiction

---

Robert J. Pranger is Director of Foreign and Defense Policy Studies at American Enterprise Institute for Public Policy Research, Washington, D.C., a position he has held since July 1972.

A native of Wisconsin, Dr. Pranger was educated at the University of California at Berkeley, where he received his Ph.D. in political science in 1961. He was elected to Phi Beta Kappa at the University of California.

Before coming to the American Enterprise Institute for Public Policy Research in September 1971 as Resident Scholar in International and National Security Affairs, Dr. Pranger was Deputy Assistant Secretary of Defense for Policy Plans and National Security Council Affairs in the Office of International Security Affairs (ISA) from late September 1970 until August 1971. Prior to this he had been Deputy Assistant Secretary of Defense for Near East and South Asian Affairs in ISA from June 1969 until late September 1970. He was twice awarded the Department of Defense Meritorious Civilian Service Medal.

From 1960 to 1971 Dr. Pranger held teaching positions in political science and political theory at the University of Illinois (1960-65), University of Kentucky (1965-68), and University of Washington (1968-71). In addition, he has taught at the University of California, Berkeley, and the University of Maryland, College Park.

in this way, nuclear war in the Middle East will never occur in real life.

Beyond its ramifications for the Middle East this story may also be helpful for exploring ways to slow down or halt nuclear proliferation in the wider international community. It is assumed here that whatever it is that compels nations to go to war, atomic warfare should be avoided at all costs. The burden for this control of nuclear proliferation cannot rest solely on the fragile foundation of national decision-making, particularly where nations are engaged in regional conflicts of long duration.

This story does not mean to cast moral blame on tiny beleaguered countries struggling for their very survival with all means of defense at their disposal, although such states also must weigh nuclear decisions in some kind of ethical balance. Behind the proliferation of atomic capabilities for good and evil stand the nuclear strategies of the United States, the Soviet Union, and certain other major powers. These nations, with all their might, have an enormous stake in a peaceful and prosperous world community capable of preventing the kind of regional conflict that could sweep mankind into nuclear catastrophe. Some of this prevention will take the form of creative political approaches to resolving conflict, but world stability also depends, in part, on restricting the capacity of all nations to make war by either conventional or nuclear means.

Scenario

I. The Crisis

Less than one year after the American presidential election the Middle East found itself in its darkest crisis since Israel's independence. In fulfillment of a campaign promise to achieve a breakthrough for peace in the Arab-Israeli conflict, the new administration in Washington issued a call for full-scale peace negotiations in Geneva attended by all the disputants plus the Big Four, China, and the United Nations Secretary General. This summons to a dramatic conference aimed at comprehensive settlement came in the wake of widespread criticism of earlier efforts to achieve conciliation through more modest, step-by-step approaches. By making this expansive effort, a new group of American policymakers sought to improve a dangerously stalemated situation that threatened new hostilities.

As part of the prelude to the Geneva conference, a major public relations effort by Washington stressed the prospects for a historic breakthrough toward a final peace settlement in the Middle East, despite openly expressed pessimism from leading figures in Israel and the Arab world. Pessimistic forecasts were not without foundation. First, arms supplies continued to flow unabated into the region from the United States and Russia, the stream of assistance actually augmented by fulsome promises during the election that Israel would receive virtually unlimited aid. Second, even before the election, Arab sentiment had again begun to veer away from the United States for a variety of reasons including anti-boycott legislation, Congressional criticism of military sales to Persian Gulf states, and a renewal of American actions in the United Nations directed against international criticism of Israel. Finally, the large conference proved a case of too little substance too late in Middle East history. Not only had such conferences had abortive endings in the past, but time had begun to work against moderate interests in the region. Where historic conflicts continue to fester without satisfactory resolution, time is seldom on the side of conciliation. After a promising and innovative start in the various disengagement agreements after the 1973 war, Arab and Israeli policies had settled down to a more typical fractiousness. Moderates were being replaced by hawkish leaders through elections and coups. Opening on a note of false optimism, the Geneva conference would take place in a context of growing Middle East instability brought about by an imbalance between those favoring extreme forces and policies and those placing their trust in a gradual conciliation process.

Outside the immediate confines of the Arab-Israeli conflict, American policy was caught in the jaws of the same vise that had brought near-ruin to United States interests during the October 1973 war. On the one side, worldwide economic recovery was encouraging ever greater dependence of industrialized nations on Organization of Petroleum Exporting Countries (OPEC) oil, thus providing the Arab oil-producing states once again with lethal ammunition for economic warfare against Israel's supporters. On the other side, worsening American relations with the Soviet Union in matters not directly related to the Middle East (in Africa, in SALT, and in a general shift of United States emphasis toward close relations with its traditional allies at Russia's expense), corresponded to a Soviet disposition to fish in the troubled waters of Arab discontent.

For all the above reasons, ranging from shifts in domestic politics to superpower competition, the Arab states and Israel began to move their foreign policy priorities from Herculean efforts at peacemaking to more familiar (and congenial to some) realms of military preparation for a fifth and definitive round of warfare in the Middle East. The concept of a "definitive" war is significant: Movement of previously detailed, step-by-step peace negotiations into the noisy forum at Geneva would bring the coup de grace to quiet efforts at conciliation. For the Arabs, this shifting perception of priorities carried with it the ominous view that true peace in the Eastern Mediterranean would come only with Israel's extinction. With the Israelis, there would be both fear of Arab designs to achieve such a definitive settlement and at the same time a belief that Israel might finally settle matters its own way by annexing occupied territories through its superior military power. Growing coolness in relations between Moscow and Washington also found armed expression in the Middle East through the buildup of forces that could move into direct confrontation should another round of regional warfare erupt. Some of the growing sentiment for definitive settlement, encouraged by superpower bickering, echoed within the congenial chambers at the United Nations. In addition, bellicose pronouncements and preparations began to flourish everywhere that the Middle East was at issue, including the much-heralded Geneva conference designed to settle the Arab-Israeli conflict.

Under deteriorating circumstances it was not surprising for observers seasoned in the Middle East's penchant for manufacturing events to find the over-publicized talks at Geneva in trouble from the start. A formula for excluding representatives of the Palestinian refugees from direct participation was found, thus adding to the already gloomy forebodings. Predictably, events involving Palestinian attacks on Israel and other targets quickly shared headlines with the conference itself. Astonishing Israeli reprisals quickly followed. Geneva came to a standstill. In this stalemate haggling escalated over every prob-

NUCLEAR WAR COMES TO THE MIDDLE EAST

lem, and negotiators hectored world opinion in propagandistic speeches. Even simple procedural issues became intractable questions. In hastily abandoning more quiet negotiating routes for the full-throttle raceway at Geneva, the United States had formulated no clear agenda in advance and had obtained no agreement whatsoever from the warring parties as to what outcomes might be expected. Prominent attendees appeared early at the conference, no doubt under instructions from increasingly jittery Middle East capitals to make their belligerence obvious, and then retired to leave the stalemate in the hands of able functionaries. Much ado was made in Washington about dual chairmanship by the United States and the Soviet Union, as yet another step forward under détente, but this joint presence soon jelled into unimaginative performances by professional bureaucrats under orders to take sides whenever tempting opportunities might arise.

Shortly after the fanfare of its opening the Geneva conference, designed to settle the Middle East conflict, collapsed under recriminations about bad faith. Such a finale to almost a decade of American initiatives for peace in the region brought with it unmistakable signs from Israel and the Arab states that the time for talking had finally ended. Dialectics between Arabs and Jews that had begun as a contradiction in British mandate policy and had then continued as a contradiction in American postwar policy, would now finally be resolved in the kind of peace that had proved lasting in Europe after 1945: a traumatic war was necessary in order to bring one side to its knees in such a way that one or the other participant would unconditionally surrender its provocative ambitions. Arabs saw this trauma as a means of reducing Israel to at least Lebanese proportions as a military power, and perhaps even to the complete disappearance of Israel as an independent state. Israelis envisioned a homeland augmented by territories occupied in 1967 and now to be annexed, with surrounding Arab powers deterred from further attacks by a military defeat so traumatic that they would never again dream of challenging Israel's legitimacy by force. Extremists had won the day in every major Middle East capital. It remained only to see how this final contradiction between Arabs and Israelis would express itself. This expression would surely take the form of war — but what kind of war?

II. Nuclear Attack

A new year opened to the drums of war in the Middle East. Arab leaders warned the United States that their economic and military positions, supported fully by the Soviet Union, had never been stronger nor their resolve to punish Israel more determined. They stated that unless American policy were to force a breakthrough toward negotiated settlement in the Middle East by pressing Israel to leave the Arab lands it occupied in June 1967, catastrophe could descend on the Jewish state and on those who supported it. These threats were accompanied by fervent outpourings of solidarity with the Arab cause from Moscow and Peking. For its part, Israel announced that any military attack would be met with severe countermeasures far more impressive than any it had used against Arab states in the past. Such countermeasures would include attacks against cities and civilian populations should Israel's own homefront be threatened by Arab forces. Statements from Jerusalem and Tel Aviv indicated that Israel's military forces would use all means at their disposal to repel aggression, and hints that nuclear weapons were among such means came from high authorities.

Evidence that Israel possessed a nuclear capability — and even possessed nuclear weapons — had been confirmed by military experts. Of the two nuclear reactors in Israel, the one near Dimona in the northern Negev Desert, built secretly in the late 1950s with French assistance, was thought particularly well-suited for producing the fissionable plutonium necessary for nuclear bombs. Reports of Dimona's plutonium output had been variously estimated, but there appeared some agreement that the reactor could have produced at least one twenty-kiloton bomb (roughly the size dropped on Hiroshima and Nagasaki in 1945) every year since 1966 — if Israel had decided to acquire nuclear weapons. While Israeli capacity to produce nuclear weapons was fully authenticated, the question of a decision to build them was not. Yet, in the mid-1970s there were reports that Israel had nuclear weapons in its arsenal, including apparent testimony by the CIA that there existed ten to twenty such bombs, as reported in the *Washington Post* and *New York Times* on 15 and 16 March 1976, respectively. Other analyses had discussed possible Israeli nuclear deterrence strategies, and there was even some discussion that atomic weapons might be used in the Middle East. If, in fact, the United States government had detailed information on Israel's nuclear weapons programs, there was no public record of what the official American reaction had been to this information.

Actual use of nuclear weapons by Israel was thought to be highly conjectural in any case, but if Israel were pushed to the extreme point of defending its very survival, such use was considered a possible course of military action by some experts. At just what point, under what dire circumstances, use of nuclear weapons would occur was unclear. Would Israel strike its enemies with such weapons before an enemy attack (in a preemptive move) or would it wait until it could retreat no further (in a last-ditch survival effort)? Since the only two previous uses of nuclear bombs in combat were for the purpose of definitively ending Japanese resistance to American forces, it could be assumed that any subsequent use in hostilities would aim at a similar, devastating impact on enemy forces. In other words, the idea of actually using nuclear weapons in warfare would be not to demonstrate potency but to make *potential* power so real that it would decisively influence the course of events. Further, the bombs dropped on Hiroshima and Nagasaki worked well toward bringing about surrender because the Japanese could not retaliate in kind. While nuclear deterrence between the United States and the Soviet Union operated on the assumption that both possessed atomic weapons sufficient to rain unacceptable destruction on the other even if one power struck first (in so-called second-strike retaliation), the concept of successful use of a nuclear arsenal would depend on precisely the opposite situation. Presumably, only one side had weapons (or was sufficiently better endowed with them) so as to destroy an enemy which had little or no prospect of successful retaliation with nuclear forces.

As peace talks collapsed and war rhetoric escalated in the Middle East, so did intimations that a fifth round of hostilities was seen by both the Arabs and Israel as the most important armed confrontation in their long struggle. The stakes would be survival — continuance of the Arab dream of a Middle East free of Zionism versus maintenance of the very existence of the state of Israel as a Zionist entity. It was also becoming obvious that the military strategies of the adversaries would pit well-coordinated Arab attacks from all sides and even from states not adjacent to Israel against Israel's broad range of force options including the possible use of nuclear weapons. As the United States moved away from the first full year of a new administration into the midst of off-year congressional elections, the stage was being set in the Middle East for the final round of fighting between two opponents more than ever determined to deliver knock-out blows. Having lived for some three decades under the nuclear condominium of Moscow and Washington, a condominium that held mankind in a balance of terror, the world was about to enter a new era of nuclear proliferation where the *use* of atomic weapons was not solely determined within the strategic calculations of the superpowers. In the fifth round of Arab-Israeli war, Israel would drop an atomic bomb on an Arab city.

What actually prompted Israel's decision to use a twenty-kiloton nuclear weapon against a center of Arab population is unclear. Massive movements of Arab military units were plainly evident along all of Israel's borders. Joint Syrian-Palestinian units in Lebanon and on the Golan Heights, Jordanian forces coordinating their moves with Syria along the Jordan River, and massive Egyptian armed crossings of the Suez Canal into the Sinai demilitarized zone had brought full alert in Israel and the initiation of large-scale Israeli air operations against these massed armies. Algeria, Iraq, Kuwait, Libya, Morocco, Saudi Arabia, and the Sudan were moving troops and supplies into the states surrounding Israel. Fighting had begun, but the outcome was still far from clear. Arab intentions, however, were unambiguous; spokesmen declared their resolve to liberate territories occupied by Israel in 1967 and to reduce Israel's military potential to miniscule proportions in order to humiliate its defense forces. A peace dictated by Arab interests would be made following Israel's unconditional surrender. The United States could no longer be relied upon as a mediator for peace in the Middle East, but the Soviet Union stood ready to support the fight for justice by the Palestinians and Arab states. Any American intervention, the Arabs warned, would be met by total oil embargoes from the oil-producing states at a time when the United States was far more dependent on Saudi Arabian oil than it was in 1973. Saudi influence also dominated OPEC, raising the possibility that new embargoes would extend beyond the Arab producers to other nations important for American energy needs. Similar warnings were issued to Europe and Japan.

Israel's decision to use nuclear weapons in response to a massed military attack was made quickly, before the Arab forces had fully committed themselves to battle and before the United States was able to fashion any response to this new war. Targets had already been selected as possible options for an atomic bomb. The weapon would be a twenty-kiloton bomb dropped by an F-4 or Kfir fighter-bomber so as to achieve the same destructive effect as that device dropped on Hiroshima: over a relatively flat city, of some 250,000 people, the bomb would be exploded as an air burst at 1,850 feet above the central point of impact ("ground zero"). The maximum effects would be felt in the city's most densely populated sector, just as in Japan. Only one plane would be used; the target would have to be located in an Arab country with little or no air defense. Distance from Israel would be no obstacle, since Israel possessed air-to-air refueling capabilities. What was important, however, was that the city be a major Arab urban center, so that dropping this bomb would make a drastic impact on the calculations of enemy forces. A "defenseless" civilian population center, rather than a military facility or infrastructure target (such as a dam), would be more appropriate for accomplishing this end, because the whole point of using an atomic weapon against a country that cannot retaliate in kind is to dramatize how vulnerable the opponent is, and no place is an opponent weaker than in ordinary civilian life. It would go without saying that further nuclear destruction could be expected from Israeli forces if the first attack were not shocking enough. In a word, a decision as extreme as using nuclear weapons in warfare against an enemy without such capacity must spread sufficient terror to justify the magnitude of that decision.

During the morning hours, on a bright early summer day, a twenty-kiloton atomic bomb was dropped on Bengazi, Libya, as part of Israeli retaliation against the start of a massive, well-coordinated Arab attack along its frontiers. Whether the massing of Arab forces would actually lead to Israel's destruction became a moot question for Israeli decision-making. A death blow to Israel was perceived as imminent, and thus the nuclear attack was launched. Emotion may have proved a powerful factor in making the decision.

The crazed ground-rules for this round of warfare had been developed during the course of a year of deteriorating peace initiatives by the United States. No one outside the Middle East took seriously the dire warnings that escalated among the Arab states and in Israel, just as Arab warnings to the United States during 1973 were not accepted at their face value until it was too late. With the detonation of this nuclear device during the opening hours of hostilities in the Middle East, concerns expressed about the dangers of nuclear proliferation over the previous years also materialized and intensified. The United States and the Soviet Union would somehow have to respond; it was no longer possible for them to avoid new kinds of political involvement.

III. The Aftermath

Effects on the city destroyed by twenty-kiloton nuclear attack were much the same as might have been predicted on the basis of experience in Hiroshima, Nagasaki, and the extensive American atomic testing program from 1945 to 1964. The atomic bomb had both immediate and delayed effects. Within a few minutes the full impact of air blast, ground shock, thermal radiation, and initial nuclear radiation had been felt. On a longer-term basis there were lingering effects from nuclear radiation.

As at Hiroshima, some 70,000 persons were killed and another 75,000 injured within the three-mile radius outward from ground zero. In the immediate half-mile vicinity of impact, also the most densely populated section of the city, around eighty-five percent of the population was killed and most others were injured. Fatalities were divided about evenly among three major causes of death: severe thermal radiation burns, nuclear radiation, and general destruction. Medical services had been severely disrupted, thus leading to many more fatalities beyond the half-mile radius than might otherwise have occurred.

No prior experience with conventional weapons could have prepared the civilian population of this city for nuclear attack, and no provisions had been made for protection against such an attack. In any case, there was no advance warning. As at Hiroshima, the high casualty potential of nuclear weapons once again was manifest. First, because the explosive energy yield of an atomic bomb is so much higher than in a conventional explosion, destruction is greatly increased. Second, with high energy yields the overpressures and winds associated with a nuclear blast wave are so intense and of such long duration that many more injuries occur than in conventional attacks. Third, the great amount of thermal radiation released by a nuclear weapon creates a larger incidence of flash burns. And fourth, nuclear radiation injuries — both immediate and delayed — are totally absent from conventional explosions.

Within a radius of some two miles from ground zero, all structures underwent some damage, with severe destruction of buildings in a zone up to one mile from the blast center. Unlike Hiroshima, where some buildings were built to withstand earthquakes and where Japanese-style homes were flexible wooden structures (though highly vulnerable to fire), Bengazi proved more vulnerable to the shock of the nuclear blast. On the other hand, it did not experience a firestorm in the blast's aftermath.

Contamination of persons by immediate nuclear radiation was significant. Anyone not killed by other causes within about .7 miles of the blast had received lethal radiation doses; within another .3 miles from ground zero some kind of treatment, ranging from urgent assistance to clinical surveillance, was required. In other words, every person not a victim from other causes — or if injured and still alive from these causes — required quick medical treatment for nuclear radiation if he was within one mile of the blast's central impact at the time of explosion. Fallout radiation hazards were minimal, however, as at Hiroshima and Nagasaki where a twenty-kiloton air burst at 1850 feet above ground produced no casualties down range because of fallout. Animals, food, and water not otherwise destroyed in the immediate impact area were also contaminated with nuclear radiation unless well protected. Medical services were totally disrupted, and no skill in therapy for nuclear radiation existed in the city or the country as a whole. Indeed, within the Arab world there were not enough medical capabilities in either severe burns or nuclear radiation injuries to make any significant contribution to treatment of casualties resulting from this twenty-kiloton blast. How would the world react to this tragedy? In anger or compassion? Above all, how would the United States and the Soviet Union respond to this event?

Throughout the years of its nuclear defense policy the United States had generally adhered to the following formula for protecting states against outside nuclear attack: American strategic nuclear power would act as a "shield" to protect those non-nuclear states who were allies and friends from possible aggression by nuclear powers. This formula was another way of saying that the Soviet Union would not be allowed to use its nuclear might to blackmail into submission countries without such might. The concept of an American nuclear shield fitted neatly into the atomic condominium shared by Moscow and Washington. It was neither intended as a protection of non-nuclear states against nuclear powers other than the Soviet Union (and perhaps China to a more limited degree), nor designed to shield the actions of a friend equipped with nuclear weapons from Soviet wrath unless that power were an ally closely involved — and thus coordinated — with United States strategic planning (such as the NATO countries). In a word, the nuclear shield concept worked within the atomic monopoly of the superpowers, but when that monopoly was broken the shield lost its effectiveness.

While publicly and privately astonished by Israel's use of a nuclear weapon against an Arab city, the United States found itself in something of a dilemma in the aftermath of the attack. American strategic forces had been raised to worldwide alert status with the start of hostilities along Israel's frontiers, with special attention paid in this alert to Soviet activities regarding Israel. In other words, the initial United States reaction to the Middle East conflict was a typical one: A non-nuclear friend, Israel, was being extended America's nuclear umbrella according to past commitments. Within a few short hours, however, Israel's nuclear retaliation changed its status behind the American shield and caused acute embarrassment and perplexity in Washington. Arab powers angrily charged that the United States had collaborated with Israel in this bombing and threatened to retaliate immediately against Israeli civilian targets "in a similar unconventional manner" — raising the specter of either atomic or chemical weapons. By its first employment of a nuclear device, of course, Israel intimated that much more atomic destruction would occur in the Arab world if circumstances required. The United States denied all charges of complicity in Israel's attack, but found it hard not to admit that it had known for some time about Israel's nuclear weapons program.

Making matters worse for the American policy of nuclear protection of Israel, the Soviet Union threatened action — direct or indirect — against the Israelis, in keeping with its earlier warnings that it would react most strongly to any use of atomic weapons by Israel. In turn, Jerusalem drew attention to its long-range aircraft armed with nuclear bombs, an unsubtle reminder to Moscow that not even southern Russia was immune from Israeli atomic attack. Faced by Arab recriminations and dire threats to sever all relations (economic as well as political), and by Soviet warnings of draconian punishment against Israel, the United States had reached the point of possible nuclear war with the Soviet Union in defense of an Israeli attack it could not possibly approve on strategic grounds (though morally it was ambivalent). In fact, the Soviets hinted in strongly worded messages to the United States that unless Washington would agree immediately to discuss a peace settlement imposed by the superpowers in the Middle East, it would declare war on Israel and take the occupied territories itself. This action would be sponsored by the United Nations, thus leaving the United States isolated in the face of world opinion. As much as America's allies in Europe deplored Arab military activities along Israel's borders, they warned Washington that they would desert to a neutral position in any war between the United States and the Soviet Union over this issue. And most European nations promptly broke diplomatic relations with Israel in the wake of the nuclear bombing.

On the brink of war with the Soviet Union and faced with disintegration of NATO before a shot could be fired, the United States agreed to a summit conference with the Soviet Union in order to discuss an imposed peace settlement in the Middle East. Among the provisions of the final settlement, to be rigorously enforced by the superpowers, would be an arms embargo for the Middle East that eventually reduced military capabilities in the region to something more appropriate to the general size and economic capabilities of countries in the Eastern Mediterranean. While the summit met without Arab or Israeli representation, the world community joined forces in massive assistance to the victims of this nuclear tragedy. Some observers even began to speculate, as a matter of hindsight, about how this disaster might have been averted.

Reflections

In retrospect, various experts on the Middle East and on nuclear proliferation reconstructed the circumstances leading to Israel's use of an atomic bomb against an Arab city. From one very important perspective the bombing had been a crucial event that precipitated peace in the Middle East. To be sure, this peace was an imposed one that would be enforced rigorously by America and Russia in order to prevent another occurrence of a nuclear crisis that could spread to world war. Yet, Israel and the Arab states received in this settlement substantially what they had sought all along — Israeli withdrawal from the occupied lands on the one hand and meaningful guarantees for Israel's security on the other. In 1945 the actual use of a nuclear weapon definitively ended a war; in the Middle East each side gained and each side lost.

Some foreign affairs experts, however, expressed great misgivings about a peace achieved through nuclear war. Hiroshima and Nagasaki inaugurated the nuclear age in modern military planning, but these events led to stalemated deterrence postures between two great world powers instead of more nuclear war. However, the third city victimized by an atomic bomb could well have been the start of a new chapter in the nuclear era, one in which other powers might arm themselves with atomic weapons in order to achieve political goals against opponents not similarly endowed in their military establishments. This could lead to rapid nuclear arming by each nation threatened by even the slightest danger that its opponents would so equip themselves, thus causing unprecedented instability in the world order. Not everyone agreed, however, that widespread nuclear arms would be destabilizing.

With the possible advent of international anarchy in a race by many nations to arm themselves with nuclear weapons, one could scarcely speak of "stable deterrence." More ominous, perhaps, than this worldwide acquisition of atomic arms with possible intent to use such weapons would be the reaction of the two nuclear superpowers to this evolution in military affairs. The American nuclear shield concept was clearly defined and effective as long as it pertained to defense of non-nuclear powers against the Soviet Union. Israel's use of an atomic bomb brought confusion to United States strategic policy, and in turn led to ambiguities for the Soviet Union which could have sparked worldwide nuclear war between the two superpowers. These events proved — if proof was needed — that the nuclear balance between America and Russia worked best for preserving a tenuous peace where their relations were most predictable. Nuclear proliferation could exert strains on this balance by destroying the expectations in Moscow and Washington that the other would behave rationally in crisis situations affecting both. The Soviets had reacted with great emotion to Israel's nuclear bomb, and only because the United States could not count on its allies did the nuclear giants move to the conference table. Otherwise, the American response, confused by Israeli behavior, could well have called the Soviet bluff on the latter's determination to take the occupied lands with its own force. In other parts of the world, should nuclear proliferation lead to further use of atomic weapons by regional powers, the reactions of the United States and Soviet Union might be equally emotional but without mitigating factors such as ended the Middle East crisis.

Briefly, most experts concluded that whatever the positive outcomes of the use of an atomic bomb in the Middle East, the costs in human lives and bad precedents outweighed the benefits. Hence, it was important to find out how this catastrophe could have been prevented. Learned opinion discerned three major areas where improvements in policy might have averted a nuclear attack in the Middle East. First, there was the issue of what political decisions might have better eased tensions, especially in the unsuccessful Geneva peace negotiations. Second, attention was focused on the question of whether the huge military aid programs of the major powers, even though the weapons they provided were principally conventional, might have encouraged evolution of the Middle East conflict toward nuclear war. And third, the area of nuclear proliferation itself was examined to see what could have been done by the leading atomic powers to prevent the building and use of nuclear weapons in the Arab-Israeli conflict. It was thought that better understanding of these three closely related areas of policy might help forestall nuclear tragedy in other areas of the world; this was no mere academic exercise in hindsight, but an effort to reconstruct events in order to achieve better policy foresight in the settlement of regional conflicts, the supply of conventional arms, and the control of nuclear proliferation.

Cooperation Between the United States and the Soviet Union in Peace Negotiations. Would matters have gone better in American initiatives for a peace settlement in the Middle East had some other course of negotiations than the Geneva conference been chosen? Certainly events did not go well at Geneva, but Arabs and Israelis were already dissatisfied with the course of American diplomacy before the conference. Perhaps more to the point, and surely more relevant for international conciliation in general, would a more cooperative spirit between Moscow and Washington before, during, and after Geneva have averted the nuclear tragedy that struck the Middle East?

A notion of international peacekeeping in which the United States and Soviet Union would play leading roles was not part of the détente relationship between the two countries prior to the fifth round of Middle East warfare. Pressed to the brink of war with each other, the superpowers did cooperate in a peace settlement which they jointly imposed and policed. Before this point, however, rivalry was the central feature of the two powers' relations in the Eastern Mediterranean, an extension of rivalry elsewhere — in strategic arms, in Europe, in Africa, and so on. With the end of a fifth round of fighting in the Middle East it was doubtful that Soviet-American competition would end anywhere else, thus laying the foundation for future regional wars, dangerous for world peace, in which the superpowers would play prominent roles in exacerbating, not settling, local disputes. Exacerbation would take the form of diplomatic intrigue and military supplies with no guarantee that, brought to the brink of nuclear war again, Moscow and Washington would reconcile their differences in the name of mankind's survival.

After the use of nuclear weapons in a fifth Middle East war, it was the consensus of informed foreign policy opinion not directly involved with decision-making in Moscow and Washington that the superpowers could have played a more constructive joint role for peace in the Arab-Israeli conflict. The two governments were more uncommitted. Though not the only means by which future nuclear wars between regional adversaries might be prevented, it was clear to many that the détente relationship between the two nations should be extended to peacekeeping operations outside the realm of bilateral relations between the superpowers. It was felt that such peacekeeping might become the ultimate test of détente's value, rather than some other issues often cited as instances of détente's success or failure.

The first recommendation for preventing future nuclear wars in conflict-prone regions such as the Middle East might be the following. Combined with more genuine concern for regulating conventional arms assistance and with more realistic arrangements for controlling the spread of atomic weapons, better diplomatic cooperation between Moscow and Washington might avert nuclear tragedy in the Middle East and beyond. No less a standard than cooperative behavior between the United States and Soviet Union in helping to settle regional disputes should be considered a measure of détente's effectiveness as a foreign policy.

Careful Control of the Supply of Conventional Arms. By any yardstick, the Middle East had over-armed itself with sophisticated conventional weapons supplied mainly by the United States and the Soviet Union and to a much lesser extent by Great Britain and France. Aside from the substantial credits for such arms granted by the United States, Israel relied on large amounts of American economic assistance to support a domestic economy burdened by defense requirements. Egypt had mortgaged its future to large-scale military expenditures, as had Syria and Jordan. Even sizeable contributions from oil-rich Arab states to Egypt, Jordan, and Syria could not cope with either defense requirements generated by the struggle with Israel or non-defense programs that were steadily slipping behind the demands of growing populations.

A number of reasons were given for the vast influx of sophisticated arms in the Middle East. "It is not weapons that create war, but political conflicts; arms are only symptomatic of deeper problems." This argument was favored by superpower leadership and, in the United States, seconded by those who manufactured military equipment. The regional adversaries looked at their heavy arms expenditures and profound reliance on the great powers for military sustenance from the standpoint of their own national defense interests. These interests had evolved out of decades of conflict and were thus likely to emphasize the worst possible cases: One's enemies would do anything to eliminate one's very existence. This was a view held by Arabs as well as Israelis, and it served remarkably well to heighten appetites for all kinds of advanced military gadgetry. Even some friends of arms control could see a certain value to large-scale assistance in conventional arms to the Middle East, since it was reasoned that this would make Israel and the Arabs less likely to resort to nuclear weapons. Such an approach to arms control was actually encouraged by certain parties in the Middle East who warned that if their demands for conventional assistance were not met by the world's major arms suppliers, they would resort to unconventional military means. Even well-meaning persons seemed to be persuaded by this blackmail.

Some experts argued, however, that whether large numbers of impressive, sophisticated weapons encouraged war or were only symptomatic of underlying causes made very little difference as far as dangers from armed conflict were concerned. The presence of expanding arsenals could only make military options more attractive, whatever the ultimate reason that nations go to war. Meanwhile, extraordinary expenditures for defense, to the detriment of domestic development, could actually encourage warlike or so-called "garrison state" mentalities among a citizenry so deprived. And some of these same experts tended to discount the idea that more conventional armaments in the Middle East would avert nuclear war, since such arms not only made military options more attractive but also included the kind of sophisticated technology necessary to wage nuclear war. Rather advanced military means are required to deliver a twenty-kiloton atomic bomb on a target and to explode the device at 1850 feet. A good deal of the arms supplied to the Middle East in recent years had been "dual purpose" — conventional *and* nuclear — in the arsenals of the United States and Soviet Union. While most such equipment was disarmed before delivery of certain elements that would give it nuclear capabilities, these weapons were supplied to nations that had great potential for adding atomic arming devices of their own. This was especially true of Israel, but capabilities also existed in the Arab world for some form of unconventional warfare by sophisticated means, be this warfare chemical or nuclear.

Not all experts could agree, therefore, on what policies in the field of conventional arms might have prevented nuclear war in the Middle East. Nonetheless, a second recommendation for averting atomic destruction in regional wars might be the following. Major suppliers of weapons, especially the United States and the Soviet Union, should strive to control arms assistance at levels that will not bring countries to the point where they can plan for or threaten definitive settlement of their disputes by military force, even if this force be conventional in nature. Israel's decision to drop a bomb came in the context of declarations on both sides that, in this round of fighting, war would settle matters between them in a manner not achieved in the past. Outside military assistance should resist the appeals of regional clients for preponderant armed strength over adversaries and should discourage ideas that seek to use military force in order to achieve the unconditional surrender of opponents. As a corollary to this recommendation, the quality of arms supplied should be as closely monitored as their quantity, with special attention paid to regulation of sophisticated weapons falling into the "dual purpose" category.

Realistic Approaches to Nuclear Proliferation. Control of nuclear proliferation in the Middle East had been within the grasp of the United States for some years before Israel's atomic bomb was exploded in combat. Elaborate declarations and negotiations had tried to establish principles and practices of non-proliferation throughout the world. Yet, for some time the United States knew that Israel had a nuclear capability and even that Israel possessed nuclear weapons, but did nothing through bilateral channels to control the development of such arms. This prevention of tragedy was not so much a matter for world community action as for American policy. How many more times in the course of the proliferation of nuclear arms would one of the superpowers detect such a development in a friendly country and make no move to restrain it? Part of the responsibility for this atomic bombing of an Arab city would rest with the United States and with the political motivations that prevented forthright action to slow down or halt Israel's nuclear program.

Another aspect of responsibility for nuclear catastrophe in the Middle East is shared by the world community beyond the United States and Israel. Certain nations with the capacity to export nuclear technology have encouraged the expansion of national capabilities for "peaceful uses" of atomic energy. It was the French, after all, who assisted Israel in secretly constructing the Dimona reactor. The United States, while not entirely innocent itself of promoting nuclear exports, has stood helpless when its refusal to assist a country, such as South Africa, would lead immediately to an arrangement between that country and, say, France.

The international supply of nuclear technology has been approaching the same kind of frenetic competition that now exists in the field of conventional military sales. Hence, in the wake of the nuclear disaster in the Middle East, no more consensus could be found on how to prevent such future catastrophes than could be reached in the realm of arms assistance. Nonetheless, a third recommendation about how to prevent future use of nuclear weapons in combat could be made, this one pertaining to the export of nuclear technology by countries that have atomic capabilities. This recommendation is in two parts. On the one hand, national means of surveillance should be alert to intelligence that indicates the existence of nuclear weapons development programs in non-nuclear countries; and on the other hand, international means should be developed to supply, as well as safeguard, the transfer of nuclear technology. Both parts of the third recommendation would require that national states sacrifice part of their selfish interests to the welfare of a world community in which they have no small stake. In keeping an intelligence watch on national nuclear developments, a power such as the United States should feel an obligation to help control this program through its own bilateral relations with that country, no matter what the political cost. And by delegating national responsibilities for exporting nuclear technology to an international body, various states would of necessity be sacrificing possible advantages. In no other way than by national initiatives, however, will the world community become a more active force in preventing further use of atomic weapons in combat. The story of this nuclear calamity in the Middle East, fictitious though it is, would tend to underline this point.

Bibliographic Note

On nuclear proliferation and various proposals for dealing with the spread of atomic weapons, a monograph by Michael A. Guhin, *Nuclear Paradox: Security Risks of the Peaceful Atom* (Washington, D.C., 1976) gives a useful overview. Guhin also provides a selected bibliography on pages 73-77.

NUCLEAR WAR COMES TO THE MIDDLE EAST

Regarding the possibility of nuclear weapons in the Middle East, especially Israel's possession of them, the following items are informative: Robert J. Pranger and Dale R. Tahtinen, *Nuclear Threat in the Middle East* (Washington, D.C., 1975); Pranger and Tahtinen, *Implications of the 1976 Arab-Israeli Military Status* (Washington, D.C., 1976); William Beecher, "U.S. Believes Israel Has More than 12 Nuclear Weapons," *Boston Globe*, July 31, 1975; Arthur Kranish, "CIA: Israel Has 10-20 A-Bombs," *Washington Post*, March 15, 1976; David Binder, "CIA Says Israel Has 10-20 A-Bombs," *New York Times*, March 16, 1976; David Burnam, "1968 Mystery of a Vanished Ship: Did Its Uranium End Up in Israel?" *New York Times*, April 29, 1977.

The possible role of Israel's nuclear weapons in deterring war in the Middle East has been discussed in Robert W. Tucker, "Israel and the United States: From Dependence to Nuclear Weapons," *Commentary*, 60 (November 1975). On scenarios for actual use of nuclear weapons in the Middle East, see Pranger and Tahtinen, *Nuclear Threat in the Middle East*, chapter four.

Details on the effects of nuclear weapons, gathered from voluminous data covering the Hiroshima and Nagasaki atomic bombings as well as the many United States test programs from 1945 to 1964, may be found in Samuel Glasstone, ed., *The Effects of Nuclear Weapons*, revised edition, as prepared by the United States Department of Defense and published by the United States Atomic Energy Commission (Washington, D.C., 1964). Based on data from this book, an ingenious "Nuclear Bomb Effects Computer" can be obtained separately.

A concise analysis of American and Soviet forces in the Mediterranean may be found in Jesse W. Lewis, Jr., *The Strategic Balance in the Mediterranean*, with a foreword by Elmo R. Zumwalt, Jr. (Washington, D.C., 1976). Proposals for possible superpower responses to the presence of nuclear weapons in the Middle East may be found in Pranger and Tahtinen, *Nuclear Threat in the Middle East*, chapter five. General issues on détente, from a wide variety of perspectives, may be found in Robert J. Pranger, ed., *Detente and Defense* (Washington, D.C., 1976).

VII

Sabotage at a Nuclear Power Plant

JAMES J. MACKENZIE

The threat of major sabotage at a United States nuclear power plant is real and serious. Present federal security requirements are, I believe, inadequate and likely would not stop even a small group of determined and organized guerrillas. If a large operating reactor were successfully sabotaged, the results for the surrounding region could be disastrous. The lethal effects from a large release of radioactivity could extend twenty miles or more from the power plant; serious land contamination could occur over thousands of square miles.

To reduce the threat of sabotage, security measures at nuclear plants should be upgraded better to match the strength and cunning of potential attackers. Other measures are possible that

---

James J. MacKenzie is a member of the Joint Scientific Staff of the Massachusetts and National Audubon Societies. Before joining the Audubon staff in 1970 he was a research associate at MIT, in the Center for Theoretical Physics. He has also completed postdoctoral research at Argonne National Laboratory and Los Alamos Scientific Laboratory. He received his Ph.D. in nuclear physics in 1966 from the University of Minnesota.

Dr. MacKenzie is a trustee of the Union of Concerned Scientists, a public interest science group located in Cambridge, Massachusetts. He has written and lectured extensively on issues related to nuclear power, solar energy, and the energy crisis. He has testified before the United States Congress, before state legislatures and before Public Utility Commissions on energy related issues.

He has served as a consultant to the National Science Foundation on the environmental impact of solar energy. He is a member of the solar advisory panel to the Office of Technology Assessment of the United States Congress.

He was a member of the Massachusetts Commission on Nuclear Safety, appointed by the Governor, and a member of the Massachusetts Legislative Energy Commission.

He is also a trustee of the Environmental Defense Fund and serves on the energy policy committee of the National Sierra Club.

153

would reduce the probability of sabotage, such as withholding from the public information on the design of plants, and increasing surveillance of both employees and potential dissidents. These latter measures, however, would have ominous implications for civil liberties and suggest that the price of nuclear energy may include a serious abridgement of our constitutionally guaranteed civil rights.

The Threat of Terrorism

National and international terrorism in the form of bombings, kidnapings, arson, and hijackings continues unabated. In a report prepared for the State Department, the Rand Corporation documented 506 incidents of international terrorism between January 1968 and April 1974.[1] The objects of terrorist acts included diplomats, businessmen, military personnel, embassies, homes, travel agencies, factories, banks, ships, cars, buses, and airplanes. Weapons used in these attacks ranged from knives, letterbombs, and pistols to hand grenades, machine guns, and high explosives. Most international terrorists have been either never caught or never punished.

Terrorism is also a significant problem within the United States. According to the FBI, 761 bombing incidents in the United States during the first six months of 1976 killed twenty-eight persons, injured an additional 132, and caused more than six million dollars in property damage. Targets of these attacks included homes, commercial and office buildings, vehicles, and schools.

Over the past six years numerous threats have been made against nuclear power plants and other nuclear facilities in the United States. According to the Nuclear Regulatory Commission (NRC), ninety-nine incidents were recorded between May 1969 and January 1976. In almost ninety percent of these incidents bomb threats were made. Dynamite was found at one power plant; at another, shots were fired at security guards; and a meteorological tower was destroyed at a third.[2] In one inci-

---

[1]Brian M. Jenkins and Janera Johnson, "International Terrorism: A Chronology, 1968-1974" (The Rand Corporation, Santa Monica, California, 1975).

[2]Michael Flood, "Nuclear Sabotage," *Bulletin of the Atomic Scientists*, 32 (October 1976), 29.

dent in 1972 hijackers circled an airplane over a nuclear reactor at Oak Ridge National Laboratory and threatened to crash into it unless a ten million dollar ransom were paid. In several instances break-ins were attempted. But apparently no one has so far been successful in actually affecting the operations of a power plant.

Incidents of a more serious nature have been reported at nuclear facilities in other countries. In 1975 there were at least three bombings at nuclear plants in France.[3] Extensive damage occurred at one plant under construction. In 1973 guerrillas used machine guns and hand grenades in an attack on a nuclear plant in Buenos Aires. Although the attackers took over the plant, no damage was inflicted on the reactor.

Internal sabotage has also become a serious problem.[4] At one American power plant cables were cut; at another pumps were deliberately clogged. In the United Kingdom dozens of incidents have been reported including the cutting of cables and the smashing of gauges and dials. Arson has been reported at several American facilities. One fire, set by a former employee, caused several million dollars' worth of damage at a plant under construction.

Despite these threats and incidents — all relatively minor compared to potential nuclear damage — there is still a major controversy over the likelihood that American nuclear facilities, such as power plants, reprocessing plants, and trucks carrying radioactive wastes, will become the serious objects of terrorism. In 1975 the Nuclear Regulatory Commission expressed the position that present security precautions are adequate and that the consequences of most acts of sabotage would not be as large as those that could result from accidents. Testifying before the California Legislative Assembly, R.G. Page, Deputy Director of the NRC's Division of Safeguards, concluded that " . . . our present physical protection review procedures . . . are sufficient to provide reasonable assurance that the public is adequately protected against any credible act of sabotage directed at a nuclear power plant."[5] Those who argue that the probability of

---

[3]Robert A. Jones, "Danger of Nuclear Terrorism Likely to Increase," *The Los Angeles Times*, April 25, 1976.

[4]Flood, p. 29.

[5]R. G. Page, "Statement Before the Energy and Diminishing Materials Committee of the California Legislative Assembly" (Washington, D.C., 1975), p. 3.

such attacks is small generally base their conclusion on three claims: First, nuclear facilities are inherently safe because of their design features which include massive shielding, multiple barriers, and the like; second, nuclear facilities are well guarded, reducing their attractiveness to extremists; and third, many other possible non-nuclear targets are easier to sabotage, such as water supplies, fuel storage tanks, and dams. One Atomic Energy Commission-sponsored study on the subject dismissed the possibility of sabotaging a nuclear plant as being negligible. "Although sabotage with serious consequences to the public is possible in theory, the probability is sufficiently low that no undue risk to the health and safety of the public exists."[6]

Despite these official assurances a nagging suspicion lingers that reactors and safeguard procedures may not really be as invulnerable as portrayed. This doubt stems partly from the recognition that compliance with and enforcement of safeguard regulations are never perfect, and partly from the acknowledged efficiency and ruthlessness of organized crime and terrorists in achieving their goals. It is quite likely that differences in opinion on the subject of the security of nuclear facilities may be traced ultimately to differences in the perceived threat. One might agree that a nuclear plant is secure against the attack of a small, unsophisticated group while holding that the same plant would be easily overtaken by a larger, more professional gang. Such a view is expressed in the unclassified summary of a recent study on power plant security by the Sandia Laboratories of New Mexico:

> Ordinary acts of willful destruction . . . present negligible radiological risks to the public health and safety. Sabotage which could endanger the public requires a relatively high degree of technical competence, careful planning, and trained personnel. . . . Nevertheless, it appears that a sufficiently determined and able group could perform acts of sabotage which could endanger the safety of the public surrounding the plant.[7]

In 1973 one high official of the Atomic Energy Commis-

---

[6]S. E. Turner, C. R. McCullough, and R. L. Lyerly, "Industrial Sabotage in Nuclear Power Plants," *Nuclear Safety*, 11 (March-April 1970), 107.

[7]Sandia Laboratories, "Safety and Security of Nuclear Power Reactors to Acts of Sabotage," Unclassified Summary SAND 74-0069 (March 1975), pp. 7-8.

sion (AEC) gave an indication of just how endangered that public could be. L. Manning Muntzing, then Director of Regulation, conceded that a band of highly trained, sophisticated terrorists could conceivably take over a nuclear power plant near a major city and destroy it in such a way as to kill thousands — perhaps even millions — of people.[8]

Identification of Possible Terrorists

Because such sabotage is possible, it becomes critical in evaluating the risks to nuclear facilities to assess whether or not persons or groups may actually exist with both the capability and the motivation to undertake a major terrorist action against a nuclear power plant. This topic has been treated rather extensively in several recent unclassified studies.[9] These reviews indicate that saboteurs and terrorists generally fall into one of the following categories: disgruntled employees, criminals including organized crime, eco-guerrillas, foreign government agents, political extremists, and deranged persons.

It is useful to consider briefly each of these categories to speculate what their motives might be and to see how they might approach an act of sabotage at a nuclear power plant.

Disgruntled Employees. Most acts of sabotage by employees occur during times of strikes and difficult

---

[8] *The Los Angeles Times,* December 17, 1973.

[9] The following articles are particularly helpful in understanding the threat of terrorists:

MITRE Corporation, "The Threat to Licensed Nuclear Facilities," MTR-7022 (September 1975).

David Fromkin, "The Strategy of Terrorism," *Foreign Affairs,* 53 (July 1975), 683.

Walter Laquer, "The Futility of Terrorism," *Harper's Magazine* (March 1976), p. 99.

Brian M. Jenkins, "International Terrorism: A New Kind of Warfare," The Rand Corporation, Report #P-5261 (June 1974).

_____, "High Technology Terrorism and Surrogate War: The Impact of New Technology on Low-Level Violence," The Rand Corporation, Report #P-5339 (January 1975).

_____, "Will Terrorists Go Nuclear?" The Rand Corporation, Report #P-5541 (November 1975).

Michael Flood, "Nuclear Sabotage," *Bulletin of the Atomic Scientists,* 32 (October 1976), 29.

management-labor relations. Presumably the threat of destructive acts is meant to provide a strong incentive for management to make a settlement favorable to labor. Actions believed the result of disgruntled employees include the cutting of cables, the destruction of equipment on and off the site, arson, and a bomb threat.[10] In the case of sabotage an employee has the advantage over outsiders of knowing the details of plant design and operations and of having little or no problem in gaining entry. A deranged employee or one being blackmailed by an outside group could pose a threat even more serious than those already cited if only because his intentions could be more malicious.

Criminals. Criminals, and especially organized crime, represent one of the most powerful forces in this country. They are at the same time ruthless and sophisticated. They will undertake almost any operation provided there is a sufficient profit. Their principal activities in the past have been in theft, gambling, extortion, and blackmail. They have also infiltrated organized labor and gained control over 15,000 legitimate businesses.[11] Given the sophistication and care with which criminals have approached bank robberies and theft, there seems little question that they could steal special nuclear materials or take over a nuclear plant if they desired. While theft would fit their style of operations more than sabotage, the latter certainly cannot be ruled out, especially if the "price is right." Frequently, criminals are able to obtain inside help through loan sharking or blackmail.

Eco-Guerrillas. Most persons with a deep concern for the environment disdain the use of force and violence; the majority would not be expected to pose a threat to nuclear installations. However, apparently some environmentalists feel that nuclear energy poses such a threat to life that they are justified in destroying property to prevent its use. In one anti-nuclear incident a meteorological tower at a construction site was destroyed. There have also been a number of bombings in the United States and Europe attributed to anti-nuclear groups. It is conceivable that such a group would attempt to take over a power plant or steal special nuclear materials suitable for making a

[10] M. Flood, p. 29.

[11] MITRE Corporation, p. 62.

SABOTAGE AT A NUCLEAR POWER PLANT

bomb simply to demonstrate the inadequacies of existing regulations and safeguards.

Foreign-Government Agents. Espionage and sabotage by foreign governments are apparently more common than most people realize.[12] Many of the diplomatic personnel stationed in the United States as well as in other western countries routinely gather and transmit intelligence information. Such information is used as a basis for sabotage in both peace and war. For example, in 1971 a Soviet intelligence agent defected from the KGB to the West. He revealed Soviet plans to sabotage vital British installations during peacetime despite the apparent good relations between the two countries. Other Soviet plans have been uncovered to sabotage — frequently through third-country agents — power plants, water supplies, and communications in Bolivia and Pakistan. Acts of sabotage such as these could be difficult to trace to the Soviet Union and may be considered as a form of economic warfare designed to weaken local governments by exacerbating their economic problems.

Political Extremists. Many types of potential saboteurs would fall within this category. Brian Jenkins, a Rand Corporation analyst who has studied terrorism in depth, suggests a few possibilities: anarchists, leftists, rightists, racists, and separatists.[13] Although they differ radically in their ultimate goals, political extremists have much in common in their tactics. Because of their training, dedication, and numbers, they pose perhaps the greatest sabotage threat to operating nuclear facilities.

To appreciate the threat that extremists pose, one need only review their actions over the past few years. In many countries terrorism has become the only apparent vehicle of political change. In South America extremists have conducted programs of bank robbery, bombing, kidnaping, extortion, and murder. In their attempts to achieve what they believe to be a more just society, they have unwittingly transformed democracies into military dictatorships. Internationally, terrorists, especially Palestinian groups, have waged campaigns of sabotage, skyjacking, murder, and assassination for over ten years. Their victims have included both Jews and non-Jews, women and children.

[12] *Ibid.*, pp. 2-10.

[13] Jenkins, "Will Terrorists Go Nuclear?", p. 3.

Between 1968 and 1974 over 500 persons were killed in terrorist incidents. In the process virtually every kind of transportation vehicle and building was attacked.

Terrorist groups are typically small in number. The political effects they achieve are far out of proportion to their membership or political power as traditionally measured. Their strength derives primarily from their ability to instill fear in a population through violence. Through sensational acts they seek to exaggerate their own strength and importance and to provoke the governments in power into repressive overreactions which will eventually lead to their downfall.

Unlike terrorists of the 19th century, many modern groups are indiscriminate in their attacks. Random violence with innocent victims achieves more publicity and causes more alarm than carefully directed assassinations. And publicity through terror is the most effective lever for change available to extremists.

If one realizes their goals of achieving publicity and terror, one can more easily understand why extremist groups might turn to nuclear sabotage and blackmail. The public has become extremely sensitive to the dangers of radiation, and even a hoax could cause widespread alarm and fear. There are, of course, other non-nuclear targets such as oil tankers, aircraft, and chemical plants that could be more easily attacked, but it seems clear that for the extremist a nuclear takeover would automatically guarantee both widespread publicity and a powerful bargaining position for blackmail.

Deranged Persons. The actions of a deranged person or a group of political nihilists are difficult to classify or predict. Conceivably, such persons could act from anti-nuclear, anti-business, or anti-United States motives. They might well feel no constraints whatever against causing large numbers of casualties. While a single insane individual would have difficulty in overcoming normal security measures at a nuclear plant, a group of armed zealots might not. Finally, unless an adequate psychological screening program were in effect, it would be possible that an employee of a utility could become deranged while working at a reactor. Depending on his technical background and motives, he might have opportunity to cause great damage at a nuclear facility.

SABOTAGE AT A NUCLEAR POWER PLANT

In the foregoing we have established that a credible threat of terrorism exists for nuclear facilities. We have also identified the kinds of groups and individuals believed capable of attempting an act of sabotage. In the following story we present one possible chain of events that could constitute an effective and damaging act of sabotage. The events and setting depicted here are completely fictional.

The Scenario

The Clear Lake Nuclear Power Station (CLNPS) was constructed on the western end of Clear Lake, a large and deep body of water located in the central part of the country. The area was ideal for a power plant. The region immediately surrounding the site was still relatively undeveloped, though occasional clusters of new houses were beginning to appear among the farms that dominated the landscape. The regional Edison Company had little problem in establishing a sufficient buffer zone around the plant as required by federal regulations. There were only two major population centers within ten miles of the plant: Reading, a university town on the north shore, and Kent, a moderate-sized manufacturing center on the south shore.

The CLNPS, a boiling water reactor, had a generating capacity of 1150 megawatts, making it one of the largest in the world. After a few months of shakedown operations the unit operated remarkably well, generating electric power virtually without incident.

The political events that eventually led to the disaster at Clear Lake originated six thousand miles away in South America. The United States government, at the urgent request of a repressive military government, had sent weapons and supplies to help suppress revolutionaries threatening civil war in Argentina. The reaction to these moves in the United States was quick and predictable. The deep divisions that had split the nation for more than ten years appeared once again. Editorials were written condemning and praising the action; speeches were delivered in Congress both for and against the shipments; and increasingly bitter and violent demonstrations were held across the country.

The security precautions at the Clear Lake nuclear plant complied fully with the requirements of the Nuclear Regulatory Commission. NRC Regulatory Guide 1.17 required onsite, armed, uniformed guards to protect the plant, as well as security alarms that would sound in at least two continuously manned stations. The plant also met the requirements of the standard set by the American National Standards Institute (ANSI), "Industrial Security for Nuclear Power Plants."[14] The ANSI standard was written in 1973 and its recommendations were essentially followed at all American nuclear plants. The standard described identification procedures for employees and visitors, search procedures at entrances, patrol schedules and procedures, access policies for different areas of the plant, and the like. The ANSI standard, however, was designed to protect only against single employees and small groups of unorganized individuals. The protection against organized assaults, such as by paramilitary groups, was left to the federal government and so went unprovided.

In Argentina continued skirmishes between government troops and the nationalists had gradually escalated to full-scale fighting. The Soviets, through Cuba, were supplying the nationalists with weapons while the United States had completed two more large shipments of supplies to the junta struggling to retain power.

At the Clear Lake nuclear plant the evening shift had just come in. It was January 12 and a long, bitterly cold night was beginning. As the two security guards were completing their log entries, a telephone repair truck drove up to the main gate. One of the guards went over to the truck. "Call home," he was told, "and then do exactly as we say if you want to see your wife and daughter alive again." The shaken guard telephoned his home; there was no answer. As he hung up the phone, four armed men entered the security center and directed the guards to page the plant supervisor to the front gate. He too was told to call his home. Again there was no answer. If everyone did as he was told, the four men warned, no harm would come to either the plant or the two families.

Fearful for the lives of the kidnaped families, the guards, now disarmed, opened the main gate. The truck rolled up to the

[14]American National Standards Institute, Inc., "Industrial Security for Nuclear Power Plants," ANSI N18.17-1973.

SABOTAGE AT A NUCLEAR POWER PLANT

plant's entrance. The two guards, the supervisor, and the four gunmen entered the plant. The Clear Lake Nuclear Power Station had been taken over without a shot being fired.

The New Liberation Army (NLA) had planned the takeover of the Clear Lake plant for several months. The layout of the plant, including descriptions of the emergency core cooling systems, was available in the public library at Reading. Through a program of surveillance the NLA had established the work patterns of the guards and supervisor. It was a simple matter to kidnap the two families in the dark after the guard and supervisor had left for the plant. Stealing the telephone truck allowed the four men to approach the plant without causing any concern.

Once inside, the four gunmen established their operations center in the control room of the plant. The reactor operators were told to keep the plant operating at full power.

Ransom demands were soon made. The NLA gunmen telephoned the television stations in Reading and Kent and informed them of the takeover. Only if all of their demands were met, they stated, would the power plant be freed and the hostages released. If their demands were not met, they would destroy the plant, killing themselves and their hostages, and causing a meltdown of the core and a widespread release of radioactivity.

Their demands were difficult indeed. First, the American government was to deliver fifty million dollars in cash to the revolutionaries fighting in Argentina. Second, the government was to supply the revolutionaries with food, medical supplies, and weapons. And third, the NLA gunmen were to be given safe passage to a third country that was sympathetic to the nationalists' cause. Only after the NLA members had safely arrived in this third country would the families of the guard and the supervisor be released.

By the next morning the news of the takeover was on the front page of every morning newspaper and on every radio and television newscast. The FBI, state and local police, along with a small army of reporters, surrounded the plant. No attempt was made to rescue the hostages. Meanwhile the FBI launched a massive manhunt to learn the whereabouts of the kidnaped families. The President of the United States met with the Secretary of State, top national security experts, and with officials of the Energy Research and Development Agency (ERDA) and the Nuclear Regulatory Commission to determine whether the demands could or should be met, and if not, what the likely consequences would be.

On the afternoon of January 13 the NLA issued an ultimatum that their demands be met by the following noon or else they would begin sabotaging the plant. Following recommendations made to the State Department by experts on terrorism, the government made no official response or comment. A policy of wait-and-see had been adopted. Meanwhile civil defense and army units had been mobilized and plans were prepared for the possible evacuation of Reading and Kent.

At 11 a.m., January 14, the federal response to the terrorist demands was made public. The United States would grant safe passage to the terrorists to any place in the world in exchange for the release of all hostages, but neither money nor supplies would be sent to the revolutionary forces. This compromise was immediately rejected by the NLA. The federal rejoinder was that a final compromise would be offered by noon, January 15.

During the entire period of negotiations the FBI and other officials worked on several schemes to overpower the NLA gunmen. Digging a tunnel into the plant was considered and rejected because of the noise, visibility problems, and lack of time. A "trojan horse" — using perhaps an ambulance or fire truck — was the preferred means of infiltrating agents but there was no plausible rationale for using one. Federal officials finally decided that the best means of recapturing the plant was through a low-keyed, nighttime infiltration using highly trained commandos. A squad was assembled and briefed on the layout of the plant and the likely location of bombs. They were to attempt to regain control over the plant during the early morning hours of January 15.

The plan of infiltration was straightforward. Teams of two men each were to approach the plant under cover of darkness. Each man was armed with an automatic weapon, grenades, and tear gas. Each had a complete set of keys to the plant. At precisely 3 a.m. they were to open their assigned doors and proceed as quickly as possible to overtake the gunmen, whether asleep or awake, and free the hostages.

At exactly 3 a.m. simultaneous explosions destroyed the emergency on-site power diesels, the switching gear carrying power into and out of the plant, and other vital parts of the power plant. All outside doors of the plant had been prewired to explosives by the NLA. The Clear Lake reactor, which had been operating at full power, immediately shut down.

A nuclear power plant that has been operating continuously for a matter of weeks has a large amount of intensely hot radioactive material mixed in with its fuel. This radioactive heat arises from the various fission products produced by the splitting of uranium and plutonium in the fuel rods. As much as seven percent of the plant's power comes from this hot radioactivity, with the remainder derived from the fissioning of uranium. When a reactor shuts down, as did the Clear Lake unit, the power generated from the splitting of uranium stops, but the heat from the radioactive decay of the fission products continues to be generated. To avoid overheating of the reactor, it is absolutely essential that the heat from the fuel rods containing the radioactivity continue to be removed. To do so requires the operation of electric water pumps. If power from offsite sources is unavailable, and if emergency on-site electric power is unavailable, there is no way to operate the pumps and no way to remove the heat.

The instant the NLA charges went off, NRC and ERDA officials knew that a mass evacuation would have to begin immediately. Fortunately, plans had been made in advance and police cars, fire engines, horns, and loudspeakers were used to awaken the residents of Reading, Kent, and other smaller towns. Previously assembled army trucks were used to evacuate hospitals, nursing homes, and jails. No one had yet established where 300,000 people were to go in the middle of the night, but since prevailing winds were from the west, residents were told via radio announcements to proceed either north or south away from the lake. Although traffic moved slowly, there was little panic.

In addition to knocking out all sources of electric power to the plant, the charges set by the NLA caused severe damage to the reactor vessel containing the fuel. Major pipes leading into the vessel were cleanly severed by shaped charges, resulting in the immediate discharge of most of the cooling water into the dry well. Within two hours the core had melted down causing a violent steam explosion which ejected half of the core through the containment. Within thirty minutes of the steam explosion a very large release of radioactivity to the atmosphere had occurred. With light winds from the west and stable atmospheric conditions, the radioactivity from the plant stayed close to the water. Clear Lake, the source of drinking water for cities and towns on the lake, was seriously contaminated. Strontium levels in the lake were five times the permitted limit for drinking water and remained above the acceptable level for several years. Fishing was not allowed for a longer period.

As winds shifted from time to time both Reading and Kent received heavy fallout. Fortunately, most residents had been evacuated by the time that the heavy airborne radioactivity arrived. There were, however, several hundred fatalities and injuries among those who refused to leave their homes during the evacuation. The cities had to remain evacuated for nearly a year until a major and expensive decontamination program could be completed. Each building, each square foot of open space, had to be meticulously cleaned and sandblasted free of radioactive contamination. Agricultural losses were huge. Large areas of land had to be scraped to reduce radiation levels. Most exposed farm animals eventually died from radiation-related diseases. Dairy farms throughout the region were especially hard hit because of iodine and strontium contamination of milk.

The power plant itself was a total loss. So radioactive that it could not be approached, it had to be simply fenced off for decades while officials tried to determine how best to decontaminate the site and dispose of the remaining structures.

The first attempted takeover of an American nuclear power plant had been both successful and disastrous.

Reflections

Improving the Security at Nuclear Power Plants

There is unlikely to be any one simple technological fix that will prevent sabotage or otherwise solve the security problems facing nuclear power plants. Given any set of security measures that one can imagine, it is always possible to postulate a gang large enough, skilled enough, and determined enough to circumvent them. As we stated near the beginning of this chapter, the most difficult task in devising a program to protect reactors is determining the maximum credible threat to protect against. The Nuclear Regulatory Commission has recently strengthened its regulations for the protection of nuclear plants.[15] The new regulations represent a step forward in deterring terrorists. They require at least five armed guards on duty at all times with orders to shoot to kill if necessary; an upgrading of physical barriers and alarm systems; more stringent search procedures for persons, packages, and vehicles; and redundant communication systems. According to the NRC, the new regulations are sufficient to prevent a take-over by several well-trained attackers equipped with automatic weapons and aided from within by a single individual. There is, however, no way of demonstrating that these, or any other regulations, are adequate to achieve such a goal.

A comprehensive set of recommendations designed to achieve further security at nuclear plants has recently been published in a study by the MITRE Corporation on the threats to nuclear facilities.[16] Several of the MITRE recommendations go beyond those adopted by the NRC. We endorse these additional measures and urge that they be considered by the NRC. If implemented, they would add further assurance that nuclear plants are secure against would-be saboteurs, both internally and from the outside.

Security and Civil Liberties

When measured on the scale of disaster that the destruction of a nuclear plant could cause, even improved protective measures such as those cited above may ultimately prove inadequate as a deterrent to saboteurs. Under these circumstances the federal government would be expected to seek new, broader powers to combat sabotage and terrorism. This would certainly be expected in the wake of a major assault at an American reactor, whether or not it were successful. We can of course only speculate on the extent and nature of the powers that the government might seek, but they could well have serious implications for the civil liberties of employees of the nuclear industry, of ac-

[15]*Federal Register*, Vol. 42, No. 37 (Feb. 24, 1977).

[16]MITRE Corporation, p. 62.

tivist organizations critical of government policies, and of the public in general.[17]

For example, in an effort to reduce the likelihood of sabotage among power plant employees the government or a utility might seek the authority to investigate the personal lives of plant workers. Their political beliefs, union activities, finances, associations, sexual activities, and communications with news media might all become legitimate areas of investigation and therefore become available for abuse. Apparently some workers in the nuclear industry have already been questioned on some of these topics with the use of lie detection equipment.[18] Workers could be dismissed or barred from utility employment on grounds totally unrelated to their trustworthiness or capabilities. Judgments in such cases could be very arbitrary, yet difficult to overturn because of the underlying justification given to protect the public health and safety.

On similar grounds, groups critical of federal energy and nuclear policies could become the objects of federal surveillance and investigation. The activities of government agencies over the past two decades have shown that a host of illegal activities have taken place ranging from break-ins to bugging, all rationalized on the grounds of national security. The constitutionally guaranteed rights of many individuals to free speech, assembly, and privacy have been systematically violated in the past. There is every reason to believe that these same rights could be compromised in the future in the name of protecting nuclear plants from possible sabotage.

Furthermore, general civil liberties could be seriously curtailed during and after sabotage at a power plant. Martial law could be declared, large-scale searches carried out without warrants, and detention and interrogations conducted without procedural safeguards, all justified to prevent a threatened meltdown at a reactor.

These warnings are not to suggest that widespread violations of civil liberties will necessarily occur as more power plants are built. But it should be recognized that a sharp increase in the number of sabotage incidents would generate

---

[17]Russel W. Ayers, "Policing Plutonium: The Civil Liberties Fallout," *Harvard Civil Rights, Civil Liberties Law Review*, 10, 2 (Spring 1975), 369.

[18]*Ibid.*, p. 397.

strong political pressures to take whatever actions are necessary to protect the public safety. One indication that events may already be moving in this direction comes from the unsuccessful attempt in 1975 of an American utility company to have a state law passed establishing for it a security police force with the powers of arresting persons anywhere in the state and having the same access to confidential records as do state and local police.

The nation has not yet made an irreversible commitment to nuclear energy. We would do well to review now — while there is still time — the complete spectrum of possible social costs of making that commitment, including especially the compromise, through terrorism, of our civil liberties as embodied in the first and fourth amendments to the Constitution.

VIII

Holocaust by Accident
LLOYD J. DUMAS

The Scenario

The Petroleum Connection

During the early 1980s terrorist and other rebel groups had become substantially more numerous and powerful in the Middle East. Even areas that had previously been relatively stable were now torn by increasingly militant opposition movements. Oppressive regimes could no longer count on long-established traditions of absolute rule, reinforced by strong police action, to maintain the status quo. It was not at all clear how successful the terrorists' attempts at bringing about revolutionary change would be, but the occurrence of such events in the strategic Middle East was considered of utmost importance by both of the superpowers and their allies.

The developed world and particularly the United States were extremely concerned because of their heavy dependence on Middle Eastern oil. Within a few years the anxieties engendered by the 1973 oil embargo had been largely forgotten, the

---

Lloyd J. Dumas is associate professor of Industrial and Management Engineering at Columbia University. He taught previously in the Department of Economics at the City University of New York and holds a B.A. in mathematics (1967), M.S. in industrial engineering (1968), and Ph.D. in economics (1972).

His publications on military related topics include "National Insecurity in the Nuclear Age" (Bulletin of the Atomic Scientists, May 1976); "Payment Functions and the Productive Efficiency of Military-Industrial Firms" (Journal of Economic Issues, June 1976); and "Economic Conversion, Productive Efficiency and Social Welfare" (Journal of Sociology and Social Welfare, Jan./Mar. 1977). He is also author of a book on energy conservation entitled The Conservation Response (D.C. Heath, 1976), and has spoken on military, economic, and energy related issues at five international, ten national, and two regional conferences since mid-1974.

171

oil had flowed freely, and the fraction of United States oil demand met by imports from the Middle East was now substantially higher than at the time of the embargo. Accordingly, the vulnerability of the United States to disruption of the oil supply from the Middle East was at least as great as it was in 1973.

The relatively rapid growth of the leftist revolutionary movement in Saudi Arabia, capped by its startling seizure of the government just a year ago, had been a real shock to the Western countries. The establishment of a Moscow-oriented government in the region's largest oil-producing country had given the Soviet Union substantial influence over more than forty percent of the Middle East's and nearly one-quarter of the world's total oil reserves.[1] It is therefore not surprising that the recent strengthening of the Marxist revolutionary movement in Iran, and the first real indications of the possibility of its success, had engendered a crisis atmosphere in the foreign policy-making branches of the United States and allied governments.

The takeover of Iran by a Soviet-dominated government would increase the percentage of Middle Eastern oil reserves under Russian influence to nearly sixty percent.[2] It would also put both Kuwait and Iraq in danger, squeezing them between two major Soviet-dominated nations. Kuwait contained an additional twenty percent and Iraq nearly nine percent of the region's oil reserves.[3] Iraq, however, had not always been on good terms with the United States, particularly since it was reported in late 1975 that the Central Intelligence Agency had, at the request of the Shah of Iran, supplied millions of dollars of weapons and ammunition to Kurdish rebels fighting Iraqi government troops.[4] Therefore, if the revolutionary movement in Iran were successful, the ultimate percentage of Middle Eastern oil falling within the Soviet sphere could easily reach nearly eighty percent, with an additional nine percent in hands less than friendly to the United States. Since this amounted to almost half of the world's total petroleum reserves, the Soviet

[1] *National Geographic* (October 1975), p. 500.

[2] *Ibid.*

[3] *Ibid.*

[4] John M. Crewdson, "U.S. Said to Arm Iraqi Kurds in '72: Official Says Shah of Iran Asked Nixon to Supply Weapons to Rebels," *The New York Times*, November 2, 1975.

Union would then be in a position economically to strangle the West — a possibility viewed as virtually an unmitigated disaster by the current administration.

Apart from its pivotal role in the oil situation, Iran's geography made its future of great importance to the Soviet Union. Because the two countries share a border hundreds of miles long, the establishment of a friendly government in Iran would provide an additional land buffer to the Russian homeland. It would also turn the entire Caspian Sea into an unchallenged Soviet lake. Perhaps even more important, it would provide Russia with ready access to an extensive warm water coastline. Finally, Russia would gain greater access to the Turkish border, and hence to NATO.

The growth of the Iranian revolutionary movement had understandably been welcomed by the Soviet Union. It had become clear that the rebels were being equipped with increasingly sophisticated Russian military hardware, apparently flowing across the Soviet-Iranian border. It was widely believed that some rebels had received training in military camps inside the Soviet Union. There had even been recent indication that Soviet military personnel may have served as advisors to the rebel forces inside Iran.

Both the United States and Iran had publicly accused the Soviet Union of interference in the internal affairs of Iran and of attempting violently to subvert its legal government. On several occasions, the Iranian ambassador to the United Nations had accused the Soviet Union of aggressive violation of its borders, and the United States had demanded that the Soviet Union immediately withdraw all its military personnel from Iran, cease violating the Iranian border, and halt its arms shipments to the rebels.

The Soviet Union repeatedly denied the presence of any Soviet military personnel within Iran, and further denied providing military training to any Iranian nationals. But it also expressed firm support for the Iranian national liberation movement, which it saw as valiantly attempting to overthrow an oppressive fascist regime supported for decades by enormous shipments of highly advanced weaponry and military technical assistance from the United States. These massive arms sales had not only maintained the Iranian elite in power, but had also succeeded in siphoning off the bulk of Iran's oil wealth while strengthening the power of the military-industrial complex in the United States. The effect had thus been, in the Soviet view, the rankest form of economic imperialism and the nearly complete destruction of Iran's capacity to use its oil as a source of wealth for its own real economic development. United States concern with the recent events in Iran, rather than being engendered by its disapproval of the alleged violations of Iranian national sovereignty by the Soviet Union, was the result of its dismay at the possible loss of its largest single weapons customer[5] and the termination of one of the more profitable of its network of exploitative economic relationships with the Third World.

The Crisis

Iran, in an attempt to cut the flow of supplies from the Soviets to the revolutionaries and to prevent further violations of its territory, massed its troops along the border. This troop buildup corresponded to a massing of Soviet troops. Reports of skirmishes along the border increased, with each side becoming more vociferous in accusing the other of incursions.

The United States stepped up its deliveries of military equipment to Iran. The number of American personnel in Iran tied to arms programs, already estimated at 60,000, was rapidly increased. The White House, defending this influx of advisory personnel against growing Congressional opposition, argued it was necessary to insure the proper utilization of highly advanced military equipment purchased by the Iranian government from the United States, and thus to guarantee the continued independence of Iran, a matter the administration considered of vital importance to the security of the United States.[6]

---

[5]In early 1976, it was reported that "Iran ranks as the Pentagon's largest foreign customer with some $10 billion worth of arms and military services on order." (John W. Finney, "Iran May Reduce U.S. Arms Buying," *The New York Times*, February 4, 1976.)

[6]"... According to a Senate staff study ... the Iranian armed forces lacked the skills to operate the sophisticated military systems they have purchased 'unless increasing numbers of American personnel go to Iran in a support capacity.' ... The report estimated that by 1980, Americans in Iran could number '50,000 to 60,000 or higher,' mostly tied to the arms programs." (Leslie H. Gelb, "Study Finds Iran Dependent on U.S. in Using Weapons: Panel Says in Event of War

The Soviet Union accused Iran of conducting "highly provocative" aerial military maneuvers near the border and of actually shelling Soviet territory. Iran claimed its flights, solely over Iranian airspace, were purely for reconnaissance. It denied shelling Soviet territory, but ambiguously claimed the right to use military force to disrupt ". . . illegal movements of supplies intended to sustain and strengthen terrorist forces" operating within Iran. Furthermore, the Shah accused Russia not only of shelling Iranian territory, but also of preparing to invade his country and forcibly establish a "communist puppet regime" in Iran.

After a particularly serious border incident in which a number of Russian troops were killed, the Soviet Union demanded that the United States ". . . halt arms shipments to Iran, and immediately withdraw *all* American military personnel." It argued that since Iranian government troops were equipped with American weapons and directly supported by American personnel, the United States must bear a large part of the responsibility for the deaths of the Russian soldiers, continued shelling of the Soviet homeland, and attempted violations of Soviet airspace. The statement also demanded that the Iranian troops immediately pull back at least twenty-five kilometers from the border, terminate their shelling of Russian territory, and end aircraft maneuvers in that buffer corridor.

The Soviet Union then issued a strongly worded warning that if the United States did not halt arms shipments and withdraw its military personnel from Iran, the Soviet Union would respond to any further serious provocations by taking whatever action it deemed ". . . appropriate to the defense of the Soviet homeland," not only against Iranian forces but also against those of the United States. In addition, there was indirect reference to recent intimations by Iran that it had developed nuclear weapons and would use them in the event of an invasion. The wording referred to the complicity of the United States in the possible development of nuclear weaponry by Iran, warned that any use of such weapons against the Soviet Union by Iran would result in the "complete devastation of that nation," and implied that such an attack might be logically considered to

---

America Would Face Risk of Becoming Involved," *The New York Times*, August 2, 1976.)

have originated in the United States.[7]

At this point, a debate began within the United States government. The State Department argued that the weight of opinion in much of the Third World was apparently with the Iranian rebels. However, if the Shah were able to put down the rebellion without direct assistance, his continued rule would be widely accepted. Though the NATO nations supported the United States' basic position, they were extremely concerned over the confrontation between the massed Soviet and Iranian troops, and it was not clear that their support would be solid if that confrontation were escalated. Furthermore, the Soviet Union clearly saw itself as defending its homeland against attack, and hence its threat had to be considered deadly serious and highly credible. Therefore, the State Department recommended that the United States persuade the Iranians to pull back their troops immediately an intermediate distance, temporarily embargo the shipment of new weapons to Iran while continuing to supply ammunition and parts, and begin the paced withdrawal of ten percent of the American military advisors. Coupling this partial compliance with Soviet demands with a strong and direct warning to the Russians not to attempt an invasion of Iran should defuse the immediate situation, the State Department thought, and still make it clear that the United States was not acceding to Soviet demands and was strongly committed to preventing Russian aggression in the Middle East.

The Defense Department, on the other hand, took the position that the Soviet Union purposely massed its troops along the Iranian land borders in order to force Iranian troops to concentrate there. The ongoing Soviet harassment of the Iranian troops, border incursions, and shelling of Iranian territory were intended to continue to divert the attention of the Iranian troops from the activities of the revolutionaries, and to manufacture border incidents serious enough to justify a full-scale Russian invasion if necessary. However, the presence of Iranian troops had had a larger-than-expected effect in aggravating the problems of supplying the rebels, so the Soviets were trying to

[7]"A special Iranian Government program to train nuclear engineers (at M.I.T.) has stirred some controversy on the Massachusetts Institute of Technology campus." (John Kifner, "Iranian Program Debated at M.I.T.: Training of Atom Scientists Called Dangerous by Some and Blessing by Others," *The New York Times*, April 27, 1975.)

force at least a temporary pullback of the Iranians.

In the Defense Department's view, the only way the Russians could be convinced to back down was by a show of strength. Therefore, the United States should step up arms shipments, maintain the flow of advisors, press for a buildup of NATO troops along the eastern border of Turkey, and begin maneuvering its forces into the Persian Gulf and the Eastern Mediterranean. In addition, Russia should be warned that the United States would brook no interference with its right to supply the means of self-defense to a legally constituted sovereign government that requested such assistance, and that it would respond in kind to any Soviet attack against the United States or any of its allies.

In the end, the Department of Defense position was essentially adopted by the White House, although it was decided to avoid NATO involvement. The President had often argued the necessity of bargaining from strength and felt that even the appearance of backing down in the face of Soviet threats would be a disastrous precedent, not to mention personal political suicide. All the United States military forces were placed on worldwide nuclear alert.

The Soviets responded by placing their own forces on nuclear alert and by repeating their previous warnings that the United States was risking war if it did not stop supplying military support to Iran. The Russians stated that they would not tolerate continued "wanton attacks" perpetrated with American weapons and support.

Secret negotiations between the United States and the Soviet Union were begun in an attempt to break the stalemate. The United States offered some concessions in reducing the supply of weapons and freezing the level of advisors in exchange for a reduction in the numbers of Soviet troops massed directly on the borders. However, the internal situation in Iran suddenly deteriorated, the offer was withdrawn, and negotiations were broken off.

With this, the Soviets issued a clear ultimatum: Either the United States immediately halt the shipment of weapons to Iran and begin withdrawal of its military personnel within forty-eight hours or the subsequent failure of the Iranians to withdraw from the border and cease their provocations would result in the Soviet Union's taking direct and strong measures against the United States as a demonstration of Soviet resolve.

The United States decided that the best way to disentangle the situation without appearing to back down was to convince the Iranian government to withdraw its troops and concentrate their attention on the revolutionaries, who were likely to be best thwarted by such a concerted attack. The Iranian government, however, refused, arguing that reducing troop strength on the border would allow a resumption of arms supplied to the rebels. It argued that the Iranian rebels were running short on weapons and ammunition and would collapse if resupply could be seriously retarded. The United States found itself in a position in which the only threats it could use to force the Iranian government to withdraw the troops — namely a cutoff of arms supplies and/or advisor support — were not credible, since the United States would appear to be giving in to Russian demands if these threats were carried out.

Thus, the situation became a high-tension, three-way stalemate.

The Accident

The crew of the nuclear missile submarine *U.S.S. Blackstone* had nearly completed their long, routine underwater patrol when the crisis began. Their expectation of long-awaited reunion with family and friends was replaced by a feeling of excitement generated by the combination of uncertainty and danger. Now the prolonged crisis was beginning to produce some small but perceptible strain.

The Captain, acting on the basis of somewhat ambiguous evidence that the *Blackstone* was being followed by an unidentified vessel, decided to take the ship down to the limits of its normal safe-diving depth as part of an evasive maneuver. He gave the order and the *Blackstone* began to dive.

The officers carefully watched the depth gauge as the submarine dove deeper and deeper into the sea. But, unknown to anyone aboard the *Blackstone*, the gauge which the officers were watching intently was faulty.

Elsewhere on the submarine, men at other stations watched as their own depth gauges indicated that the ship was exceeding its safe-diving level and rapidly making its way toward crush depth. Immediately they warned the officers that their gauges showed they were diving too deep. The officers watching the faulty gauge ordered the dive to continue. Suddenly cracking noises were heard.[8] The officers ordered the ship to rise, but the damage already done to its structure and systems caused the submarine to fail to respond. As the ship plunged deeper, the water pressure built to a level which crushed its hull, sending the *Blackstone* to the bottom.[9]

As the submarine sank toward the bottom, a Submarine Emergency Communications Transmitter (SECT) buoy was released. This buoy was designed to be released automatically from a damaged submarine, to rise to the surface, and to transmit whichever of a number of coded emergency messages was appropriate to identify the nature of the trouble. As the SECT buoy broke the surface, it began transmitting the message indication (falsely) that the submarine had been sunk by enemy action.[10]

The signal was received by United States defense communications and the Pentagon was notified. The Joint Chiefs ordered verification procedures to be undertaken and they informed the President of the apparent sinking of the *Blackstone*.

---

[8]On March 27, 1973, the United States nuclear submarine *Greenling* dove far below its safe test depth during exercises in the Atlantic, because of a faulty depth gauge. According to a reporter for the *Portsmouth Herald* (of New Hampshire), a man identifying himself as a sailor aboard the *Greenling* told him anonymously that a confrontation had occurred between the officers and men as the former ordered the dive to continue while they watched a faulty depth gauge, despite warnings from other crew members watching other gauges that showed the *Greenling* was diving too deep. The sailor claimed the officers did not order the ship to rise until after cracking noises were heard.

The Navy officially reported that the ship had indeed dived below safe depth because of a faulty gauge. But the officers had ordered the ship to rise after they had compared depth gauge readings. No warnings were given to them and no cracking sounds were heard. ("U.S. Submarine Escapes After Diving Below Safety Level," *The London Times*, May 4, 1973.)

[9]The United States nuclear submarines *Thresher* and *Scorpion* sank in the Atlantic on April 10, 1963, and May 21, 1968, respectively. (Majorie Hunter, "Scorpion Wreckage Found Off Azores," *The New York Times*, November 1, 1968.)

[10]On at least two occasions during 1971, SECT buoys were accidentally released from Polaris nuclear missile submarines. In both cases, the buoys began transmitting the coded message indicating that the submarines had been sunk by enemy action. However, the submarines involved were able to surface and cancel the emergency message. (L.D. Malnak, sworn affidavit, Washington, D.C., January 10, 1974.)

A check was made as to whether any similar incidents had occurred elsewhere in the system. The President decided to await the results of these communications, not wanting to exacerbate the situation by making any accusations, much less by taking direct retaliatory action, before he was as sure as he could be that the incident had, in fact, occurred.

The tension was extraordinarily high. The President listened to the words of his various advisors, but realized that the final decision — and the final responsibility — were his alone. He had not slept much in the last few days, and was beginning to feel the strain. He was becoming impatient with the delay, as the enormity of the situation bore increasingly down on him.

It was nearly an hour after the receipt of the original message about the *Blackstone* before the verification report was received.[11] The report was somewhat ambiguous, stating that the *Blackstone* had apparently been sunk, and that Soviet antisubmarine warfare forces were known to have been in the area. However, it could not be accurately and independently verified that the *Blackstone* had actually been destroyed by enemy attack. The report went on to say that no communications had been received indicating any possible attacks elsewhere, and that positive verification communications with most major installations and force groups confirmed this.

Because it would have taken months to pin down the exact cause of the *Blackstone* disaster,[12] it was decided the United States must act on the assumption that the *Blackstone* had been purposely destroyed by the Soviets as their promised demonstration of determination to enforce their demands. The Hot Line was activated and the United States sent a message to the Kremlin charging the Russians with the deliberate destruction of the missile submarine *Blackstone*, and warning that the United

---

[11]As of 1971, the United States Defense Communications System required an average of 69 minutes to transmit a "flash" (top priority) message, as, for example, the message transmitted by the American ship *Liberty* when it was attacked by Israeli forces in 1967. United States Congress, Investigating Subcommittee, Committee on Armed Services, House of Representatives, *Review of Department of Defense World-Wide Communications* (Washington, D.C., 1971).

[12]When the United States nuclear submarine *Scorpion* sank in the Atlantic in May of 1968, five to seven months were required to find the ship and verify that it had not succumbed to "foul play." (William Beecher, "Photos of Scorpion Discount an Attack," *The New York Times*, January 3, 1969.)

HOLOCAUST BY ACCIDENT

States would be forced to take retaliatory action unless the Russians publicly acknowledged and apologized for their action and immediately withdrew the bulk of their troops from the Iranian border as a gesture of conciliation. The Soviets replied that they knew nothing about the sinking of any United States missile submarine anywhere, and that the United States should not be so foolish as to think that it could force Russian compliance with its demands by manufacturing such an incident. They further warned against any attempt at retaliation for the alleged submarine loss, and again denied any knowledge of the incident, and accordingly any responsibility for it. Furthermore, they repeated their demands for an immediate halt to United States arms shipments to Iran and a withdrawal of advisors.

The United States did not reply immediately. Instead another internal debate ensued concerning appropriate response. The situation was extremely confusing. On the one hand, the Russians had made clear, public statements that they would take direct action against the United States as a demonstration of their determination to enforce their demands. On the other hand, they had just denied responsibility for the sinking of the *Blackstone*, precisely the sort of demonstration to be expected. It was clearly an act which would be considered of major significance, yet it did not threaten United States retaliatory capabilities and involved only a limited loss of life with absolutely no civilian casualties. Hence, it was a perfect limited counterforce strike, which did not force retaliation.

The State Department argued that it would make no sense for the Soviets to make such an attack and then deny responsibility for it, if the attack were supposed to be a demonstration of resolve. The United States must consider the possibility that the sinking of the *Blackstone* was an accident, and that if Soviet forces were involved, they may have either destroyed the *Blackstone* accidentally or acted without authorization from the Soviet high command. They concluded that the United States should take no action. If the sinking of the *Blackstone* were intended as a demonstration, it would thus fail. Therefore, the Soviet Union would be forced to repeat the demonstration, at which time it would be crystal clear that that was what they were attempting to do, and the United States could then reply appropriately. If the incident were not due to an authorized Soviet attack, it would not be repeated, and the United States would thus avoid pushing the Soviet Union unnecessarily into a retaliation which could escalate into a general nuclear war.

The Defense Department argued that SECT had been fitted with a number of safety devices to prevent its accidental release and transmission. Furthermore, in the unlikely event that the buoy had been accidentally released, the *Blackstone* would have surfaced to cancel the message. This, combined with the presence of a large Soviet anti-submarine warfare group in the area, made it extremely likely that the *Blackstone* had, in fact, been sunk by the Russians.

The denial of responsibility by the Soviet Union was, in the Defense Department's view, intended to generate confusion and prevent decisive military action, thus allowing the Russians and the Iranian revolutionaries to solidify their positions. Reports from Iran indicated a rapidly deteriorating situation. If the United States allowed itself to be frightened or confused into inaction, if it did not intervene decisively and force the Russians to back down, then the fall of Iran would soon be a *fait accompli*, and the powerful "oil weapon" would be in Soviet hands. No delay was permissible. The Defense Department maintained that the United States should make an immediate retaliatory strike against a limited Soviet counterforce objective, and rapidly increase the flow of its military personnel and equipment into Iran. This would call the Russian bluff, deter an invasion, and bolster Iranian forces sufficiently to bring about the defeat of the revolutionaries.

After hours of discussion, the President, who appeared to be leaning toward the State Department view, decided that it would be best for everyone to get some rest and to resume the debate the next morning. He believed that, given the strain and sleeplessness of the last several days, the value of doing so far outweighed the risk involved in a few hours' delay in making a decision. The meeting was accordingly adjourned.

A Failure of Communications

It had been many hours since the last Hot Line communication and the Kremlin still had not received the American reaction to its denial of harming the *Blackstone*. It was, however, clear that the flow of United States arms to Iran was continuing unabated. Suddenly, the ominous silence was shattered by a communication from the Soviet radar warning system indicating that a missile attack had been launched against the Soviet Union. The Kremlin was told that the target appeared to be the Russian Arctic naval facilities near Murmansk and possibly also the White Sea port of Archangel.

The Soviets immediately activated the Hot Line and demanded to know why the United States had launched a missile attack against the Soviet Union. They repeated their denial of responsibility for the sinking of the submarine and warned that they would retaliate in kind. The United States denied that it had retaliated for the *Blackstone* incident, insisted that it had absolutely no knowledge of the alleged missile attack, and warned the Soviet Union that any attempt to justify a further attack on United States forces by manufacturing such an incident would fail. The United States would retaliate immediately in response to any Russian attack.

The Kremlin, infuriated both at the wantonness of the attack and at the similarity in language between the current denial of responsibility for the missile barrage and its own earlier denial of responsibility for the *Blackstone* sinking, ordered the immediate launch of a Russian missile attack against United States naval bases in Puget Sound and at San Diego. About ten minutes after the attack had been launched, it became clear that radar warning of the missile attack against Murmansk and Archangel was false. The radar system had simply malfunctioned.[13]

Unable to destroy its missiles so far into their flight, the Kremlin once again activated the Hot Line, explained that its warning radars malfunctioned, warned that it had launched an attack against the United States, and gave what trajectory information it could.

The American warning system had already picked up the attack. But within a few minutes nuclear explosions completely destroyed both San Diego and Seattle. What had not been leveled by the blast was burning as fire storms raged through

---

[13]A number of false radar warnings of attack have apparently occurred. The most spectacular of these (of which there is public knowledge) is undoubtedly the warning of a massive missile attack against North America transmitted by the Ballistic Missile Early Warning System station at Thule, Greenland, to the central defense room of the North American Air Defense Command. It took some fifteen to twenty minutes to verify that the warning was false. Apparently the radars had echoed off the moon. (*Boston Traveller*, December 12, 1960.)

the surrounding areas. Nearly three million people were dead or dying.

The President vowed that the Soviets would pay for this first attack on the United States mainland in close to two centuries. He ordered a limited nuclear strike against the Soviet Union. The port cities of Baku, Odessa, and Vladivostok were destroyed. More than two and one-half million Russians were killed. The Soviets, angered by this devastating reply to what they had told the United States was an accidental strike, counterattacked. Casualties climbed into the tens of millions, as a larger nuclear attack was launched against the Soviet Union. The Soviets launched a still larger counterattack, and the conflict escalated into a general nuclear war.

Epilogue

More than three hundred million human beings were dead. Every city of size in both the United States and the Soviet Union lay in rubble. And in the smoldering ruins below and the poisoned atmosphere above lay the seeds of the destruction of human society, if not humanity itself. The ecology had been unbalanced. The rotting corpses bred disease; water supplies were contaminated; disease-carrying and crop-destroying insects, highly resistant to radioactivity, multiplied rapidly out of control as their predators died far more readily of the effects of the deadly nuclear radiation. Without a transportation network, there was no fuel, no medicine, no pesticide, no chemical fertilizer. Those who survived the direct effects of the nuclear war would likely die in raging epidemics, freeze with the coming winter, or starve as the heavily energy-dependent agricultural systems collapsed and insects attacked local crops.[14]

Nearly three-quarters of the earth's protective ozone layer was destroyed, vastly increasing the amount of dangerous ultraviolet radiation reaching the earth's surface.[15] As a result, anyone exposed to sunlight for more than ten minutes experi-

---

[14] For an excellent discussion of these kinds of interactive effects, see Tom Stonier, *Nuclear Disaster* (New York, The World Publishing Company, 1964).

[15] National Research Council, *Long-Term Worldwide Effects of Multiple Nuclear-Weapons Detonations* (Washington, 1975), pp. 5-6.

enced severe, blistering sunburn.[16] It was thus extremely difficult for farmers around the world to work in the fields.

The high levels of ultraviolet radiation also contributed to the further unbalancing of the ecology, damaging both animal and plant life. These effects, combined with the spread of disease and insect plagues, caused worldwide starvation and death.

Reflections

Analyzing the Scenario

There are three critical elements in this scenario: (1) a major intense international political crisis, (2) specific accidents involving weapons and their associated systems, and (3) an inability to verify the accidental nature of the incidents with sufficient speed. Each of these elements plays a different key function in making the scenario "work." The accidents, in this case the sinking of the *Blackstone* and the false Soviet radar warning, serve as triggering events. The inability to verify accurately the accidental nature of these events quickly and with relative certainty, however, is what puts pressure on the actors to consider them to be genuine attacks. But it is their occurrence during an international crisis that ultimately makes them credible as the result of purposeful enemy action.

It is technically conceivable that an accidental nuclear war could be generated without the crisis background. For example, a false warning of a substantial attack against several United States nuclear weapons or warning systems, coupled with false positive verifications that the attack had occurred and that the targets had been destroyed, could trigger an accidental war. However, the likelihood of so many serious system failures and accidents occurring together is probably extremely small. But the occurrence of triggering events during an international crisis drastically lowers the threshold for their credibility and enhances their effectiveness, and therefore dramatically increases the probability of accidental war.

---

[16]Philip M. Boffey, "Nuclear War: Federation Disputes Academy on How Bad Effects Would Be," *Science*, October 17, 1975, p. 249.

The crisis brings the superpowers into confrontation in a situation in which both perceive themselves to have vital national security interests in the outcome, and the ambiguities are such that each can legitimately maintain a fundamentally different view of the other's motivations and intentions. In the fall of Saudi Arabia and the growth of the leftist revolutionary movement in Iran, the United States perceives a Soviet power play to gain control of virtually all of the Middle Eastern oil reserves so that it can disrupt the West's economies at will. It sees itself as protecting its supplies of a vital economic resource upon which its economy is still largely dependent. The Soviet Union, on the other hand, perceives that the United States is trying to kill off an indigenous revolutionary movement in Iran in order to continue to control an extremely valuable commodity while maintaining a militarily powerful, pro-Western government on the Soviet border. Such a government serves as a constant implied threat, providing a convenient staging area for espionage activities as well as possible future military adventures. It sees itself primarily as defending the Soviet homeland against present and likely future attack, and secondarily as seizing an opportunity to break decisively the Western stronghold in the Middle East. The step-by-step building up of tension follows directly from these conflicting viewpoints which allow each side not only to see the stakes as being extremely high, but also actually to believe that it is in the right.

Furthermore, the Soviets attribute to the United States a greater degree of control over Iranian policy than it actually has — a common mistake in the international arena. This ultimately puts the United States in a position in which it is held responsible for the failure of Iranian troops to withdraw from the Soviet border, despite the fact that it has tried unsuccessfully to bring about such a pullback. And interestingly, the United States' ability to coerce the Iranians is hamstrung by the very nature of the other Soviet demands which destroy the credibility of its possible threats against Iran.

The nature of the accidents that play a key role in triggering the war is also of particular importance. In the first place, they are highly plausible events based on system malfunctions of a type that have occurred repeatedly, though infrequently, in the past. The sinking of the *Blackstone* was ultimately caused by the malfunctioning of a single gauge, combined with a relatively brief delay in reaction attributable to a common human failing — the tendency of those in authority to persist in chosen actions as a demonstration of their authority, despite the protestations of underlings that the actions are inappropriate. False radar warnings, of the type which afflicted the Soviet system, have in the past been caused by external events as diverse as flights of geese and the rising of the moon. It is a virtual certainty that some have also been caused by quirks in the internal electronics of these highly sensitive, highly complex warning systems, as well as by mistakes made by the human operators of the system.

A second important feature of these accidents is that both of them are wholly internal to the military systems of one of the superpowers. Typically, it is thought that in order to generate a retaliatory response to an accident, that accident would have to involve both actors — for example, the accidental launch of a Soviet missile against a target in the United States. But, as this scenario points out, an accidental nuclear war can also be generated by failures of a nation's own weapons and allied systems without the involvement of any enemy forces or targets in the event at all.

This is extremely important because it implies that very unspectacular, almost routine failures (e.g., the failure of a depth gauge), can trigger accidental wars. These are far more likely to occur than spectacular events, like the unauthorized launch of a missile. Our estimates of the probability of accidental nuclear war must thus be significantly increased.

It should be pointed out that although this particular scenario included one accident for each side, it could be readily modified to include accidents involving only one side's forces. Therefore, the probability of a triggering event must be considered equal to the probability of a sufficient accident involving the forces of the side with the *least developed* safety procedures and the *least reliable* equipment. It is hence not enough to see to it that "we" do not have an accident — "they" must also avoid having an accident.

It should also be pointed out that serious accidents involving major nuclear weapons carrier systems have not been a rarity. Over the period 1950 to 1973, there has been an average of more than two-and-one-half such accidents *publicly reported* per year.[17] It is anyone's guess how many have actually occurred.

The failures of verification involved in the scenario are of two different types. It is extremely difficult to verify quickly the causes of accidents that produce the rapid sinking of ships at sea, particularly submarines. Unless there is an "eye-witness" or sufficient time for two-way communication, one must often locate the sunken ship before verification can be completed. Even in the case of a surface vessel, many hours may be required.

With submarines the verification problem is almost infinitely more difficult. The ability of modern nuclear missile submarines to remain submerged for extended periods of time, among other things, makes them extremely difficult to track — or even to find. This, in fact, is clearly their greatest advantage as a strategic weapons system. In order to exploit this advantage fully, logic requires that they neither follow pre-determined courses, nor communicate frequently — particularly during periods of military alert. Hence, not even the Navy would be expected to know the precise location of its missile submarines during most of their time at sea. Verification is further complicated by the inability of submarines to communicate over long distances while they are submerged. This is the reason for SECT and similar systems.

The problem of verifying the truth or falsity of a radar attack warning is different in at least two important respects. First, the location involved is known, stationary, and on or above the surface, thus making communications far simpler. Second, even those stationed at the place(s) of origin of the warnings may not know whether a malfunction has occurred. They themselves may have to follow verification procedures that consume many minutes of precious time. Since the *maximum* warning time available for certain types of missile attack is only fifteen to thirty minutes, even relatively rapid verification may be far too slow. Those receiving such warning of a significant attack may thus be faced with a choice of either verifying or responding. Doing one may preclude the other.

---

[17]Lloyd J. Dumas, "National Insecurity in the Nuclear Age," *Bulletin of the Atomic Scientists,* 32 (May 1976), 27.

This is particularly true in the case of an apparent counterforce attack, i.e., an attack aimed by one side against the weapons of the other side in order to destroy part of the attacked nation's retaliatory capability. In this situation, the best way for the nation being attacked to prevent its weapons from being destroyed is to launch them before the attacking missiles arrive. Thus, a nation that espouses a strategic military doctrine relying heavily on engaging in counterforce attacks merely serves to magnify the probability that its rival will adopt a strategy of "launch-on-warning." But a launch-on-warning strategy implies a much-reduced time available for verification of the accuracy of warnings received, and hence sets the stage for a real retaliatory response to a false warning, as in the present scenario. Beginning with the appointment of James Schlesinger as Secretary of Defense during the Nixon administration, the United States has more and more publicly supported the adoption of a counterforce strategy.

One further aspect of the scenario deserves special attention. Since its installation in 1963, the Moscow-Washington "Hot Line" has been hailed as a major device for preventing accidental war. Yet in the course of this scenario the Hot Line is activated several times, precisely for the purposes for which it was designed, and still a devastating accidental war occurs. This is not to say that such a direct communications link is useless — it is just to say that we would be extremely foolish to rely heavily on such devices.

Preventing Accidental Nuclear Disaster

We begin with two simple, basic premises: (1) No system designed or operated by human beings is infallible. (2) The more opportunities an event is given to occur, the more likely it will occur. The first premise guarantees that there will always be malfunctions of varying degrees of severity in all military systems. Accidents involving nuclear weapons and nuclear weapons carriers, false warnings, failures of communication, and the like will continue to occur as long as the systems in which they occur continue to exist. Failing the total elimination of these weapons and their systems, we can never be one hundred percent certain that a nuclear weapon or weapons carrier accident will not trigger an accidental war.

But even if we are unable to insure that accidental nuclear disaster cannot occur, we can still ask what steps will be effective in substantially reducing its probability. It is here that the second premise comes into play.

Because there are more chances for something to go wrong, in general the more complex any system or subsystem is, the more likely it is to experience a malfunction. Unfortunately, modern weapons carriers and associated communications and warning systems are inherently complex. While there is undoubtedly room for simplification of design, the nature of the demands commonly placed on these systems is such that the possibilities for design simplification are likely to be fairly limited. Therefore, it is highly unlikely that simplification of design by itself will drastically reduce the probability of accidental war.

On the other hand, it is possible to reduce the probability of certain types of malfunctions that are particularly dangerous (e.g., accidental detonations, unauthorized launches) by designing in a number of layers of redundant safety systems, though doing so generally does tend to increase the probability of other types of malfunctions because of the contribution to complexity. However, requiring the incorporation of such systems can not only add enormously to the cost of the system, but may very well cripple its effectiveness in rapidly performing the military functions for which it was designed and built. Clearly if there is any reason to build a nuclear weapons-related system in the first place, there is no point in building one so encumbered by redundant safety devices that it cannot be quickly put into action. Such a system would be militarily unusable in this era of fifteen-minute response times. Thus, this approach too has only limited potential.

Furthermore, even if we do succeed in reducing the probability that a given weapon or weapons-related system will be involved in a dangerous malfunction, the security gains we have registered will be rapidly overwhelmed as the number of such weapons and systems increases, and as they are deployed in more and more geographically diverse locations. The former effect occurs because each additional system built represents, in effect, additional opportunities for something to go wrong. For example, if we replace three weapons, each of which has a one in ten chance of accident, with seven new weapons, each of which has only a one in twenty chance of accident, the probability that at least one accident will occur *increases* from about twenty-seven percent to about thirty percent.

The geographic dispersion effect occurs primarily because greater diversity of locations typically implies that more people will be involved in the weapons control and release process, heightening the chance that an emotionally disturbed, mentally ill, or otherwise unreliable individual will enter the picture, with all the implications that has for increasing the probability of a triggering event. That this sort of human reliability consideration is a real problem is illustrated by the fact that some 3647 people with access to United States' nuclear weapons or responsibilities in the nuclear release process were disqualified because of drug abuse, mental illness, alcoholism, discipline problems, and the like in 1972 alone.[18] In addition, greater geographic dispersion will also increase the complexity (and accordingly reduce the reliability) of the communications and control systems required.

The net conclusion to be drawn from this is really quite simple: Despite incremental improvements achievable by safer design, ultimately more weapons in more places mean more chance of a nuclear weapons system malfunction that could either produce a limited nuclear disaster or trigger a full-scale accidental nuclear war. Hence the simplest, least expensive, and without question most effective way of reducing the probability of such an event is to reduce the size and geographic dispersion of nuclear weapons stockpiles and nuclear weapons-related systems and forces.

Partial nuclear disarmament would also tend to reduce the tension associated with serious international political confrontations. Since it seems highly unlikely that such periodic confrontations will disappear as long as the nation-state system itself continues, about the best we can hope for is to reduce their frequency and intensity. It is unclear whether even substantial nuclear disarmament will affect the former, but it is almost inconceivable that the reduction in perceived threat that it implies will not reduce the latter. Therefore, partial nuclear dis-

---

[18]United States Congress, Subcommittee on Military Applications, Joint Committee on Atomic Energy, *Military Applications of Nuclear Technology* (Washington, D.C., 1973), pp. 6-9.

armament would have a dual effect in reducing the probability of accidental nuclear war.

But would not partial disarmament reduce the military strength and hence the national security of the United States? Might it not even increase the probability of accidental nuclear war by making each side more nervous about protecting its smaller nuclear deterrent forces?

Currently, both the United States and the Soviet Union possess thousands upon thousands of city-destroying nuclear warheads, and many more of somewhat smaller destructive power. These weapons arsenals give each nation the capability of destroying the other many times over. Since, despite all the money that has been spent on military research and development, no one has yet come up with a technique for killing a human being more than once, most of the destructive capability embodied in these weapons stockpiles has no military value. As long as these stockpiles are large enough to guarantee that sufficient destructive power would survive an attack to assure the annihilation of the attacker, a nation governed by rational leaders should be deterred from launching such an attack.[19] Thus, the excess in these arsenals above the minimum stockpile required for deterrence adds nothing to military strength, much less national security. In fact, through its contribution to the likelihood of accidental nuclear war, that excess actually reduces national security.[20] Hence, its elimination would tend to improve national security, not degrade it.

The possible tendency of smaller deterrent forces to make both sides more trigger-happy, as it were, can be easily overcome by relying on relatively invulnerable deterrent forces, such as nuclear missile submarine fleets which are virtually impossible to destroy, and will remain essentially invulnerable into the indefinite future. In addition, the forceful renunciation of the counterforce doctrine and all military research and development relevant to its implementation would further drastically reduce the incentive for dangerous hair-trigger operating procedures.

[19] It is unlikely that any size stockpile would be sufficient to deter an irrational national leadership.

[20] For a much more detailed, though still partial development of this argument, see Lloyd J. Dumas, "National Insecurity in the Nuclear Age."

In the end, then, some substantial degree of nuclear disarmament is clearly the best way and possibly the only effective way of reducing the probability of a catastrophic accidental nuclear war. To the extent that they can be achieved, mutual disarmament agreements should be negotiated. But if these negotiations prove to be as intractable in the future as they have been in the past, the unilateral elimination of a substantial part of the completely militarily useless and security-reducing excess in the nuclear weapons stockpiles should be undertaken. We cannot allow ourselves to be stalemated — not if we want to be sure that the scenario presented here remains only a frightening fable.

The Future

IX

Facts, Morals, and the Bomb

CHARLES C. WEST

If all that has been said in this volume so far is true, and all that has been forecast is possible, what is the hope for peace? It may seem diversionary at this point even to raise the question. Surely the danger is clear and we have analyzed it enough. What need of further reflection on the trends of world conflict when the threat of destruction hangs over all of us here and now? Should we not close with a call to action and a program to carry it out?

There is truth in this urgency, but there is also a problem. Twenty-five years ago, in East Berlin, I was sitting in on an intense student debate — about the division of Germany into Soviet and western spheres, about socialism and private enterprise, and about freedom and the ways it was threatened — when an ardent young Communist broke in. "What's the use of discussing all these things," he cried, "when, if we don't launch a campaign for peace, we may at any minute get an atomic bomb on our heads?" He meant, of course, the bomb the Americans then had, and which the Soviet Union had not yet developed. He had a point; the problem with it was that not one person in

---

Dr. Charles C. West is Stephen Colwell Professor of Christian Ethics at Princeton Theological Seminary. Dr. West received his B.A. from Columbia College, New York, his B.D. from Union Theological Seminary, New York, and his Ph.D. in ethics from Yale University in 1955. His dissertation was published under the title Communism and the Theologians.

Ordained in the United Presbyterian Church, Dr. West went to China in 1947 and spent three years there as a missionary in Peking, Hangchow, Shanghai, and Nanking. He also served as instructor and chaplain at Cheeloo University and Nanking Theological Seminary.

Dr. West has been active throughout his life with the World Council of Churches, both as a fraternal worker in Germany with the Gossner Mission and the Kirchliche Hochschule in Berlin, and as associate director of the Ecumenical Institute of the World Concil of Churches at Bossey.

A former president of the American Society of Christian Ethics, Dr. West has published four additional books including Ethics, Violence and Revolution and The Power to be Human.

ten of his audience believed that *that* was the most important danger they faced.

His predicament is not unlike ours today. The threat of a catastrophic nuclear war is real. If it should come, all the other issues that arouse our passions — liberation for the oppressed, the just sharing of the world's wealth, control of technological power, and freedom for the human spirit — would be buried in its rubble. What is more, the control of this nuclear threat is a moral science only indirectly related — indeed at times opposed — to the pursuit of our other goals. But the problem is that billions of people in the world today do not believe that this is the greatest danger they face. They often do not trust our perception of the common predicament, colored as it is by the power and wealth we hold and which they are largely denied. Indeed some of them think that *we*, not the bomb, are the danger. Their perspective may be limited, but so may ours. In any case their hopes and fears, their struggles and points of view, are part of the context, along with us and our concerns, in which the issue of the power of nuclear weaponry is set.

This in itself, however, would not be enough to make us rethink our problem. If only the interests of certain other peoples were involved, the moral technology that has produced mutual assured deterrence and the nuclear umbrella would surely be expanded to include them. Nuclear monopoly by the great powers *and also* firm security guarantees for smaller nations; détente between the Soviet Union and the Western powers, *and also* aid and trade concessions for Third World development; strict safety limits on the breeder-reactor and waste disposal procedures, *and also* greater attention to the energy needs of poorer peoples — all of this is in theory possible. But it does not go to the heart of the problem. We who have the power remain ourselves the planners. We try to control the solutions to the difficulties our science and technology have produced. This is a false perception of the situation we are in. We are in fact playing a critical scene in the whole drama of human (and indeed of natural) history, but we are neither the authors nor the most important actors. It is about the meaning of this drama that we must ask if we are to know how creatively to interpret our roles. And since we do not know the whole script or the finale — in fact our actions may even change the scene — we must make our inquiries in a dialogue with God and with the

FACTS, MORALS, AND THE BOMB

other actors who have different perceptions and different concerns.

The dialogue, I suggest, has two levels: First, it is a dialogue about the style and the claims of our knowledge about the reality in which we are engaged. What kind of truth has been revealed by the science that produced nuclear fission? How is it related, both in method and content, to truth known in other ways from other sources? How can we discern some coherent picture, human, natural, spiritual, social, and scientific, of the history in which nuclear weaponry is one element and nuclear war might be an event? How can we test our discernments?

Second, it is a dialogue about the moral character of the world in which we live and the response it demands of us. What is, in fact, the governance which places the awful dimensions of science-based technological power in context, and how does it enforce itself? What consequences can be drawn from it for human responsibility in exercising or renouncing power, including nuclear power? How does this power relate to other powers in life, divine and human? How is our power curbed and directed?

Let us take a look at these in turn.

I. The Question of Truth

It is amazing how one gets used to an apocalypse when it has been around for thirty-one years. Even though the danger is a thousand times worse now than in 1945 (destructive power is now measured in megatons rather than kilotons of TNT), and the picture has been filled out in all its horror by scientists and the public media, it is still hard to recapture the sense of impending doom which the mushroom cloud over Hiroshima produced. For too brief a time people reached for categories beyond science and even beyond morality to grasp what was going on.

"We have gone too far" was one spontaneous reaction I remember from the debates around Columbia University during that fateful summer. We thought we had trespassed on knowledge reserved for God alone, and the result could only be our destruction. The theme of that response is an old, even a pre-Christian one — Pandora's box, Prometheus' punishment, Icarus' crash for trying to fly too high, Phaeton thrown from the sun-chariot he could not control. But for a world of science-based technology it was a new discovery.

"Our generation is able to listen with fresh attentiveness to those passages in the New Testament which speak about the end of history," preached a professor from Union Theological Seminary in New York. "We can understand their urgency for we also carry on our activities with a haunting sense that time may be running out."[1] The text he used was one seldom heard until then in the pulpit of a mainline church:

> For the mystery of lawlessness already is at work, restrained just now by one until he be removed. Then the lawless one will be revealed, whom the Lord Jesus will destroy by the spirit of his mouth, and bring to nothing by the shining of his presence. (II Thess. 2:7-8)

This too was an old Biblical motif, but for conventional American Christianity, a new reality.

Nor were the scientists themselves unaffected. Enrico Fermi's wife reported a sense of guilt among the physicists at Los Alamos, and J. Robert Oppenheimer put it yet more sharply: "In some sort of crude sense which no vulgarity, no humor, no overstatement can quite extinguish, the physicists have known sin; and this is a knowledge which they cannot lose."[2] For the next few years the *Bulletin of the Atomic Scientists* was a source of urgent prophetic judgment about the modern world in a style that had once been reserved for theologians and social reformers.

In short, the basic question which the first atomic explosion raised among those who experienced it most deeply was not about engineering, whether physical, social, or even moral, but about reality. What is the character of the knowledge which physics has obtained of the inner secrets of the atom? That it is immensely powerful is clear. But is it the power of God, or is it demonic? Are the theories that nuclear scientists have developed coherent with Truth in any universal sense or are they divisive attempts to organize a part of reality against the whole? "After all," replied Fermi to those who questioned dropping the atomic bomb on Japan, "the thing's superb physics!" But not

---

[1] David E. Roberts, *The Grandeur and the Misery of Man* (New York, 1935), p. 177.

[2] Quoted in Robert C. Batchelder, *The Irreversible Decision* (New York, 1961), p. 112.

FACTS, MORALS, AND THE BOMB

even all physicists were satisfied with that answer.[3] Is the beautiful mathematical harmony of atomic theory with all its consequences for nuclear armaments as well as its beneficial uses an expression of the peace of the universe, or is it part of the logic of the lawless one?

Familiarity has dulled the edge of questions like these today, but the experience of science-based technology has generalized them as well. Environmental apocalypse is a distinct possibility. Genetic control of life looms down the road. Pandora's box is open. Where are we now in the history of the universe, having let loose these powers? How should we respond to them, we who after all are only Pandoras and not gods? Prometheus is loose. His fire is radioactive and brighter than a thousand suns. Where is Zeus when we need him?

There are several answers to questions such as these. Let us examine three.

Scientism

The first, and perhaps the most prevalent reply is to reject the questions themselves, and to live with the consequences of the rejection. In this view, the scientific method itself is the only reliable means of obtaining objective information about reality, however many problems this information may raise for human life. It must proceed by its own rules as a first enterprise. The control of its results for human welfare, and their meaningful interpretation by philosophers and theologians, must follow after. If control fails and meaning is lost, this is not the fault of science but of human beings in other fields of endeavor.

It is not surprising that this position survives even the threat of nuclear catastrophe. It is the very basis of the modern scientific enterprise and all its achievements. It rests, however, on some definite assumptions, going back to the fathers of modern science, Galileo and Descartes, which produce the split view from which it suffers.

a. The first is the assumption that only quantifiable qualities, measurable by definite instruments in repeatable experiments, are of the essence of things: height, weight, speed, direction, and the like. Not what the eye sees or the emotions appreciate is real, but the forces and proportions which the in-

[3]Robert Jungk, *Brighter Than a Thousand Suns* (New York, 1958), p. 202.

struments measure. Only here is publicly verifiable objective knowledge to be found. The rest is private and subjective.

For a long time the full implications of this assumption did not emerge. Galileo was dealing after all with visible objects — the planets in the sky or balls on an inclined plane. The mechanical world-view of Sir Isaac Newton could still be grasped by a model. Even early modern theories of the atom presented a picture to the mind something like a miniature solar system. It was not until the layman began to hear about curved space from Einstein or learned from quantum mechanics about the complementarity of wave and particle concepts of light, that what had been meant all along became clear: Reality, this school believes, is in the mathematical equations which express the interactions of things, not in the things themselves.

b. The second is the assumption that the universe runs by laws, which have nothing to do with human faith, hopes, or values. They are laws with their own geometric consistency, their own balance of forces, and their own tendencies over eons of time. The human mind can discern them, but human destiny is irrelevant to them.

This axiom too was obscured at first. Early modern scientists such as Kepler and Newton assumed that they were exploring the mind of God in discovering the regularities of his creation, and that this same God had revealed himself in Jesus Christ. This was, however, a non-functional piety. The God-hypothesis was not, as Laplace later put it, necessary to the system. No purpose, no causal will, was implied in the determinism by which it works. What is more, to add a modern insight, the laws themselves are descriptions of statistical generalities, not of individual behavior. As with throws of the dice, chance in each specific case leads inexorably to necessity as the cases multiply.

c. There is also the assumption that a thing is explained when we know *how* it works. Not truth in any sense that guides or controls us, but power which we can control is the result of scientific investigation. This is an outrageous statement to many scientists, even today. It was curiosity, not lust for power, that made Pandora open her box. It was desire, even reverent longing, to explore the truth of things as it objectively is, to unlock the secrets of the universe in order to admire them — that drove scientific research in its pure form. Technology has another root — the need to solve the problems of production, to increase profit and improve the conditions of life. But the two, as Carl Friedrich von Weizsäcker has put it, have grown from separate roots into one trunk and their leaves form one huge crown.[4] In fact the knowledge that science delivers is information about structures and forces which are objects for the human subject and can therefore be manipulated by him or her. This result is rooted in the scientific method itself.

Again, this was not clear at the beginning. Descartes was sincere in asking how the clear ideas of the mind can be known to correspond to the qualities of matter in extension, and he was sincere in his answer that God, who made both mind and matter, does not deceive. But the answer did not hold. Modern science is permeated by the skepticism of Hume and Kant: The human reason contributes its own categories to the organization of sense impressions. It can never know the object as it is in itself, but only phenomena which categories of understanding and instruments of measurement define. This relativism is reinforced still more by the character of experiments in modern micro-physics. That which is to be measured is itself affected by the investigator and his tools. The best that can be found is a relation between them under certain conditions. "The scientific law," writes von Weizsäcker, "becomes more and more only an indication in regard to the possibility and the result of experiments; a law concerning our ability to produce phenomena."[5]

Science, however, can indeed "produce phenomena." As its vision of the universe fades into abstract relativity, its discovery of power sources for human use continues every day. Confidence in the scientific method nowadays is rooted here, in the technological fruits it produces. "If you ask what makes the Siamese twins of science and technology the idols of our time, the answer ought to be: It is their trustworthiness."[6] In a world whose ultimate meaning is obscure, here at least is a method which organizes chaos, which bends natural forces to human control, which produces what security, peace, and prosperity we enjoy.

[4]C.F. von Weizsäcker, *The Relevance of Science* (London, 1964), pp. 11-12.

[5]C.F. von Weizsäcker, *The World View of Physics* (London, 1952), p. 200.

[6]*The Relevance of Science*, p. 14.

So the priests of scientism would argue. They recognize that there are problems, even prospects of catastrophe. Some propose, with B. F. Skinner, to extend technology to human behavior itself. Others, like Jacques Monod, would project the "ethic of objectivity" inherent in the scientific method into a self-transcending, self-sacrificing style for the whole of life. But in any case, they would say, nothing is gained by a romantic escape from the one means of discerning objectively what forces work upon us and how we may cope with them.

What is wrong with this perspective? Its great strength is clearly that it is rooted in the practice of a community which directs all its members to an objective goal. The search for truth wherever it leads and regardless of its consequences, respect for established facts, the willingness to admit mistakes or ignorance and to leave questions unanswered, the public democratic character of research, and the readiness to build upon and acknowledge the work of others — all these are disciplines that have given integrity to science through the years. Why cannot we trust them to prevent nuclear catastrophe as well?

There are, I think, three reasons. First, the scientific method, just because of its stringent objectivity, fails to grasp the reality of human power and the way it makes use of the facts which science brings to light. Technology has its own roots, its own motivations and its own aims. They are in human nature and they follow patterns determined by human decisions and desires. In fact this power invades even the laboratory to influence the focus and direction of research itself. The most vivid illustration of this is the mistaken fear of such distinguished scientists as Leo Szilard and Albert Einstein that the Nazis might be the first to develop an atomic bomb, which led them to urge upon the United States government the massive program which led to Hiroshima. But there are many, many others, often less dramatic. Not only for the sake of national security, but also for commercial advantage, scientists have been brought to deny the public character of their research and to keep its results from one another. Technological power is not a secondary quality, in Galileo's sense, to be dealt with in the private and subjective realm. It helps to determine where science shall direct its investigation, what problems it shall solve, and what truths it shall discover. The scientific method has no means for discerning or controlling this dimension of reality.

Second, the scientific method provides no tools for critical analysis of the social role and bias of the scientist himself. No wonder that some, like Skinner, imagine themselves as the managers of human nature and others as the last custodians of objective truth, while their prescriptions as to what is technologically and scientifically feasible for the less-developed world are met with responses ranging from annoyance to fury, by those who are negatively affected by their enterprise. The scientific method is not dialogical, however communitarian it may be within its premises. It does not learn truth by encounter in which the whole person is challenged and changed. There are analogies, to be sure, as Michael Polanyi has pointed out, between conversion from one major theory to another and conversion to a new social ideology or religious faith. But these are analogies only. They do not help the scientist to see his whole activity in the context of a human interaction that relativizes, judges, and perhaps changes his work.

Third, the scientific method as we have described it excludes by definition the very range of truth which could give meaning to the whole of life. The dull, colorless mathematical universe of which not even a mechanical model can any longer be made, and which goes its way indifferent to all that is human, is the direct result of a reductionist premise in research, not a description of reality. In fact it is constantly being violated, as Polanyi once again shows, by science itself in its discernment of esthetic patterns of order among phenomena.[7] If there is a creative reality which can give meaning even to the phenomenon of nuclear fission, we must seek it through the synthetic imagination which is also a way to truth.

Organicism

With this we come to the second answer to our question. An organicist takes issue with scientism at just this point, with a perspective that is outspokenly metaphysical — out of process philosophy — drawing models from biology more than from physics. The way back from the edge of disaster, from this point of view, is to perceive in time the organic, even psychic, continuity of all reality from the electron through the highest forms of life to the stars in their galaxies, as the whole strives through

---

[7]Michael Polanyi, *Personal Knowledge* (Chicago, 1958), chapter three.

its creative spontaneity at every level to realize higher goals. In the words of a biologist-advocate:

> There is an eros reaching forward to values not yet realized. Eros is met by the lure of possible values not yet concretely real in my experience. Eros requires agape to give it direction. So too, eros is required in order that agape be appropriated by the recipient. Part of the implicate order of the universe is this realm of values which presses on us as possibilities from which we choose and are chosen. It is real. It is influential. It is personal. To be grasped by it is to feel a claim.[8]

The assumptions of this point of view oppose those of scientism at all three basic points:

a. Knowledge begins with the perception of the organic wholeness of things, including their qualities of beauty, meaning, and value. The synthetic moment should come first, the analytical second, in understanding reality. In fact quantifiable aspects of things, reducible ultimately to mathematical terms, are the abstractions; the whole in its creative interaction with other wholes is the reality. It is the higher synthesis that makes sense of the parts. This means that true knowledge does not come through the refinement of the experimental method, its instruments or rational processes in the first place, but through intuition of and participation in the living process of which we are all a part. "Mechanism is an abstraction from organism; to fail to see this is to reify process. In process thought all entities are organisms influenced by past events and anticipating future ones. They are both subjects and objects."[9]

b. The laws by which the universe works are developmental and move all reality toward the creation and realization of value. Human life and destiny are the highest emergents on the scale, but there is an inward continuity of all existence. There is a creative freedom which runs through the entire process, modifying but respecting the order of things which is itself dynamic. Frederick Ferré suggests three basic forms of this interaction: "The balance between growth and death — that maintains healthy organisms at proper scale and within finite limits . . ."; "the balance between local differentiation of function and

---

[8]Charles Birch, "What Does God Do in the World?" *Anticipation*, No. 22 (Geneva, 1976), p. 42.

[9]*Ibid.*, p. 43.

holistic mutuality of connection ..." in ever more complex organisms; and "the balance between necessity and spontaneity" in the creative self-determination of life at ever higher levels.[10]

Contrary to scientism, this philosophy does require God as a working hypothesis, or at least as the logical completion of the argument, but a God of a particular kind. He is the divine *in* the process, not the creator of it. He influences, but does not dispose. His character and spirit work in and with the world to bring forth its true meaning, but the world on all levels has its own freedom. Evil therefore can happen. In fact some disordering that seems evil may be part of a creative process out of which higher order will come.

c. A thing is explained, not when we know how it works and can tap its power for our purposes, but when we know its organic connections, both inner and outer, and can relate it to new visions of order on higher levels. There is no division between truth and power. They seem to divide only when power is perceived in a partial or a distorted context, and therefore misunderstood. This misunderstanding can have disastrous consequences of course, as can all misdirections of creative freedom. We could destroy much of our world with nuclear weapons. But the truth of the universe is organic, creatively harmonious, and guided by love. This is the context in which human freedom and power have their meaning. To sense this continuity with all that is, and this purposeful direction, is to understand reality in a way that redirects the will to power.

Thus argue the proponents of process philosophy. They speak their message more vigorously to the ecological crises of our time than to the danger of nuclear war, but it can apply to both. It has certainly one great strength: It reminds us that we begin our thought and our actions — our science and our technology — within a relationship with the very reality we study and manipulate. This relationship has a living form which includes God, nature, our neighbors, and ourselves. To abstract from it may give certain forms of useful information and release certain powers, but it is not the way to truth. There is another.

The great weakness of this point of view, however, is the

---

[10]Frederick Ferré, *Shaping the Future* (New York: 1976), p. 113.

encompassing vagueness of the way it points. First of all, whence come the standards by which one can distinguish whether a given development is creative or destructive? When is a given wholeness organically valuable and when monstrous? With one voice the process believers seem to say that nature itself provides the standards. The balance of growth and death maintains healthy organisms at the cost of some. We need not regret those lost. The balance between differentiated species and their ecological harmony, between freedom of mutation (in body or spirit) and the requirements of an organic system, can be disturbed somewhat for the sake of a creative new adjustment, but not too much. But with another voice these same believers speak of development as a spiritual reality, of higher forms of human and divine love moving the system toward its goals. In this process persons as such are valuable and changes may be fundamental. A mixture of biological models, humanistic ideals, and Christian assumptions sounds here in such a way that one can rarely say which voice carries the tune. The result is little clear guidance from this perspective about the very issues that concern us most in this book: the control of nuclear armaments and the question of the use of nuclear fission for the production of power.

In the second place process thought is a more metaphysical guide to possible order in life than a method for grasping and directing the powers of life. The method of science-based technology is still overwhelmingly scientistic, and process philosophy has not come to grips with the power that method has produced. Its God is too weak to cope with such a challenge and its organicism leaves too small a place for a nuclear explosion.

Third, we face again the nagging question: Whose vision of creative unity prevails and by what forces can it be realized? Process philosophy is an anti-revolutionary point of view in its organic, developmental style. It emphasizes the continuity of human and non-human nature and the rights of the latter as well as the former. Is this the perspective of the secure and the rich making their own experience universal once more?

Social Determinism

The question of social determination is the thrust of the

third response to the questions with which we began. It found its most provocative expression in Karl Marx and its philosophical base in Hegel, but it has since become the common possession of many sociologists of knowledge and, more important, the spontaneous reaction of many outsiders to the control of science by political and economic powers. Scientific knowledge, in this perspective, is, like all other perceptions of reality, a part of the struggle of human beings to master nature, to produce the means of their livelihood, and to struggle against other classes that oppose their welfare and interests. In Marx's terms, consciousness is determined by social existence. It is therefore the function of a relationship and not simply objective, but the relationship is one of dialectical conflict with other classes and with the material world. Knowledge therefore is fundamentally technological. Humanity in fact is created by solving problems of production. This capacity distinguishes man from ape. The basic relation between humans and nature is antithesis or contradiction (to use Hegel's words), which must be overcome as man humanizes nature by his productive action (synthesis). This dialectical movement *is* reality. True science is to discern its movements and to serve the human struggle.

All of this is distorted however, in this view, by the human conflict, which centers on the control of economic power. Because of this, humanity is divided into opposing classes, each with its own perception of reality, dictated by its interests and the conditions of its struggle to prevail. Natural science is drawn into this conflict, indeed is produced out of it, and therefore is distorted as well. The real catastrophe toward which the world is heading is a revolutionary upheaval in which the dispossessed will take over the power which had exploited them. This becomes catastrophic in a special way, even the most optimistic of revolutionaries admits, because nuclear weapons may be used in the conflict. The source of the evil development of nuclear physics into bombs and missiles, however, is the social conflict.

This means, finally, that science-based technology, as truth and power, will find its proper place and unity only in the context of a humanity liberated from exploitation, in which the centers of oppressive power are destroyed. Only then will a free and universal rationality prevail.

This perspective has one fundamental virtue which the other two have lacked. It recognizes that our perception of scientific truth and our use of technological power both are conditioned by the social conditions of our existence and the conflicts which arise there. Lust for power and craving for security give direction to research and development more than the powerful and secure will admit. Economic interest has enormous power over the whole scientific-technological enterprise, even to political decisions about nuclear weaponry. In short, even scientific knowledge and visions of organic harmony are ideologically biased. They are not relative only to the conditions of experiment and the instruments of measurement. The scientists know that much. They are not dependent only on the insight of a valuing community. The process believers see that. They are distorted because they grow out of the struggle of dominant groups in society to secure their status and enhance their power, or of suppressed groups to achieve their liberation. It is not surprising that the outsiders in the power struggle see this most clearly. Third World peoples and poorer folk in the technologically developed nations are constantly having to bear the consequences of decisions made in the power centers of technology, often at their expense. They are constantly being told that scientific knowledge itself dictates these decisions. Not surprisingly they are constantly demanding things which the science-technology establishment regards as dangerous foolishness — such as nuclear power plants where local sources of energy would suffice, or even nuclear weapons.

The social determinists raise a critical question about the way the whole scientific-technological enterprise perceives reality and responds to it, which we may not forget. They do not, however, answer the question. They are right in pointing out the way class interests distort our understanding. Their hope for a pure human consciousness emerging already among the poor and the oppressed is an illusion. Ideal humanity is the substitute for God in this perspective. But this god continually fails, just as soon as the outsiders gain some part of power, wealth, or position. It drives its believers out of dialogue with real human beings, poor or rich, into communion with an abstraction.

Where are we, then, in our search for a truth which will have the power to place the awful fact of nuclear fission and its consequences in a meaningful context? Let me suggest four convictions that grow out of the debate so far, but go beyond it.

First, knowledge of the external world is a relationship and an interaction. Whether in physics, biology, sociology, or politics, knowing includes, as Michael Polanyi has put it, an act of appraisal. It involves the risk of a personal commitment which is a form of communion. In a real sense the truth discovers and claims the investigator in a way that goes far beyond the data and gives them form. In Polanyi's own words:

> Intellectual commitment is a responsible decision, in submission to the compelling claims of what in good conscience I conceive to be true. It is an act of hope, striving to fulfill an obligation within a personal situation for which I am not responsible and which therefore determines my calling.[11]

The objective side of this personal knowledge is its claim which has the force more of a relationship discovered than of a fact defined. It requires a continuing dialogue about the whole structure of the relationship. The subjective side is the personal commitment, the affirmation which can never be replaced by absolute, impersonal certainty.

This may seem remote from the problem of controlling nuclear armaments, but it is fundamental to any ethos which might put them in context. The nuclear physicist, the missile technician, the military strategist, and the politician all are operating in a real world where their knowledge is relational in this sense. When Galileo, as von Weizsäcker has pointed out, set forth his revolutionary theories, he was not simply drawing conclusions from observations. He was proclaiming a new belief about the behavior of the physical world, which was out of harmony with the structure of understanding which then held the physical, moral, and spiritual universe together. He claimed the right to do so regardless of the consequences for that universe, because this truth had laid its claim on him, and he was sure he would be vindicated.[12] He is the archetype of the modern scientist, and his relation to the world beyond his science is archetypical as well. There is no longer an Inquisition, but the prospect of nuclear physics being used to destroy the world, or genetic biology manipulating future human life, is even more

---

[11]*Personal Knowledge*, p. 65.

[12]*The Relevance of Science*, pp. 104ff.

frightening. To break the hold of one world view on the whole range of truth was right. But today the crucial question for the modern Galileos is the reverse: What is the relation of truth in science to truth in politics and truth in theology? How do the relations bear on truth *in* each field? To take this question seriously is the beginning of an attack on the promise and the menace of nuclear power.

Second, knowledge is power, and the natural sciences are not equipped, by the limitations of their method, to understand the relation between power and truth. A responsible concern for truth itself, as the whole context of the power which science has produced, will drive the scientist therefore into politics, economics, philosophy, and theology, as it will drive professionals in these other fields to come to grips with scientific theory. Belief in a basic structure of reality has broken down in almost every field: in physics with the loss of the mechanistic model, in politics with the breakdown of natural law, in philosophy under the attacks of existentialism and linguistic analysis, and even in theology as God comes to be known more as act than as being. Across the board the critical question has come: How are the powers our various disciplines discern related in a meaningful and promising way? Here is where integration of truth must be sought.

Third, knowledge is ultimately a dialogue with God, even in the natural sciences. Of the three perspectives we have explored, scientism is the most honest with itself about this dimension. The organicists set forth what characteristics God may have in order to fit their vision, and thereby deprive him of the otherness which makes dialogue possible. The social determinists show with devastating insight how religion provides an illusory reality which deflects people from facing and coping with the powers before them. But they evade the issue by imagining a liberated humanity which will be the source of ultimate truth and power. The God problem inherent in the search for truth is this question: Whence does One reveal himself who is totally other than our human powers, ambitions, plans, fears, and visions, and who therefore can confront us as an authority not an echo for our truths, a transformer not a legitimator of our power? In this world where the truths that science discovers open up apocalyptic visions of destruction because of the way the power they release is used by man, no less a God can convince us that he matters.

The rigorous scientists are at least realistic about this. The universe, they say, has no meaning, except that which we give it by intelligent planning. We are alone with our science-based technological reason to cope with whatever powers we raise out of the atom, the gene, or the sun, and whatever forces organize our society. But this throws an overwhelming burden upon the scientist and the technician, a burden not only of responsibility but of guilt.

Von Weizsäcker dramatizes the problem with the story of his only conversation with the great Swiss theologian Karl Barth. Von Weizsäcker said to Barth that he could trace a direct line from Galileo to the atomic bomb, the line defined by the science of physics. What is more, having lived through Nazi propaganda he could see communications technology — the radio and its elaborations — as an even greater threat, manipulating the human mind. "I ask myself sometimes," he continued, "whether I must not give up scientific research altogether, because to stop at any point seems as if I were willing the cause but not the effect." He added that he realized the enterprise would go on even if he withdrew from it. The problem of controlling its demonic power would have to be faced in another way. To turn away from the search for destructive and therefore false and misleading truths has some effect. He did, in fact, produce a political sensation by making, with other German physicists, a statement refusing to take part in any German research on nuclear weapons. But all this does not answer the question: Where is the ultimate truth and power in this situation, and what is the scientist's responsibility thereto?

At this point von Weizsäcker records Barth's reply, and his own reaction to it:

> Mr. von Weizsäcker, I know that the answer I give you is insufficient. I know no better one, so I will give you what I can. If you believe, what all Christians say but in truth almost no one believes, that Christ is coming again, then you may, indeed you must, continue to do natural science. If not, then you have no right to do so.

"The answer," von Weizsäcker continues,

> is, if you like, mythical. But this answer expressed something that greatly helped me. It expressed that the problem is not in an isolated sphere that has nothing to do with theology. Rather the only confidence in which I can move in natural science is rooted nowhere else than in a truth about which theologians too often tend to say that it has nothing to do with natural science.

> When I think further along this line, it leads me back to the question of our place in history. When a Christian says that Christ will come again, he is speaking of the history of salvation. But salvation history is history. If Barth was saying something relevant here, he forces us to ask about the place of natural science in the history in which Christ has lived, in the history of which Christians say that in it he will come again.[13]

On this basis von Weizsäcker continues to be a physicist. No simple comfort is given. No wrong is hereby excused. But physics with all its fruits is placed in a context, a dialogue with ultimate reality, that authorizes it, gives hope for it, and directs it toward meaningful ends. The theologian and the physicist, along with the politician, the sociologist, and others, will still be in tension with one another. Some theology will continue to seem to the scientist constricting and outmoded. Some physics will continue to sound like heresy to the theologian. But the tension lies within the one history in which God is the principal actor, and the ultimate dialogue is with him.

Fourth, truth, even in the sciences, is the product of a dialogue with other human beings in the context of their experiences, cultures, struggles, and needs. What has been said about the social determination of the scientific enterprise can be given a positive meaning when we accept this bias as an invitation to dialogue and mutual correction. What knowledge is it most important to seek? Where should the priorities be in research? Until now those with wealth and power have determined not only the answers to these questions but to a large degree the content of what is discovered. Nuclear fission was driven to successful completion by the defense needs of a great power. Its adaptation to electric power production is largely spurred by the increasing demands of wealthy nations for energy. Scientific arguments for the safety and economy of breeder reactors over against other possible energy sources are often valid and convincing, but never quite as valid as the proponents maintain because of the social interest which produces them. What new truths would be discovered if the needs and interests of a poorer or less-centralized economy were determin-

---

[13] I draw this account by von Weizsäcker from two sources which I have combined. The first is a lecture given at the Conference for Natural Scientists and Theologians at the Ecumenical Institute, Bossey, Celigny, Switzerland, 1958. See the Report of this Conference, p. 25. The author repeated the story more briefly in *The Ecumenical Review*, 28 (April 1976), 162.

ing the research and if the scientists themselves shared that social experience? What different directions would technology take?

At the moment an almost automatic selection process removes scientists from the context of poverty and oppression. The dialogue between the two worlds is therefore far too much at cross purposes, as if out of different universes. Physics itself, energy research, military technology, and all the related work of science must be done by poor people, in small and exploited nations and races, struggling to find prosperity and peace. Then the broader dimensions of truth will emerge.

II. The Question of an Ethos

The truths which nuclear physics has revealed about the inner workings of the atom have turned out to be power, not structure, and have forced us into a critical dialogue both with God and with the outsiders among our neighbors about the historical meaning and direction of this power. With this we are already into the question of moral reality. Is there such a thing? Nothing is easier than to draw up moral codes for peace and justice — beginning with a ban on nuclear weapons and a plan for the redistribution of wealth and productive capacity among the peoples of the world — but is there somewhere a power that can enforce such codes, and correct the self-interested bias which creeps into our formulation of them? What is the moral power, if any, with which human powers must reckon?

Once again, each of the perspectives we have described has a different answer, and each answer is an expression of faith, a wager against the future. For the scientific manager hope lies in a moral technology for the limitation of nuclear weapons within an assured mutual deterrence, and in a technology-based world economic development that will spread also to the poorer peoples without threat to the prosperity of the developed. For the organicist all nature brings forth the values which we need only to recognize in order to adjust our powers to its creative harmony. For the revolutionary it is the struggle for power and liberation by the outsider that brings peace and justice to birth and overthrows the powers of destruction, which now prevail. Over against all of these — and sometimes from within their camps — the Christian, here above all, must talk of God. What does it mean, in an age of nuclear power, to speak of divine power and purpose? Let me make just two suggestions.

1. First, and centrally, there is the theme of Karl Barth's reply: This is a history in which Christ will come again. This is relational, evocative language. Some would call it symbolic or mythical. It is no more so than the scientist's assumptions about reality, the idea of an organic, value-creating universe, or the hope of a liberating people's revolution, but like them all it takes on meaning as it makes sense of the power struggle in which we are all involved. It does so, I believe, in at least three ways.

a. In the center of the universe, giving it meaning and direction, is the power of God in Jesus Christ. Ultimate reality is in this sense personal. Human concerns matter in the scheme of things. The laws which describe the interaction of the stars in their galaxies or the sub-atomic particles are set in this context. So also are the structures of technology and the power they organize, even the power of nuclear fission. There is no need to manufacture heroic pictures of the humanity we will try to preserve in spite of the indifference of the universe to our concerns. We do not have to reduce our hopes to the level of an organic continuity with all of life. The struggle for liberation does not have to get lost in the solidarity of some impersonal collective. The real power is already set forth, in the character and work of the risen Christ. Here is the point of reference for understanding where we are.

This has been dimly but almost universally recognized in modern humanity by the way we use the words *justice* and *peace*. There are theoretical possibilities of peace in a world of nuclear armaments based simply on human power: a totalitarian rule engineered by technology and secured by a nuclear weapons monopoly, or a balance of deterrents among a few nuclear powers and denial of nuclear capacity to the rest, for example. We know they will not work, not just because of technical unfeasibility, but because peace is meaningless unless it embraces the needs and hopes of human beings in their personal interaction with each other. In other words peace depends on helping people to their justice, and the model of justice is the calling and the promise of God in Christ, with all the freedom, hope, and responsibility it involves. The human search for justice is a ferment that breaks down every power structure. It may work perversely, as when the poor riot and destroy the economy which exploits them but on which they still depend, or as if some dominated people should try to achieve their freedom by nuclear blackmail. But it cannot be suppressed because the power of God is its source.

b. There are powers in this world which have their own logic, their own aims and pretensions. This is a world in which Christ was crucified. Yet these same powers are within creation. They have their places and their functions in the divine purpose. The risen Christ in one sense fights against these powers. In another sense he is their meaning and manager.[14] They are rebellious and destructive, but the object of the battle with them is to bring them back to their true function in a Christ-directed universe. The Christian is therefore called on in the New Testament to resist them (Ephesians 6:12), to tell them about the wisdom of God (Ephesians 3:10), to submit to them in their proper function (Romans 13:1), and to take part in Christ's reconciliation of them through the cross and resurrection (Colossians 1:20).

The power which comes from the splitting of the atom can well be called one of these. So also can the power of military and industrial technology that makes use of nuclear fission. The structure this technology creates has its own logic which is a curious mixture of perceiving God's purpose for it and the desire to make itself God. The job of the Christian is to help it sort things out.

How much deterrent capacity does the United States need to prevent nuclear war from breaking out, and in what branches of weaponry? There is a logic of absolute security which would answer this question on the basis of an enemy's utmost capacity to inflict damage. There is another which would evaluate an enemy's intentions, interests, relations, and capacities as a whole, including the possibilities of lessening tensions and creating new relations of mutual dependence.

What should be done about the proliferation of nuclear weapons capacity among nations other than the great powers?

---

[14]I am here too briefly summarizing New Testament use, especially in the Pauline letters, of the term *exousiai* — powers or authorities. For a fuller treatment see G.B. Caird, *Principalities and Powers* (New York, 1956), or Heinrich Schlier, *Principalities and Powers in the New Testament* (London, 1961).

There is a logic for which the overriding issue is control over an increasingly uncontrollable process, and effective deterrent influence over every government with a bomb. There is another that seeks to work in an insecure situation for structures of international justice and mutual support that would reduce the force and meaning of nuclear weapons.

One could develop these cases and mention others, but the point is clear. We live in a world where the certainty of power control is never given. When we search for it, we ourselves are destroyed by it. Apocalypse means revelation. It may be that the principal job of the witness to Christ in a world where the powers will have their way regardless is to reveal the catastrophe ahead. But this may never be done except in the midst of a struggle to turn them from that catastrophe toward their constructive functions. God has a purpose for the powers that seem to dominate us and our history. They can never be as utterly destructive therefore as their own logic would demand, or as irredeemable as their own motives would suggest.

c. There is a terrible moral risk in working with nuclear physics, weapons technology, or any other of the powers of this world. One cannot, as von Weizsäcker clearly saw, evade guilt for what is done, even by withdrawing from it. The advocate of unilateral nuclear disarmament is no less responsible for the consequences of his position — if he can make it prevail — than the proponent of parity or superiority in nuclear weapons. To work with power is to take actions which coerce others, which may be based on wrong judgments even if on good motives, and which are bound to be unjust to some even if they are right on the whole. For the scientist, the technician, the politician, or the businessman to know that the final judgment on his work and on the world is that of the redeemer who does not excuse but forgives makes it possible to bear the responsibility of living with nuclear power. Because there is this forgiveness, and because it is reflected in the business of this world, mistakes can be corrected, wrong policies can be repented of, and broken relations can be healed. It is possible for the perpetrators and the victims of the Hiroshima explosion to work together for peace. It may be possible even after some future nuclear catastrophe to begin together again. And meanwhile it is possible to admit and correct mistakes before they become catastrophes, and to build an ethos in which even the powerful are willing to be corrected.

2. We have spoken so far of power. Let us look for a moment at the question of order. Knowledge, we have said, is a relationship with the object known — with God and with other people who come from different perspectives and experiences. The order this knowledge reflects is relational as well. It is a covenant built on the faithfulness of God who calls people into community with him and with one another, and who brings physical creation into the fellowship as well by making human beings responsible for taming it and bringing forth its fruits. The law which gives form to this covenant is no more nor less than the character of this God — his justice, his mercy, and his love. There is no other structure to the world than this. Other constructions may be built of course — theories of the atom, national states, multinational corporations, class theories of society, and many more. These constructions may be useful for their purposes for a time, but their relation to the covenantal structure of the world as God makes it depends on how far they are able to reflect the divine character in their own ethos, however indirectly.

The phenomenon of nuclear armament, from the atomic theory out of which it came to the organization of weapons systems for national defense, seems the ultimate challenge to this. It has its own laws. They express a different order — that of national security in a world of assumed organized hostility, itself equipped with nuclear weapons. What is more, it is part of a worldwide proliferation of arms, conventional and nuclear, of alarming proportions. Here is a growing dependence on physical force alone as the true order of the world, which not even its futility and probable catastrophe seem able to deter. Is there any evidence that the God who works through covenant has any influence on this trend?

The signs may seem small, but they are there. SALT itself, despite meager results for disarmament, is one. The two great nuclear powers have realized that they must set up structures of mutual consultation on matters of strategic defense aimed at each other. It is a small beginning of a covenant relation. The seriousness with which the United Nations is taken, especially as an instrument for making the concerns of the Third World known, is another example. The ecumenical fellowship in mission of the Christian Church, as it finds itself holding in one community partisans of opposing peoples, is still another. From here one could extend the list to thousands of small, sometimes personal acts which build relationships across old battle lines and break down structures of exploitation and domination.

This is the fabric of world order. In relationships between states it expresses itself in agreements which promote the flow of trade, of culture, and of people between them, and which compromise their interests where they conflict. The more this happens, the less significant is the nuclear arsenal. Between the rich and the poor world it is a matter of hearing and responding to the needs and hopes of those outside the structure of economic and technological establishment, so that they may become full partners in the world community. The more this is done, the fewer will be the countries trying to assert themselves with armaments, nuclear or conventional.

There is, in short, no final security for governments or any other structure in this world. There is something much better — hope and promise in new covenants based on new relations of mutual trust and help. Armaments there will continue to be. No human order was ever maintained without some coercion. But they play a role *within* covenantal relations and are dependent on them. National security is an important but a relative thing in the whole fabric of the relationships through which the nation lives. The art we must learn is the building of these relationships with the restrained use — and sometimes the renunciation — of the power God has given us, including nuclear power.

X

What Can be Done: Some Practical Steps

THOMAS A. HALSTED

The scenarios presented in this book are neither fanciful nor farfetched; one or more of the events described is *likely* to happen, possibly before the end of this century, unless people and governments take a radically different approach to the control of nuclear weapons and nuclear war. Yet not only do we — particularly we Americans — reject the notion that these nightmares could become reality; we tend to support the very actions and attitudes which will make them happen. The United States has taken the lead in promoting the worldwide spread of nuclear energy, until very recently with inadequate controls over the accompanying spread of technology and facilities which could make it all too easy to turn peaceful nuclear programs into nuclear weapons. It has whetted appetites for large, modern, super-sophisticated military forces through a billion-dollar-a-month program of arms sales, often to unstable regions of the world, without adequate thought to the long-range consequences — including the possibility that recipients will find

---

Thomas A. Halsted has been active in the field of public affairs, in particular arms control and disarmament, during most of his professional life. He studied for his B.A. at George Washington University, and after service in the U.S. Army, joined the Bureau of Intelligence and Research of the Department of State. In 1966 and 1967, he worked in the United States Arms Control and Disarmament Agency, and from 1967 to 1971 he was national director of the Council for a Livable World. He also served as a legislative assistant to Senator Alan Cranston of California, and since 1972 has been the executive director of the Arms Control Association and Arms Control program director for the Carnegie Endowment for International Peace.

Mr. Halsted has published widely in newspapers and magazines and has lectured and appeared on radio and television on various topics related to nuclear arms and disarmament.

221

their appetites for nuclear weapons increased along with those for high-performance conventional arms.

America has carried on a costly and dangerous nuclear arms race with the Soviet Union, reaching levels of nuclear overkill out of all proportion to any definition of security needs. And as technology constantly strives to improve the reliability, accuracy, and killing power of nuclear weapons, strategists develop new counterforce rationales to justify their use. By their example, the nuclear superpowers are increasing, not reducing, the likelihood that other nations will see nuclear weapons as the answer to their security needs, and will by acquiring them in increasing numbers bring closer the day that one or another of the dreadful scenarios described above is at last played out.

We have been unbelievably lucky that no nuclear weapon has been used in war in over thirty years, despite the thousands that are deployed around the globe. And it is indeed more by pure luck than good management that we have thus far averted the outbreak of nuclear war or the theft of nuclear weapons or nuclear materials by terrorists. Lloyd Dumas reminds us in chapter eight that "the more opportunities an event is given to occur, the more likely it will occur." As the number of nuclear weapons continues to grow, and as more means of using them to fight wars rather than deter wars are devised; as the number of nations that elect to acquire a nuclear weapon option increases; and as the number of opportunities for diversion of nuclear materials from nuclear power facilities grows, the chances increase that our luck will run out before long.

We may have a little more time to take the steps necessary to avert disaster. But until people and their leaders see that nuclear catastrophe is not only possible but even probable, they are not likely to act with the sense of urgency and bold imagination necessary to stop it. That sense of urgency is not yet sounding in the voices of more than a handful of world political leaders and thinkers.

Three years ago a group of eminent theorists on national security and disarmament met to discuss the possibility of "nuclear war by 1999." Their conversation makes chilling reading. Their conclusions:

> Nuclear war in some form is likely before the end of this century.
> It will probably occur as the direct result of a proliferation of

nuclear powers and weaponry. The more people who have such weapons, the more probable their use.

Existing political systems and the policies they generate fail to provide curbs on, or alternatives to, the proliferation of nuclear weapons. Nations continue to increase their armories in the name of self-protection.

To survive in such a world, nations may have to surrender much of their sovereignty. But a new kind of world government would involve the abandonment of many democratic values. Nuclear war is a more likely prospect.

People are complacent about the threat of nuclear war. We have different fears. The horror of the first atomic bomb explosions is fading from our memories.[1]

One of the participants in that discussion, George Rathjens, speculated that "perhaps our best hope is that we will learn a lesson from the first major *nuclear* disaster so that our complacency will not lead us to many more such wars before the end of the century...."[2]

I hope he is wrong. It seems to me just conceivable that the right political decisions can be made without the world first enduring the horror of a nuclear war; furthermore, it is not altogether clear that the world would react constructively to such an event. Surely, then, we should not rely on the potential cathartic effect of the next use of a nuclear weapon to bring us to our senses.

We must look, therefore, at both the long- and short-range actions that must be taken, at three levels: what governments must do collectively; what steps the United States government could take unilaterally; and what citizens can do for themselves to support and promote these government actions.

The International Agenda

First of all, we must accept that a non-proliferation strategy is at best a holding action. Over the long run, what is needed is not an effort to slow the spread of nuclear weapon capabilities (the present approach). Certainly it is not one of learning to live in a proliferated world either. (This is increasingly the subject of research by the United States government, which is beginning

[1]"Nuclear War by 1999?" *Harvard Magazine*, 78 (November 1975), pp. 19-25.
[2]*Ibid.*, p. 23.

to devote more effort to contemplating this phenomenon than it is to stopping it.) Rather we must consider "de-proliferating" — developing a conscious program dedicated to the eventual *elimination* of nuclear weapons from the earth. This can be viewed as a utopian goal, but the alternative — to which we are now tending — is madness. If we have indeed only two basic choices, let us opt for the visionary one. It is the best hope. President Carter has called for "the ultimate . . . reduction of nuclear weapons in all nations of the world to zero."[3]

What can the international community do to forestall disaster and pave the way for nuclear disarmament? The list which follows is by no means all-inclusive, but it addresses both the most urgent problems and the solutions which seem politically most attainable, albeit difficult. Most of the proposals in this inventory are already on many other agenda for action. My purpose here is to list those I think could have the most profound effect, and to comment on their feasibility and effectiveness.[4]

1. Limiting Access to Nuclear Materials

a. International control of peaceful uses of nuclear energy: Over the past two years members of the nuclear "suppliers' club" (the United States, the Soviet Union, Great Britain, Canada, France, Japan, and West Germany, and more recently the Netherlands, East Germany, Italy, Sweden, Belgium, Czechoslovakia, and Poland) have been holding private meetings in London to attempt to reach agreement on common policies governing the supply of fuels and facilities for nuclear power programs around the world. Their meetings were triggered by India's detonation in 1974 of a "peaceful nuclear device" using materials diverted from a Canadian-supplied research reactor on which there had been inadequate safeguards. They were given further urgency by the 1975 transaction whereby the Federal Republic of Germany agreed to build a complete nuclear fuel cycle for Brazil. The deal involves not

---

[3]Response to Arms Control Association Questionnaire. See *Arms Control Today*, 6 (October 1976).

[4]For a more exhaustive discussion of these and other non-proliferation strategies, see Thomas A. Halsted, "Nuclear Proliferation: How to Retard It, Manage It, Live with It," Aspen Institute for Humanistic Studies, P.O. Box 2820, Princeton, New Jersey 08540.

only elements necessary for a peaceful nuclear power program but also components which are widely viewed as unnecessary for Brazil's power program but potentially useful for a future nuclear weapons program, should Brazil opt for one.[5] Subsequent French negotiations with South Korea and Pakistan to sell them fuel reprocessing plants further stimulated concern about the need to establish agreed controls on such sensitive facilities, which can reduce from months to days the time necessary to convert irradiated reactor fuel rods into weapon materials. During the 1976 United States Presidential campaign, Jimmy Carter pressed for a firm United States policy which would discourage the growth of a "plutonium economy" by deferring plutonium reprocessing and recycling; a few days before the election President Ford presented essentially the same recommendation. Early in 1977 President Carter announced the details of his plutonium and nuclear export policies and asked Congress for enabling legislation.

But, as Herbert Scoville has pointed out earlier, nuclear export policies are not the only non-proliferation strategies; indeed, they may not, in the end, be politically very effective. They deal, after all, only with capabilities to acquire nuclear weapons, not with incentives. Those governments which want to obtain nuclear weapons may find it slightly more difficult to do so with more stringent "suppliers' club" controls, but they are likely, if anything, to have their incentives increased to "go it alone." And other governments wanting to acquire an independent peaceful nuclear program may well resent the implication of the suppliers' restrictions that they have suspect motives. The Carter position on nuclear exports includes a self-imposed moratorium on construction of reprocessing plants in the United States as well as on their export abroad; at least in this respect the United States cannot be accused of a discriminatory supply policy.

b. Reducing dependence on nuclear power: The Eisenhower "Atoms for Peace" program of 1953 signaled the inauguration of a broad-scale sales effort to promote the use of nuclear power as a cheap, efficient, and modern way to generate electric power. Through the sales efforts of the nuclear energy industry in the

---

[5]See Norman Gall, "Atoms for Brazil, Dangers for All," *Foreign Policy*, Summer 1976, pp. 155-201, and William W. Lowrance, "Nuclear Futures for Sale: To Brazil from West Germany, 1975," *International Security*, 1 (Fall 1976), pp. 142-166.

United States and elsewhere, abetted by the International Atomic Energy Agency (IAEA) which saw that measures to facilitate as much as possible the access to nuclear energy would be the only way to persuade would-be members of the IAEA to accept the accompanying safeguards, appetites for nuclear power plants were generated throughout the developing world. Belatedly, realization that both the safety and security problems are more serious than first anticipated and a growing awareness of the weapons potential of peaceful nuclear programs have led to a reappraisal of the wisdom of the nuclear power sales pitch of the past twenty years. Furthermore, higher investment costs than earlier anticipated have sharply lowered industry expectations of profitable markets, both at home and abroad, for nuclear energy in the years ahead. Nevertheless, the number of nuclear power plants in being, on order, or being planned today is still sizeable — 454 plants, in forty-one countries, with a planned output capacity of 343,000 megawatts.[6] This represents a sizeable number of potential candidates for further proliferation problems.

Higher costs and public opposition to nuclear power programs may mean that fewer of these plants will be built, but meanwhile there is little public effort being made to explore either promising alternatives to nuclear power or the benefits of energy conservation, particularly in the United States, the premier waster of energy resources. National leadership for energy conservation and exploration of alternatives to nuclear power in the United States could have widespread international effects.

2. Inching Toward Disarmament

The nuclear weapons nations, as suppliers of nuclear materials and technology for peaceful programs, have routinely described their non-proliferation policies only in relation to nuclear export policy, while declaring that the policies concerning their own nuclear weapons and safeguards are their own business and nobody else's.[7] Thus they have rejected the argument that there is a compact in the non-proliferation treaty whereby

[6] See the Aspen Report.

[7] Thomas A. Halsted, "Report from Geneva," *Arms Control Today*, 5 (June 1975). See also William Epstein, *The Last Chance, Nuclear Proliferation and Arms Control* (New York, 1976), pp. 244-258.

the governments being asked to give up the nuclear weapon option are entitled to see some compensating sacrifice on the part of the nuclear weapon states — even though such a sacrifice is explicitly called for in Article VI of the treaty, which commits the parties to work toward "effective measures relating to the cessation of the nuclear arms race ... and to nuclear disarmament." Progress in this area has been almost nonexistent. Yet as long as there is none, the nuclear weapons states continue to flaunt a double standard before the world: They deny nuclear weapons to others while continuing to demonstrate a belief that nuclear weapons are usable and that nuclear war may indeed be fightable and perhaps even winnable. Some of the long-overdue actions the nuclear weapons states should take are:

a. A Comprehensive Test Ban (CTB): A treaty ending all nuclear testing would be seen by the rest of the world as the first positive sign that the United States and the Soviet Union are willing to accept real restraints on their nuclear weapon programs. It would signal as well a recognition that new kinds of nuclear weapons are not going to be developed. The two treaties signed in 1974 and 1976 which allow both countries to continue testing weapons underground up to 150 kilotons (more than ten times the size of the Hiroshima bomb) and to conduct "peaceful nuclear explosions" up to 1.5 megatons have been widely viewed as a sham. President Carter called them "wholly inadequate" during his election campaign. No serious obstacle other than bureaucratic inertia and military unwillingness to give up anything stands in the way of a complete test ban. Even if no treaty were immediately possible, unilateral United States abstinence from further testing would not undermine United States security and would be likely to provide a stimulus for others to join. The time for a CTB is now.

b. Strategic Arms Limitations: The United States-Soviet SALT negotiations have been under way since 1969. With the single exception of the 1972 treaty banning all but minimum deployment of antiballistic missiles (ABMs) SALT has stopped no important military programs on either side. In fact, since SALT began, the United States has added more nuclear weapons to its inventory than the Soviet Union now possesses and has begun development of strategic cruise missiles; Russia has introduced new generations of intercontinental missiles, missile launching submarines, and medium-range bombers.

Both are embarked on weapons improvement programs which will increase the likelihood of nuclear war between them. If SALT is still worthwhile, it must be made more productive. Sizeable reductions in numbers of strategic nuclear delivery vehicles on both sides should be coupled with severe restrictions on means of improving remaining weapons; further improvements in accuracy and other means of improving counterforce capabilities should be stopped. In every conceivable way, modernization of strategic forces should be frozen. And what cannot be accomplished by negotiations should be addressed by unilateral initiative aimed at encouraging reciprocity.

In March 1977 the Carter administration offered a comprehensive and sweeping SALT proposal to the Soviets. While it was initially rejected by them, it contained many important features which may form parts of future SALT agreements.

It is often argued that such steps will not affect the decisions of others to "go nuclear," as their security concerns are not the threat from the superpowers, but rather from their neighbors. I disagree. As in the case of the Comprehensive Test Ban, positive commitment by the superpowers toward nuclear disarmament on a bold scale cannot help but have an important exemplary effect. And coupling such disarmament with an end to a qualitative arms race which can only lead to highly destabilized developments will provide further security assurances to others.

c. Withdrawing nuclear weapons from abroad: The United States has "tactical" nuclear weapons deployed around the world — over 7000 in Western Europe alone. American nuclear weapons in South Korea are so close to the Demilitarized Zone that a North Korean attack on South Korea would almost certainly involve American nuclear weapons. The Soviet Union has nuclear-capable forces in Eastern Europe, probably involving some 3500 warheads.[8] Though American military doctrine contemplates the possibility of keeping a "tactical" nuclear war limited in scope, Soviet military writings do not subscribe to any comparable doctrine of restraints; they call for all-out war. President Carter in his campaign several times observed that he doubted that a tactical nuclear war could be kept from escalating into a full-fledged intercontinental exchange. Thus tactical

[8]*The Military Balance, 1976-1977* (The International Institute for Strategic Studies, London, 1976), p. 103.

nuclear weapons are a misnomer; they are likely to increase, rather than deter, the likely outbreak of all-out nuclear warfare. The number of United States tactical nuclear weapons could be cut in half immediately, and the rest gradually eliminated.

d. Conventional force deployments: Both through negotiations and by unilateral action, further reduction of tensions and increased stability could be brought about by reducing and, in some cases, entirely eliminating overseas deployments of military and naval forces. United States ground forces should be withdrawn entirely from South Korea and significantly reduced, with corresponding reductions of Soviet forces, in Europe. The United States and Soviet Union should both withdraw naval forces and close down naval support bases in the Indian Ocean, making it a "zone of non-intervention," and consider early steps to reduce their naval force deployments in the Mediterranean.

e. Controlling conventional arms sales: The international traffic in conventional arms is uncontrolled. Both in quantity and quality of equipment, the traffic has escalated each year to the point that United States arms orders alone are now more than twelve billion dollars annually, or one billion dollars a month. It will be many months before the more restrained Carter administration approach results in any reduction from this level. The next closest competitor, the Soviet Union, accounts for roughly one-sixth of the American total. Proponents of continuing sales of sophisticated arms to willing recipients argue that among other benefits such sales can reduce incentives for those recipients to acquire nuclear weapons. The nuclear/conventional weapons tradeoff is also evident in cases where sales of conventional arms have been made contingent on the recipient's foregoing critical elements of the nuclear fuel cycle. This apparently was the case when Pakistan was negotiating for A-7 attack planes at a time the United States was trying to persuade Pakistan to withdraw from a contract with France to acquire a nuclear reprocessing plant.[9] The second example seems to be the wrong solution to the proliferation problem; the first is based on faulty reasoning, particularly as more and more dual-capability aircraft (able to carry both nuclear and conventional weapons) are included in transfers of

[9] George C. Wilson, "Pakistan Bomber Purchase Cleared by Defense Department," *The Washington Post*, November 16, 1976.

"conventional" weapons. Furthermore, such customers as Iran and Saudi Arabia, literally able to buy more military equipment than they can handle, may sooner or later conclude that their already ultra-modern forces lack only the nuclear ingredient to make them truly powers to be reckoned with.

A drastic reduction in the scale and complexity of arms transfers would seem to be in order. Until President Carter announced a reversal of United States arms export policy in May 1977, there had been little official enthusiasm for such a step in any of the supplier governments. In some of them, notably France and the United Kingdom, arms sales constitute an important part of the export market. While some suppliers argue that arms exports will increase stability in unstable regions, such sales are more likely to increase both the likelihood and intensity of conflict. But most arguments for continued sales at high levels seem short-sighted and self-serving, especially when balanced against the cost of raising the levels of violence should wars break out and of potentially stimulating nuclear appetites. Suppliers and customers should seek agreements in critical regions to lower the levels of sales and, if possible, to eliminate certain classes of weapons altogether. The United States has begun to take the lead in opening negotiations toward this end with the Soviet Union and with American allies.

f. No-first-use policies: The United States has never been willing to declare that it would not be the first to use nuclear weapons in some circumstances. The United States has argued that such a declaration would undermine the confidence of its allies and has rejected as propaganda a recent Soviet proposal for a NATO-Warsaw Pact no-first-use agreement. Yet if we are not willing to declare that we will not use nuclear weapons even against those whom we have asked to give them up, what security assurances have they gained by forgoing them? Perhaps it could be argued that would-be nuclear powers are not worried about the superpowers using nuclear weapons against them, but rather they are worried about their neighbors. Nevertheless, failure to enunciate a no-first-use policy is one more example of a "do as I say, not as I do" approach to nonproliferation policy.

3. Other Multilateral Actions

a. Nuclear free zones: Regions free of nuclear weapons have been proposed from time to time, and in three instances have been established with some degree of success: in Antarctica, on a seabed, and in Latin America. The latter case has not yet been fully implemented; the treaty establishing the Latin American Nuclear Free Zone requires the participation of countries outside the region which have territories within it, and that the nuclear weapons states undertake not to use or threaten to use nuclear weapons against parties to the treaty. France has not agreed to the first condition, and the Soviet Union has not accepted the second. Consequently, though twenty Latin American states have ratified the treaty, two of the most important, Brazil and Chile, have conditioned their full participation on full implementation by all outside powers to whom the treaty applies, while neither Argentina nor Cuba is a party to it. Thus until France and the Soviet Union ratify the necessary additional protocols, and Argentina and Cuba complete the ratification process, the treaty will be only symbolic. Nevertheless, it sets an important precedent, and provides hope that other proposals for nuclear free zone agreements, in Africa, South Asia, and even the Middle East, which have been discussed in recent years, are not out of the question.

b. Special United Nations session on disarmament: An *ad hoc* United Nations Committee on Disarmament which met in 1976 recommended, and the General Assembly adopted, a proposal that a special session of the General Assembly be convened in 1978 to discuss disarmament problems. For years proposals for a World Disarmament Conference have been put forward, only to be put off for lack of support by the superpowers whose representatives have expressed doubts that such a large conference would be anything more than a propaganda forum where they would be castigated for their slow progress in arms control and disarmament. Nevertheless, the case for convening as large a forum as possible, with a suitably constructive agenda, is strong. Arms control and disarmament are everybody's business, not the private preserve of the United States and the Soviet Union. Furthermore, such a forum could provide an opportunity for an important dialogue on the implications of nuclear weapons. Such discussions, it is argued, could serve to play down the presumed prestige of acquiring nuclear weapons, and perhaps to highlight the increased risks that acquisition of nuclear weapons might entail — provided only that considerably more evidence is shown than now exists of United States and Soviet willingness to move toward real nuclear disarmament. Otherwise, any such exercise in nuclear education is bound to fail.

c. The non-proliferation treaty: Finally, despite its imperfections, efforts to preserve and strengthen the 1970 Treaty on the Non-Proliferation of Nuclear Weapons (NPT) must continue. One hundred nations have now become parties to it. There are important holdouts, and many of its parties are dissatisfied with the discriminatory manner in which it has been implemented. Nevertheless, no member has withdrawn from the treaty, and all are committed to the convening of a second review conference in 1980. The NPT cannot stop further proliferation by itself, but it is not wholly without value. And a world without the NPT, or one in which parties begin to withdraw from it, would be a far more dangerous place than it already is. The NPT is a symbol that nations can still make an effort to stave off nuclear disaster. It will survive, and be improved upon, only if steps such as those outlined above are taken.

The Role of the United States

I have contended above that the United States is the leader in the arms race. If the United States were to take bolder steps to discourage proliferation, begin the process of nuclear disarmament, and narrow its definition of an adequate defense, its actions would have a telling effect on attitudes and decisions in other countries.

The attitudes of America's political leaders shape and are shaped by those of the public. This commonplace observation is perhaps more clearly borne out in the area of defense and security concerns than in any other field, for the public has almost nowhere to turn for guidance on these matters than to political leaders — and military leaders — in Washington. Thus a strong commitment by the leaders of the United States government to arms control and disarmament could bring about profound changes in public attitudes.

The role of Presidential leadership cannot be overemphasized. The President can rally the people for war, even for unpopular wars. And with the will to do so, he can rally the people for new peace and disarmament initiatives. One need only recall the support President Kennedy mustered in 1963 for the Limited Test Ban Treaty, in a commencement speech at American University in which he made clear his commitment to bring about such a treaty, a scant six months after the United States and Soviet Union had stood at the brink of nuclear war over Cuba.

To sustain a new dedication to work seriously for disarmament requires not only Presidential commitment, but acceptance at all levels of the government that arms control and disarmament are integral parts of national security policy. This requires that the director of the Arms Control and Disarmament Agency (ACDA) be given an equal voice to those of the Secretaries of State and Defense, to the Joint Chiefs of Staff, and to the President's National Security Advisor, whenever questions of national security policy arise, and, most importantly, that those officials have a sense of commitment to disarmament objectives equal to that of the ACDA director.

Suggestions that this sort of governmental commitment can only be brought about through the creation of a new "Department of Peace" strike me as steps in the wrong direction. A new separate department asked to be responsible not only for disarmament, but also for development and perhaps of other humanitarian foreign policy programs as well, would only relieve other agencies and departments of responsibility for what should be the entire government's concern. The Arms Control and Disarmament Agency, created in 1961 to conduct research and negotiations in support of disarmament policies, performs those roles in close cooperation with other agencies. It could be argued that many of its functions could have been done as well by a team of first-rate experts in the White House; but the agency now exists and to abolish it would be a step in the wrong direction. Furthermore, a body of talented professionals on some issues — nuclear proliferation problems, for example — exists in ACDA which is unmatched in expertise and dedication anywhere in the world.

The Congress is already playing a growing role in arms control matters, but the impetus for much of it has stemmed from a sense of frustration at the hands of an executive branch which has attempted to bypass Congress on arms sales, nuclear exports, and new weapons development. The executive branch needs to view Congress as an active partner in developing and pursuing effective new policies, not as an antagonist. This is particularly true at a time when new leadership is taking control of key committees as well as party leadership in both houses.

One new program in which the Congress played a leading role in 1975 and 1976 was the development of an imaginative and potentially important new mechanism for evaluating military programs: the arms control impact statement process. Under new legislation, certain weapons programs must be subjected to analysis of their impact on arms control and disarmament policies and negotiations, and the result of this evaluation submitted to the Congress along with any request for funding. In principle, the idea should forestall the commitment to new weapons systems and strategies which would be likely to complicate or set back arms control progress. In practice, however, it has been a dismal failure. In 1976 the Defense Department submitted eleven impact statements, the Energy Research and Development Administration another five, on the day that the Senate was considering the Defense appropriation. The statements were not only so late as to be useless, but they were so devoid of information that Senator Humphrey declared that the two departments had violated the law, and Senators Sparkman and Case sent them back to the executive branch for revision. Such revision is unlikely, as is any more responsive performance on the part of relevant executive agencies in future years unless continued pressure is brought to bear on seeing to it that the process works as intended. Both the new administration and the Congress need to see to it that the process is lived up to, both in letter and in spirit.[10]

Military procurement and deployment decisions should be made not only with their implications for arms control and disarmament in mind, but with the nation's real defense requirements as the principal justification. Plans, well underway, to equip strategic forces with the B-1 bomber, the M-X ICBM, cruise missiles, and the Trident submarine would be radically altered if the essential criterion were truly defense of the United States and its important allies, and not a need to keep defense industries operating and to "stay ahead" of a worst-case projection of Soviet military prowess. Troop levels in Europe are kept

[10]See Betty Goetz Lall, "Arms Control Impact Statements: A New Approach to Slowing the Arms Race?" *Arms Control Today*, 6 (July/August 1976).

high as a bargaining chip for the stalled negotiations on mutual and balanced force reductions there; tactical nuclear weapons deployed around the world are more likely to get us into war than deter one. The need for many present overseas installations, such as naval bases in the Indian Ocean, is highly questionable if the defense of the United States is our principal military mission.

Certainly the United States should have adequate conventional defenses, including adequate means of warning of an attack, but this requires neither far-flung overseas deployments nor attempting to match and overmatch, dollar for dollar, gun for gun, tank for tank, and missile for missile a Soviet Union equipped with inferior-quality armaments, backed by a faltering and inefficient economic structure, and faced by other enemies and internal security problems for which the United States has no counterpart. An administration willing to redefine national security to give adequate weight to arms control and disarmament should also be able to redefine national defense to mean defense of the nation's true interests and that alone.[11]

Strong government support for an aggressive arms control and disarmament program will require, but will also bring about, shifts in present public attitudes about military programs and about disarmament.

While some politicians give lip service to the idea of disarmament, few of them dare to use the word itself and are at pains to explain how each timid step in arms control will not cause the military strength of the nation to weaken. At the same time many of them are willing to accept the judgments military men and their supporters pronounce, almost without question.

This is painfully true in Congress. A majority of Congressmen are poorly informed on military matters, inadequately staffed, and overworked. When they must make a judgment on a defense problem they seek out "the experts," who almost invariably are the members and staffs of the military committees and the proponents of the military programs themselves from the Pentagon and the arms industry. Even when they are dubious about the need for a weapon program they tend to support it on the ground that "it is better to err on the side of safety." What if Congress made its decisions this way on questions of health

[11]See Walter C. Clemens, Jr., "America Already is 'Second to None'," *The Washington Post*, November 15, 1976.

care, public education, or aid to cities? Of course we need a military establishment, but we don't need to gratify its every desire.

Accordingly, we need more balance in the information given to the public about arms control and disarmament matters. One way to accomplish this is to greatly increase the budget of the Arms Control and Disarmament Agency (ACDA) for public information, for its publications, for convening regional town meetings and bringing civic leaders to Washington, and for more extensive use of radio and television — in short, all the mechanisms that are regularly used for Pentagon public information programs.

ACDA could be strengthened in other ways. In addition to increasing its public affairs role, ACDA could be made more independent from the Department of State. By statute its director reports to both the President and the Secretary of State, but because it is physically housed in the State Department building and staffed in part by foreign service officers on loan from the department, the department's influence tends to be greater, and many people tend to look upon ACDA as an appendage of the State Department. Study should be given to establishing a separate ACDA career service. At present the agency's staff is a mixture of civil servants, active duty military officers, and career foreign service officers on loan from the State Department. Many of these are competent and dedicated professionals, but their first loyalty must necessarily be to their parent service, and many of them view their ACDA tours as undesirable detours from a career pattern in another field.

ACDA could also perform an important educational function of potentially great value: Just as foreign military officers are brought to the United States for specialized military training, senior government officials, including military officers, could be trained in ACDA-managed institutes on arms control and disarmament problems.[12]

What Can Concerned Citizens Do?

The United States will not play a leading role on the international scene, nor will it put its own house in order, without sustained and informed public support for more effective pro-

[12]*Harvard Magazine*, p. 23.

grams in arms control and disarmament. Particularly in this area, citizens tend to feel that there is little good they can do beyond handwringing and supporting "causes." With only rare exceptions, the public has neither expressed nor effectively used widespread concern about military excesses, war, or the threat of war in any political way. Yet I believe that a strong undercurrent of support for peace and progress toward disarmament is more widespread than public opinion polls show. Recently they have suggested growing public concern about increasing Soviet military strength, and a resolve to keep America "Number One."[13] Until the advent of the Carter administration the information available to the public on these issues was so one-sided, largely the product of a newly invigorated cold-war propaganda campaign abetted by responsible government officials from the President on down, that poll results showing a growing public hawkishness were no surprise. Although there is now a different official attitude in Washington, it will take a major educational effort to soon reverse such results.

The same poll respondents, if they could be assured that arms control measures would enhance our security more effectively than more armaments, would support such measures enthusiastically. And when, as rarely happens, major events or programs remind the public that nuclear war could really happen to them, the response is overwhelming. Examples include the public reaction to plans to build and stock fallout shelters in the early 1960s; widespread concern about radioactive fallout from nuclear testing, leading to the adoption of the 1963 Treaty Banning Nuclear Weapons Tests in the Atmosphere, in Outer Space, and Underwater; and the "bombs in the backyard" scare of the 1969-1970 antiballistic missile debate, which mobilized community opposition to the proposed ABMs wherever they were to be deployed.

The threat of nuclear proliferation seems far away, however. How to give more effective voice to public concern about it?

There is a temptation, already in evidence, to couple concern about proliferation to concern about nuclear power plant

---

[13]For a presentation and analysis of these trends, see the Potomac Associates, *The Pursuit of National Security: Defense and the Military Balance* (Washington, D.C., 1976), pp. 24-39.

safety. This seems to me to be the wrong approach. Nuclear power deserves, and is beginning to receive, more careful public scrutiny in recent years. There are many reasons, and I have presented some of them above, to question whether any further commitment to nuclear power makes sense, and to press for alternatives such as solar power. But the chief target for those concerned about nuclear proliferation is not nuclear energy, which to a large extent can probably be managed, at least in the United States, to make the risks of proliferation quite small. It is, rather, the continuing pursuit of security through military programs which are out of all proportion to national needs.

There are talented individuals and effective organizations throughout the country which can help the concerned public develop effective political action. There are public officials and candidates for elective office who would take more forthright stands against military excesses if they knew they had both public backing and access to information and effective arguments to give voice to their convictions.

Community action and self-education on disarmament can be fostered through specialized committees and associations, which focus the energies of like-minded individuals and also serve as the focal point for much of the more effective political action, and through more broad-based existing community activities. Churches, PTAs, and service organizations all can provide forums for discussion of disarmament and national security problems.

Citizens interested in obtaining information or the services of speakers can contact a number of specialized organizations for this purpose. Some of these are membership groups; others exist principally to serve as a talent bank for advising Congress and government officials and for providing resource materials to the public. Some representative organizations specializing in arms control and disarmament are listed in the Appendix, as are some more broadly based groups which are occasionally concerned with these issues.

The next few years offer a great opportunity to bring about important changes. They also are years of increasing peril, as much of this book has forecast. One thing is certain, and Edmund Burke said it best: "All that is necessary for the forces of evil to win in the world is for enough good men to do nothing."

Appendix
ORGANIZATIONS CONCERNED WITH ARMS CONTROL AND DISARMAMENT

Listed below are some of the effective organizations which devote all or most of their attention to arms control, disarmament, and defense issues. Some are active lobbies; others are engaged solely in dissemination of information, through magazines, newsletters, and other publications.

Arms Control Association
11 Dupont Circle, N.W.
Washington, D.C. 20036

Carnegie Endowment for International Peace
345 East 46th Street
New York, N.Y. 10017

Center for Defense Information
122 Maryland Avenue, N.E.
Washington, D.C. 20002

Coalition for a New Foreign and Military Policy
120 Maryland Avenue, N.E.
Washington, D.C. 20002

Council for a Livable World
100 Maryland Avenue, N.E.
Washington, D.C. 20002

Council on Religion and International Affairs
170 East 64th Street
New York, N.Y. 10021

Federation of American Scientists
307 Massachusetts Avenue, N.E.
Washington, D.C. 20002

APPENDIX

Friends Committee on National Legislation
245 2nd Street, N.E.
Washington, D.C. 20002

Members of Congress for Peace Through Law
201 Massachusetts Avenue, N.E.
Washington, D.C. 20002

New Directions
2021 L Street, N.W.
Washington, D.C. 20036

SANE
318 Massachusetts Avenue, N.E.
Washington, D.C. 20002

United Nations Association of The United States of America (UNA/USA)
345 East 46th Street
New York, N.Y. 10017